S0-BYX-444

TAX PLANNING FOR INVESTORS
**The Eighties Guide to Securities Investments
and Tax Shelters**

TAX PLANNING FOR INVESTORS
The Eighties Guide to Securities Investments and Tax Shelters

Jack Crestol, CPA, J.D., L.L.M.

and

Herman M. Schneider, CPA, J.D., L.L.M.

Both Tax Partners of Coopers & Lybrand

DOW JONES-IRWIN Homewood, Illinois 60430

ISBN 0-87094-298-0
Library of Congress Catalog Card No. 82-71350

Printed in the United States of America

1 2 3 4 5 6 7 8 9 0 K 9 8 7 6 5 4 3

Preface

The investor's primary objective in investing in securities is to make a profit: buy low, sell high. Unfortunately, however, getting the *most* profit from a year's security transactions is not a simple matter of buying low and selling high, because the tax laws determine how much of the profit can be kept.

The informed investor measures his or her economic gain or yield in terms of aftertax dollars or the amount of additional cash available after considering all expenses including income taxes. It should be emphasized, however, that although the informed investor should be highly conscious of tax factors, he or she will rarely allow these tax factors to affect an economic decision. A short-term gain taxed at ordinary rates is still superior to a long-term capital loss, no matter how heavily the gain is taxed. Nevertheless, in many instances taxes can be minimized with little or no economic effect.

To aid investors in their understanding of how security transactions and other types of investments are taxed and the kind of planning measures necessary to maximize the aftertax gain, this book was first issued in 1966 and revised in 1967, 1970, and 1978. It has again been revised to reflect new developments, including the Tax Reform Act of 1976 (1976 TRA), the Revenue Act of 1978 (1978 RA), and the Economic Recovery Act of 1981 (1981 ERTA), and now provides in Section I a list of tax saving opportunities and in Section II a summary of the tax rules an investor needs to know to plan effectively. This book is not intended to show investors how to realize economic gains in securities transactions, but rather how to obtain the best tax advantages in recognizing gains or losses. To this end, tax savings opportunities are discussed in the form of objectives, such as postponing tax recognition of gain, converting short-term gains into long-term gains, and the like. For example, the investor may be able to convert a short-term gain into a long-term gain and also defer the tax until the following year by writing an in-the-money Call, while at the same time achieving his or her intended economic objective.

The provisions of the Economic Recovery Tax Act of 1981 will affect all investors, but will have an extra beneficial effect on high-tax-bracket individuals who are taxed up to 70 percent on their investment income or who benefit from the 50 percent maximum tax on personal service income. The principal changes affecting investors are (1) decreased tax rates, including reduction of maximum tax rate on investment income to 50 percent; (2) decrease in the maximum tax rate on net capital gains from 28 percent to 20 percent; (3) restricted use of tax straddles; (4) tax preferences will no longer affect the maximum tax on personal service income; (5) reduction in maximum alternative minimum tax rate to 20 percent; (6) reduction in maximum estate and gift tax rates to 50 percent and increase in annual gift tax exclusion from $3,000 to $10,000; and (7) greater tax benefit can be obtained from use of tax shelters. These and other changes will be discussed in detail in the text.

The Tax Equity and Fiscal Responsibility Act of 1982 was passed while this book was being printed. Accordingly, the authors were unable to provide a discussion of its new provisions, but they must be considered when reading this book. Below is a summary of the provisions that will affect investors. Unless otherwise indicated, they generally will apply to taxable years beginning after 1982.

1. One of the provisions that was deleted from the Senate Tax Bill would have reduced the holding period for long-term capital gains from one year to six months, effective for sales and exchanges after June 30, 1982. Another tax bill has been adopted by the Senate which would also reduce the holding period for long-term capital gains to six months. (See 32.02.)

2. The prior alternative minimum tax and add-on minimum tax (see 57 and 58) will be combined into one alternative minimum tax. All of the existing tax preference items have been retained, except for adjusted itemized deductions and amortization of child care facilities. Thus, in addition to the 60 percent deduction for long-term capital gains, the new tax preferences include:

a. The interest and dividend income exclusion up to $100.
b. The all savers' certificate exclusion.
c. The 15 percent net interest exclusion which will take effect in 1985.
d. The bargain element on exercise of incentive stock options.
e. Excess mining exploration and development expenses.
f. Research and development expense.

In computing the alternative minimum, the tax preference items are added onto adjusted gross income (AGI). The only allowable deductions will be charitable contributions, medical expenses in excess of 10 percent of AGI, casualty losses in excess of 10 percent of AGI, personal housing interest expense, investment interest expense to the extent of investment interest income, and the estate tax deduction. Thus deductions for taxes, other interest expense, investment, and other miscellaneous deductions, are not allowed in computing the minimum taxable income. A flat 20 percent tax rate will be imposed on the minimum taxable income in excess of $30,000 for single returns ($40,000 for joint returns).

3. The rule requiring original issue discount on corporate bonds to be included each year in income in equal amounts over the life of the bond has been amended for obligations issued after July 1, 1982. (See **43.09(b)**.) Original issue discount will now have to be computed by both the issuer of the bond and the bondholder on an accrual basis. This will result in less original issue discount in the earlier years and greater amounts of discounts in the later years. Thus, while the intent was to decrease the corporate debtor's deductions in earlier years, bondholders will also report less income in the earlier years. Moreover, the original issue discount rules will be extended to certain noncorporate obligations.

4. The practice of stripping coupons from the bonds and then either selling the bonds at a loss or accelerating income by selling the coupons will be prevented by the new provisions. (See **9.06** and **43.09(e)(f)**.) Effective for sales after June 30, 1982, a seller will have to apportion the bond tax basis to the stripped bond coupons and the bond principal which is based on their respective fair market values. This will deny the seller a loss on the sale of the stripped bond. In addition, buyers of stripped bonds or coupons will be subject to the new original issue discount rules. These rules require buyers to currently report income instead of deferring income until disposition of the property and will prevent the purchaser of stripped bond coupons from converting

ordinary income into capital gains by selling the coupons before they mature.

5. A 10 percent withholding tax will be imposed on dividends and interest received after July 1, 1983, from corporate and certain governmental securities. An exemption will be allowed for annual interest payments of less than $150. Additional exemptions are provided for persons over 64 with a tax liability for the year of less than $2,500 (married) or $1,500 (single), and for persons under 65 with a prior-year tax liability of less than $1,000 (married) or $600 (single). Interest payments made by individuals will generally be exempted. The withholding tax will reduce an investor's income since the withheld amounts will not be available for further investment. Investors making estimated tax payments should reduce the amounts by the estimated withholding tax on dividends and interest.

6. Another Senate tax provision, which would have prevented the tax-free reinvestment of utility dividends, has been deleted from the 1982 act. (See **52.02**.)

7. Investments in tax shelters will also be adversely affected by the 1982 act. In addition to toughening the alternative minimum tax, the benefits of ACRS depreciation deduction and the investment tax credit have been reduced. The scheduled increases in ACRS depreciation for 1985 and 1986 have been eliminated. Furthermore, an investor must reduce the basis of the property by one half of the amount of regular, energy, and certified historic structure investment tax credit. In lieu of a reduction in basis, an 8 percent tax credit can be elected (4 percent for 3-year property). Additional penalties will also be imposed for abusive tax shelters. (See **67**.)

This book is concerned primarily with the federal tax liabilities of an individual filing an income tax return on a cash basis. Although many of the ideas presented and the discussion of the relevant income tax provisions may also apply (with or without some modification) to nonresident aliens, traders, dealers, partnerships, trusts, estates, and corporations, the text does not consider such possible application. However, there are separate chapters summarizing the tax effects for nonresident alien investors, corporations, trusts, estates, and other types of investors. In addition, the discussion is confined primarily to transactions in securities of publicly owned corporations, and, although many of these provisions apply also to closely held corporations, it does not consider the special tax provisions relating to closely held or related corporations. In all the examples, it is assumed that the investor files a tax return on the calendar year basis. Furthermore, for the sake of simplicity, a capital gains tax of 20 percent is used, although for many investors the effective tax rate will be lower. Unless otherwise indicated, all examples are applicable under the Economic Recovery Act of 1981.

For practical reasons, state and local tax liabilities are not considered herein. Such liabilities are usually small in relation to federal tax liabilities, are deductible in computing the federal tax liability, and are frequently computed on comparable bases. The investor is warned, however, that situations may arise where state or local tax liabilities may be large enough to influence an investor's tax planning. Each investor should acquaint himself with the nature and magnitude of such taxes as they apply to him.

For the convenience of the reader, the discussion of tax savings opportunities is cross-referenced to the discussion of tax principles. Official authorities are referred to in footnotes and indexed in the appendix, and both a detailed word index of subject matters and a detailed table of contents are provided. Many readers will prefer first to scan the tax savings opportunities for interesting suggestions and then to read the sections of Section II that apply.

The authors wish to acknowledge their appreciation of the invaluable assistance of their associates in the offices of Coopers & Lybrand. In particular, James B. Fish, Jr., CPA, and Warren G. Wintrub, CPA, assisted in preparation of the earlier editions and/or this revision.

The authors would also like to thank JoAnn Skaferowsky and Marcia Henry for their help in preparing the manuscript for final copy.

Jack Crestol
Herman M. Schneider

Contents

Tax Savings Opportunities

¶1

1 INTRODUCTION

The ideas discussed in this section are intended to present the investor with alternative legitimate methods of casting a transaction so that the investor can either reduce his tax liability or defer the tax to another year. Many of these ideas have been sanctioned by court decisions or by Treasury regulations or rulings. However, the investor should be aware that the Treasury may attack tax savings transactions on various grounds, sometimes despite court approval of the transaction.

The trading in Listed options on several exchanges has become a very popular form of investment. However, for many sophisticated investors, Unlisted options are still being utilized. Accordingly, portions of this section dealing with options will cover all options, but certain sections will be applicable to only Unlisted options. Under such circumstances, such limitations will be clearly indicated.

The illustrations generally do not take into consideration the transaction costs (i.e., commissions, applicable transfer taxes, and so forth). Accordingly, such costs must be considered in the overall economics of the transaction.

It is appropriate at this point to reemphasize the importance of the economics of a transaction, aside from the tax considerations. The courts and the Internal Revenue Service more and more have been looking into the pretax economics of the transaction. The investor will be denied the tax benefits of a transaction he enters into solely for tax reasons with no expectations of ever realizing a profit on the transaction.[1] However, the existence of economic profit

---

[1] Goldstein, 364 F2d 734 (CA-2, 1966),
Cert. Den.

potential should be sufficient. Notwithstanding, the Internal Revenue Service had ruled prior to the Economic Recovery Act of 1981 (1981 ERTA) that the short-term capital loss generated in a commodity straddle transaction results in no real economic loss and is not deductible.[2] This position of the government fails to recognize the total economic and profit potential of commodity straddle transactions, but is indicative of the emphasis that is being placed on "pre-tax economics." Accordingly, the economic and profit potential of the tax saving opportunities discussed below must be considered.

2 POSTPONE TAX RECOGNITION OF GAIN OR LOSS

The transactions discussed below will postpone the recognition of the gain or loss, but will not change the character of the gain or loss when recognized for tax purposes. Several of the ideas have general application, while others are limited to specific types of investments.

.01 "Short Against the Box"

An investor can sell a security but defer the recognition of gain until the next year by selling short an equal number of shares and covering the short sale in the following year with the shares originally held. This is commonly known as "selling short against the box." Ordinarily, the long-term or short-term nature of the gain will be determined at the time of the short sale and therefore will not be affected by the deferral. However, in the case of securities held for more than one year, care should be taken to ensure that long-term capital gain treatment will result. The amount of tax on the gain will depend on the taxpayer's other income, other tax preference items, and the tax rates in effect in the year in which the gain is recognized. Deferral of the gain, therefore, may result in a higher or lower effective tax rate on the gain, and should be taken into account in determining whether or not to go short against the box. A deferral of gain may be particularly effective where there will be a prospective tax rate reduction or an investor has a change in economic status (e.g., retirement from his position). By delaying long-term capital gains until after retirement, there may be a drop in overall income.

> **Example (a).** An investor may wish to protect his profit in stock acquired on November 1, 1981 for $20 per share, and which is selling on

---

[2] Rev. Rul. 77-185, C.B. 1977-1, 22.

December 1, 1982 for $50. Instead of recognizing a $30 per share long-term capital gain in 1982, the investor could sell short the stock at $50 and defer the closing of such sale until January of 1983, at which time the long-term gain of $30 per share (less transfer fees and taxes) will be recognized. If the stock was acquired on December 15, 1981, so that the holding period of the stock was not more than one year at the time of the short sale, the gain recognized upon the closing of the short sale would be a short-term capital gain. (See discussion of short sales, **37.**)

Example (b). *Alternative minimum tax:* T's itemized deductions (interest expense, charitable contributions, and so on) for the current taxable year exceed 60 percent of adjusted gross income and he has already realized long-term capital gains in the current year. He wishes to realize additional gains but does not want to increase his alternative minimum tax for the year. By selling short and closing the short position in the following year, he will minimize his alternative tax for the current year and defer the gain in the short sale until the next year when he expects to pay a lower effective tax rate on the gains.

The short against the box transaction can also be utilized when an investor has a gain on a Listed option and wishes to defer the gain into the succeeding year.

Example. On September 10, 1982, T purchased one ABC Call February 55's for a premium of $600. On October 15, 1982, the Call is selling for $2,000 and T wishes to lock in the gain but defer the short-term gain until 1983. T could write (sell) the identical Call for a premium of $2,000 and effectively be in a short against the box position. In February of 1983 both positions will be collapsed, thereby resulting in a $1,400 short-term gain in 1983.

A short sale may also be used to sell a depreciated security but defer the recognition of the loss until the next year. Ordinarily it is more advantageous to deduct the loss in the current year. However, under certain circumstances, it may be more beneficial taxwise to postpone recognizing the loss. The following are some examples where the losses should be postponed.

Example (a). *Excess deductions:* T's deductions exceed his income, including $3,000 of capital gains, by $5,000. On December 1, T wants to sell a stock and realize a capital loss of $2,000. There would be no tax benefit if the capital loss is recognized in the current year because there is no taxable income and the excess deductions cannot be carried to another year. (See **20**.) A short sale of the stock will enable T to apply the capital loss against his income in the year the sale is closed.

Example (b). *Long-term loss and short-term gain:* In 1982, T has realized $10,000 of short-term gains and $10,000 of long-term losses. He expects to realize short-term gains and long-term gains in 1983. T has suffered a $6,000 loss on a stock acquired late in 1982 and wants to sell it before there is a further drop in its value. By selling the stock short and closing it early in 1983, T can offset his 1982 long-term losses against his short-term gains and offset the postponed $6,000 short-term loss against his 1983 short-term gains. If he recognized the loss in 1982, the loss would be applied against his 1982 short-term gains. However, only $4,000 of the $10,000 long-term loss could be offset against the remaining 1982 short-term gains, $4,000 of the loss would be applied against $2,000 of his 1982 ordinary income (see **32.03**) and $2,000 of the long-term loss would be offset against 1983 long-term gains. T would obtain an additional $2,000 deduction in 1982, but at the expense of having $6,000 more of short-term gains in 1983 and only a $2,000 reduction in long-term gains.

Example (c). *Income averaging:* As a result of the income averaging rules (see **63**), T can pay a low tax on his capital gains in 1982. T expects short-term gains in 1983 and expects to pay a much larger tax on his 1983 gains. T has incurred a $5,000 loss on a security and wants to sell it before there is a further decline. By selling short in 1982 and closing in 1983, T can obtain a greater tax benefit from the loss.

Under certain circumstances, the broker may release to the investor a substantial portion of the funds arising from the short sale or allow the purchase of other securities with the purchasing power created because of such short sale. However, interest will ordinarily be charged when the funds created by the short sale are used. The investor should determine the policy of his broker in this situation before making the short sale. It may be possible to keep both positions open for a long period of time, have the use of the funds or additional purchasing power during this period, and still avoid recognition of gain.

With the repeal of the basis carryover provision, it is possible during the interim period to avoid tax on the unrecognized gain if the investor died before the short sale was closed. A determination should be made whether closing the short sale before or after death would result in a savings of overall taxes.

.02 Acquisition of a Put

The investor can defer the recognition of any gain on his stock and still minimize the possible reduction in the amount of his gain by acquiring an option to sell the stock (a Put). The advantage of this method as compared to the use of a short sale, discussed above, is that in the event the stock continues to rise, the investor obtains the benefit of such rise. However, the cost of acquiring this insurance against decline is normally in the area of 10 to 15 percent of the value of the underlying security. This varies in accordance with the period of time that the option will run, the volatility of the stock, and supply and demand for the Put. A tax disadvantage under either method is that, if the underlying security is held less than one year at the time of the short sale or acquisition of the Put, any gain on subsequent sale will generally be treated as short-term, since the holding period of the stock will not begin until the short sale is covered or the Put is exercised, expires, or is disposed of. (See discussion of short sales in 37.03(c).)

It is not expected that Listed Puts will have a duration of more than nine months and accordingly, long-term capital gain potential on the sale of Listed Puts will not be available. However, Unlisted Puts for more than one year will be available and can be utilized to accord the investor potential long-term capital gain treatment upon ultimate sale.

> **Example.** Assume that an investor owned stock acquired July 1, 1982, at $20 per share, and she purchased on December 1, 1982, a one-year, 10-day Unlisted Put at $50 for the equivalent of $5 per share. The investor then has the right to "put" or sell the stock to the writer of the option at any time during the period for $50 per share, regardless of the then selling price of the stock. If the market value of the stock rises, for example, to $75 per share and the investor wishes to close out the transaction, she can sell the stock in the open market, recognizing a $55 per share, short-term capital gain (the stock was held for less than one year at the time the Put was acquired). She would try to sell the Put prior to the end of the one-year period, realizing a short-term loss of approximately $5 per share, in lieu of merely letting the Put expire, in which case the loss would be long-term.

If the investor had sold short the stock at $50 per share in lieu of ac-
quiring the Put, she would have limited her gain to $30 per share. Thus,
for a cost of approximately $5 per share, the Put insures a minimum gain
and allows potentially substantial gain possibilities for the one-year period
in the event of a rise in the stock market.

If the market value of the stock should fall, for example, to $30 per
share by December 2, 1983 (Put held for more than one year), she would
sell the Put for the equivalent price of approximately $20 per share ($50
option price less market value of stock of $30) and, therefore, recognize
long-term gain of approximately $15 per share ($20 per share proceeds less
$5 per share cost of the Put). The stock would then be sold for $30, resulting in a capital gain of $10 per share which is given *short-term* treat-
ment even though the stock was held for more than one year. This occurs
with respect to the gain because, at the time of the acquisition of the Put,
such shares were held for less than one year, thus bringing in effect the
short sale rules. If the stock were instead sold for $15 per share, a *loss*
of $5 per share would be treated as *long-term,* since the short sale rules
would not be applicable.

.03 Deferred Delivery Under New York Stock Exchange Rule 64(3) (Seller's Option)

A discussion of the seller's option is to be found in 5.02. Selling
via this route will enable the seller to take advantage of the current
market price and still defer recognition of gain and add up to 60
days to his holding period. Thus, a seller who has held a security for
from 10 months to one year can convert a short-term gain into a
long-term gain without further exposure to market risk.

.04 Year-End Sales

A cash-basis investor selling stock toward the end of his taxable
year may control which year the gain is to be recognized. When stock
is sold in the "regular way," as is the case in most instances, the settlement day will be the fifth business day following the trade date.
A loss will be recognized in the year in which the trade date falls, but
a profit is not taxable until the subsequent year in which the settlement date falls. The cash-basis investor may cause the gain to be recognized in the year of the trade by making the sale "for cash." (See
5.02 dealing with deferred delivery under N.Y. Stock Exchange
Rule 64(3) for possible postponement of gain for up to 60 days.)
For example, assume that an investor has recognized a $10,000 long-

term capital gain and a $10,000 short-term loss in the current year and on December 29 has sold stock which will result in a short-term gain of $11,000. Under the regular rules the $11,000 short-term gain will be recognized in the subsequent year and the $10,000 short-term loss will offset the $10,000 long-term gain in the current year. By making the sale for cash, the $10,000 short-term loss will be applied against the $11,000 short-term gain instead of against the $10,000 long-term gain. The result will be that the investor will be accelerating the time the $11,000 gain would ordinarily be taxed, but he has reduced his overall tax liability on his stock transactions by converting $10,000 of the $11,000 short-term gains into long-term gains.

When Listed options are sold "to close" (i.e., long position is sold), the settlement day is the next business day. The rules concerning the year of recognition are the same as with stock sales as discussed above.

The following table illustrates these rules:

Stock	Cost	Selling amount	Gain (loss)	Date of sale	Terms	Year transaction recognized for tax purposes
A	$10	$15	$5	12/30/82	Regular way	1983
B	10	15	5	12/30/82	For cash	1982
C	10	5	(5)	12/30/82	Regular way	1982
D	10	15	5	11/15/82	Deferred delivery (seller's option)–60 days	1983

Gain or loss on the purchase of stock to close a short sale (settlement five business days after trade date) and on the purchase of a Listed option "to close" the short or written option (settlement one business day after trade date) will be recognized on the settlement date only (see **32.02**).

.05 Transitional Rule Post-June 9, 1981 Sales

Under the 1981 ERTA an investor could have reduced the effective tax rate on long-term capital gains by postponing his sale until after June 9, 1981. Where the investor wished to sell his stock for economic reasons before June 9, 1981, but wanted to take advantage of the lower effective long-term capital gains rate for post-June 9, 1981, sales, he could have sold short ("short against the box") and closed the short sale either in the latter part of 1981 or in 1982.

Those investors who have sold property and are receiving their payments in installments cannot benefit from the lowered long-term capital gains rates unless the actual sale occurred after June 9, 1981. In addition, the lower 20 percent maximum capital gain rate only applies to the net capital gain (net long-term gains less net short-term losses) on post-June 9, 1981, transactions, or if less, the net capital gains for 1981.

Example (a). ABC stock is purchased on February 1, 1980, at $20 per share. On May 1, 1981, ABC is selling at $30 per share, but the investor expects the price of the ABC stock to fall. If the ABC stock is sold on May 1, the investor will pay a higher effective tax rate on the capital gains. However, if the ABC stock is sold "short against the box" on May 1, 1981, at $30 per share and the short position is closed in the latter part of 1981, or in 1982, the capital gains would be subject to lower capital gains rates and the seller has avoided any economic risks. (See **32.02** for applicable rules.)

Example (b). Assume an investor realizes net short-term gains of $100 before June 9, 1981. After June 9, 1981, the investor realizes $80 of net long-term capital gains and $50 of net short-term losses. Although the investor has realized $80 of net capital gains (and $50 of net short-term gains) for 1981, the net capital gains after June 9, 1981, is $30 (net long-term gain of $80 less net short-term losses of $50). Therefore, only $30 of net capital gains qualifies for the reduced capital gains rates.

.06 Installment Sale of Securities in a Private Transaction

An investor who has a large security position with substantial unrealized appreciation, and is negotiating a sale thereof in a private transaction, with part or all of the sale price to be paid after the end of the current year, should consider the availability of the installment sales method of reporting the income realized as a way of deferring part or all of the capital gains tax. The proceeds received after the close of the year now will qualify for installment sale treatment even if payments in the year of sale exceed 30 percent of the selling price. The contract should provide for a minimum of 9 percent annual interest in order to avoid the current imputed interest tax provision. Some tender offers, where debt obligations are issued, have been arranged so as to enable the seller to use the installment method of reporting the gain. Note, however, that certain demand obligations or readily tradeable obligations received in corporate acquisitions are treated as cash payments. (See 43.10.) An installment sale with the seller's spouse, other family members, or trusts for family members may be permitted under certain circumstances. (See **50.**)

An installment sale can be used to convert interest income into capital gains by means of a private installment sale to a brokerage firm, with payment of the sales proceeds deferred for a period of less than one year.

Example (a). T purchased ABC stock for $20 on July 1, 1982, and the stock is selling for $50 a share on October 1, 1982. T sells the stock to a brokerage firm for $55, the sales proceeds to be paid nine months later. The amount of gain and the character of the gain is determined at the time of sale, but the $35 short-term gain is not reported until the sales proceeds are received on July 1, 1983.

Example (b). T purchased ABC stock for $20 on July 1, 1981, and the stock is selling for $50 a share on June 1, 1982. T sells the stock to a brokerage firm for $52 with payment and delivery to take place on August 1, 1982, pursuant to a deferred delivery under NYSE Rule 64(3). (See **5.02.**) The intent is that title passes on the delivery date. Therefore, T will realize a long-term gain of $32 when the transaction is consummated on August 1, 1982.

.07 Tax-free Reorganization

An investor in many corporate reorganizations is given the choice of receiving either cash or stock or both in exchange for his stock. Where his stock has appreciated in value, generally it is desirable to receive stock of the acquiring corporation, thereby deferring the unrealized gain until a subsequent sale of the stock of the acquiring corporation. If an investor has an unrealized loss on his stock, it may be more beneficial to ask for cash in the exchange and thus recognize the loss in the year of the exchange. Note that if there is a pro rata distribution of stock and cash to the shareholders of the acquired corporation in a tax-free reorganization, any loss on the exchange would not be recognized for tax purposes but the receipt of cash may be taxed as a dividend to the extent of any gain.

.08 Exchange of Bonds

Holders of certain U.S. Government bonds may have an opportunity to exchange such bonds for other governmental obligations without recognition of gain. The conversion of Series E bonds into other government obligations has the effect of deferring the interest element until disposition or redemption of the new bonds. Tax-free exchanges of other types of bonds are also permitted. (See **43.10** for discussion dealing with exchange of bonds.)

.09 Contribution or Bargain Sale of Securities

A taxpayer can permanently avoid recognition of gain on appreciated securities by giving them to a charity or can substantially avoid tax on the appreciation by selling them to a charity for a price equal to his basis. The charitable contribution deduction in the former situation is the market value, and in the latter case is the difference between market value and the selling price. See **24** for discussion of the benefits of charitable contribution of low basis appreciated securities.

.10 Offsetting Losses

In lieu of postponing gain on sale, an investor may prefer to offset the recognized gain by selling other securities at a loss or by entering into other types of transactions. The use of Listed options, commodities, or other types of options or securities is discussed below. In addition, an investor may prefer to enter into a tax shelter in order to obtain the desired losses. Substantial first year losses can be obtained by entering into cattle or oil transactions. Real estate shelters, on the other hand, will ordinarily throw off deductions over a period of years. (See **67** for a discussion of tax shelters.) A long-term capital gain can be offset by a capital loss in a corresponding amount or by an ordinary deduction equal to 40 percent of the long-term gain. However, an ordinary deduction may result in only a 20 percent tax savings if the alternative minimum tax is applicable. See discussion in **58**. The use of a capital loss, however, will also reduce the long-term capital gain deduction tax preference for purposes of the alternative minimum tax, but the tax preference will remain if offsetting ordinary deductions are utilized. For example, assume an investor has long-term capital gains of $50,000 and is entitled to a capital gain deduction of $30,000, which is a tax preference item. The remaining taxable gain of $20,000 can be offset by an ordinary deduction of $20,000, thereby eliminating any taxable gain. There will, however, be an outstanding tax preference item of $30,000. If a $50,000 capital loss were realized in the taxable year, the long-term capital gain would be completely eliminated and there would be no tax preference because there would be no long-term capital gain deduction.

3 INSURE PROPER TIMING AND NATURE OF GAIN OR LOSS

An investor may be in a current security position where some positive action on his part will assure him the desired tax result.

.01 Nature and Timing of Capital Losses

Investors should consider taking capital losses within the one-year short-term period in order to have the loss sustained carried forward as a short-term loss. Long-term losses sustained are carried forward as long-term losses in succeeding years and must first offset long-term gains in the year to which carried before offsetting short-term gains. (See discussion of capital loss carry-overs 32.03.) It is important where possible to arrange the year's transactions so that long-term losses are deductible against short-term gains. To the extent that a capital loss offsets a long-term capital gain after 1981, the average investor is reducing income tax at an effective maximum rate of only 20 percent. By timing to offset the capital losses against short-term gains, the investor is reducing income that may otherwise be subject to an effective maximum rate of 50 percent.

Example:	1	2	3	4
Current year long-term gain	$10,000	$10,000	$10,000	–
Current year short-term gain . . .	10,000	10,000	10,000	$10,000
Loss carry-over long-term	–	(10,000)	–	(10,000)
Loss carry-over short-term	–	–	(10,000)	–
Net long-term gain	10,000	–	10,000	–
Net short-term gain	10,000	10,000	–	–
Tax (assume 50 percent bracket)	$ 7,000	$ 5,000	$ 2,000	–

Tax savings on $10,000 long-term capital loss carry-over (compare column 1 with column 2) is $2,000. If the loss carry-over was short-term, such savings would have been $5,000 (compare column 1 with column 3). The same savings can be achieved from a long-term loss carry-over (column 4) only if there are sufficient short-term gains and no long-term gains in the year.

.02 Identification of Securities

Where part of a position in securities is sold or transferred, adequate identification should be made so as to assure proper and desired tax consequences. (See **35.01**.)

Example. Position in XYZ Co.:

Date purchased	Shares	Basis
January 5, 1975	100	$1,000
March 10, 1976	100	3,300
March 15, 1981	100	1,500
September 30, 1982	100	2,800

On December 15, 1982, the investor sells 100 shares for $3,000. By identifying the shares sold, he will recognize either long-term gain (against purchase 1/5/75 or 3/15/81), short-term gain (against purchase 9/30/82) or long-term loss (against purchase 3/10/76). The choice is his. Without proper identification of the certificates delivered, the stock from the 1/5/75 purchase will be deemed the 100 shares sold. (See **35.01**.)

.03 Worthless Securities—When and How to Take a Loss

It is frequently difficult to establish the worthlessness of a security in order to obtain a deduction. Generally, a sale for more than a nominal amount will show that worthlessness did not occur in an earlier year barred by the statute of limitations for refunds. Because of the difficulty of establishing a worthless deduction, it is preferable, where feasible, to sell the stock at a nominal price to an unrelated party, such as a broker. Where the year of worthlessness is in doubt, protective claims for refunds should be filed for each possible year. (See **44**.)

.04 Create Wash Sales

Under certain circumstances it may be desirable to create a wash sale so as to add back, to the basis of the newly acquired security, the disallowed loss and holding period. This might be the case where the investor, within 30 days after the sale of securities at a loss, realizes the disadvantageous timing of the capital transactions. (See discussion of Wash Sale Rules, **36.01**.)

Example (a). T, after holding ABC stock for 8½ months, liquidates his position in 1982 to realize a short-term loss. Subsequently, but within the next 30 days, ABC stock suddenly starts to rise. T now feels that ABC stock has potential appreciation. By repurchasing ABC stock within 30 days after the previous sale, under the wash sale provisions his loss is not recognized for tax purposes and, instead, such loss would increase the basis of the new shares acquired. What is more important is that the ABC stock will start off with an 8½ month holding period, thus according sudden substantial overall gain, long-term capital gain treatment by merely holding ABC stock for an additional three one-half month period.

Example (b). T, on January 2, 1982 purchased 100 shares of ABC stock at $100 per share (Lot 1) and 11 months later on December 2, 1982, purchased an additional 100 shares at $70 per share (Lot 2). By December 20, 1982, ABC has substantially appreciated in value and is selling at $95 per share. If T sells the 200 shares of ABC at $95 per share, he will recognize a net short-term gain of $2,000 ($2,500 gain on Lot 2 less $500 loss on Lot 1).

If instead, T sold 100 shares (Lot 1) on December 20, 1982, the $500 loss sustained is not recognized for tax purposes since T acquired 100 shares of ABC stock (Lot 2) within 30 days prior to such sale. Thus, the $500 loss would increase to $7,500 the basis of the 100 shares acquired on December 2, 1982. More relevant is the new holding period of the remaining 100 shares of ABC stock. The 11-month, 18-day holding period of the Lot 1 shares is added to the 18-day holding period of the Lot 2 100 shares. Thus, for tax purposes, the remaining 100 shares of ABC stock are deemed to have been held for more than one year and a sale of such shares on the next day, December 21, 1982, for $9,500 will result in the $2,000 net gain being treated as long-term.[3]

Example (c). T sells ABC stock and realizes a short-term loss. Subsequently, he discovers that he would obtain a greater tax benefit if the short-term loss were taken in the next year since he has realized long-term

---

[3] Code: 1223(4).

gains in the current year and expects to realize short-term gains in the subsequent year. Therefore, he repurchases the shares within 30 days and resells the stock at a loss in the subsequent year. The short-term loss is then offset against short-term gains and any excess against ordinary income, subject to limitations.

Example (d). In the above example, T realized a long-term loss on the sale, which could only be offset against long-term capital gains, or ordinary income at the rate of two dollars of loss for every dollar of ordinary income. By utilizing the wash sales provisions, he can carry the long-term loss into the next year and apply it against short-term gains.

Example (e). T sold ABC stock in December 1982 and realized a short-term loss which would be offset against long-term gains. He wishes to obtain a 60 percent capital gain deduction on his long-term capital gains. Accordingly, he washes the loss by repurchasing the stock and then realizes a short-term loss by reselling it in the following year and hopefully will be able to offset it against 1983 short-term gains or against ordinary income.

Example (f). T inadvertently sells shares to a related party and the loss is disallowed under Section 267. (See **50.**) Within 30 days he repurchases the shares and later obtains an allowable loss by selling the shares to an unrelated person.

Example (g). T owns 100 shares of ABC stock for several years at $100 per share. ABC stock is currently selling at $40 per share and T wishes to sell his investment and recognize his loss. However, the sale would produce a long-term capital loss of $60 per share. If T had sold or written a Listed Call on ABC stock and now purchases the same Call "open" (i.e., creates what is tantamount to a short against the box in Listed options) and within 30 days sells ABC stock for $40 per share, the $6,000 loss would be disallowed under the wash sales rules and would be added to the basis of the Listed Call purchased open. (The holding period of the option should also include the holding period of the ABC stock. However, this point may be irrelevant.) Thereafter, the long Call is "delivered" against the "short" Call to close. Any gain or loss on the closing of a short Call would be short-term. Accordingly, the $6,000 loss, which otherwise would have been long-term, now may become short-term capital loss (see **38.01** to **38.09** for full discussion of options and an analysis of the technical and administrative procedures concerning option trading).

Example (h). T has owned 100 shares of ABC stock for several years with a tax basis of $100 per share. T wishes to sell the 100 shares at the current market value of $40 and recognize a $6,000 loss. However, he wishes to convert the loss which otherwise would have been a long-term capital loss into a short-term capital loss. T could purchase a Call on ABC stock at a strike price of 40 and sell the ABC stock at 40. The $6,000 loss would be disallowed under the wash sale rules and should be added to the basis of the Call. In addition, the holding period of the stock should also be added to the holding period of the Call. T would exercise the Call and purchase the stock (i.e., ABC stock at $40 per share). The basis of the newly acquired stock would include the basis of the option (i.e., the disallowed loss in the stock sale, $6,000 plus the premium on the Call plus the amount paid for the new stock, $4,000). However, the holding period should completely disappear, and thus the immediate sale of the newly acquired ABC stock would result in a capital loss, which should be accorded short-term capital loss treatment. The cost of accomplishing this objective might be too significant (i.e., commission costs on the exercise of the option and on the sale of the second lot of stock, and, in addition, the premium paid for the Call).

Example (i). T has owned 100 shares of ABC stock for almost one year with a tax basis of $100 per share. T wishes to maintain his position in ABC stock even though ABC is now selling at $40 per share, but does not wish the potential loss to mature to long-term status. T purchases a Put on ABC stock. It should not matter what the striking price of the Put is nor the duration of the Put, because the mere acquisition of the Put should cause the short sale rules to apply, resulting in the loss of the holding period on the 100 shares of stock. The subsequent disposition of the Put or lapse of the Put will start a new holding period for the stock (see **37.03(c)**).

.05 Option Spreads—Create Gain and Loss in Different Taxable Years

The economic as well as the potential tax consequences of various option spread techniques have and will become more important with the increased listing of many more options—both Puts and Calls—

and with the closing of what was perceived to be a loophole by the use of commodity straddles (i.e., deferral of and possibly conversion of short-term gain).

Example. For purposes of this illustration, assume that in 1982 T has realized $20,000 of short-term capital gains from other transactions. On October 1, 1982, when ABC is selling at $50 per share, T purchases 10 Calls on ABC with an exercise price of 45 expiring January 22, 1983 (Jan 45 Calls), for a cost of $7,000 ($7 per share) and sells (writes) 10 Calls on ABC with an exercise price of 50 expiring January 22, 1983 (Jan 50 Calls), for a premium of $4,000 ($4 per share). T has invested $3,000 with a maximum possible gain potential of $2,000 if ABC is selling at 50 or more by January 22, 1983, or a maximum loss potential of $3,000 if ABC is selling at 45 or less by January 22, 1983. It is interesting to note that if ABC remains stable in price, T will make $2,000 on a $3,000 investment in 3½ months. This transaction is referred to as a *bull spread* (i.e., bullish on ABC).

Assume ABC rises to 74 by December 30, 1981, in which case the Jan 45 Call and the Jan 50 Call will be selling at approximately 29 and 24 respectively (parity). T could buy in the short Jan 50 Calls for $24,000 and recognize a $20,000 short-term capital loss in 1981, offsetting the previously recognized capital gains. In order to protect the built-in gain in the Jan 45 Calls, T could write a higher price Call on ABC, sell the Jan 45 Calls, effectively short against the box, or employ other strategies. A sale in 1983 or even on December 31, 1982 (settlement in 1983), for $29,000 will cause the gain of $22,000 to be recognized in 1983 (when the maximum tax rate is 50 percent).

.06 Obligations Issued at a Discount

An investor may elect in any taxable year to include in income annually the increase in the redemption value of certain noninterest-bearing obligations issued at a discount, such as Series E savings bonds. Thus, if it is advantageous to increase income of a given year, the election can be made. If an election is not made during his lifetime, it can be made on the deceased investor's final return. (See **19.02.**)

.07 Sale of Municipal Bonds at a Loss

Many tax-exempt bonds are selling far below their original offering price because of the increase in interest rates since the tax-exempt bonds were issued. Holders of these bonds have the choice of selling them at a loss or holding them until maturity and receiving the face value of the bonds upon redemption. A sale of these bonds gives the investor not only a capital loss, which can be offset against capital gains and to a limited extent against income, but also provides an opportunity to upgrade the investments or purchase bonds with proportionately higher yields. For example, T purchased $10,000 of 8 percent municipal bonds, which mature in 1987 and which are presently selling at 80, or $8,000 for all of the bonds. By selling the bonds T would recognize a $2,000 capital loss. The proceeds are then reinvested in 12 percent tax-exempts, thereby increasing the tax-free interest yield from $800 to $960. The current use of the capital loss plus the increased interest yield may more than offset the loss of $2,000 upon redemption of the bonds at maturity. Note that the wash sales rules do not apply to the losses where securities which are not substantially identical are acquired.

4 PROTECT APPRECIATION ON LONG-TERM POSITION WITH POSSIBILITY OF ADDITIONAL LONG-TERM CAPITAL GAINS

If the investor has held a profitable position for more than one year and wants to protect the long-term capital gain, he may consider selling the stock short against the box and simultaneously purchasing a Call. Thus, for the cost of a Call, he is both ensuring his present economic gain and will also obtain the benefit of any future appreciation in the stock.

Example. T, on June 1, 1981, purchased 100 shares of ABC stock at $20. On June 2, 1982, ABC stock is selling at $30. T could buy one Jan ABC 30 at $3 ($300) and sell short 100 shares of ABC at $30. If ABC declines below $30 by the middle of January 1983, the long position could be delivered against the short position resulting in a $1,000 long-term capital gain, and the worthless Call would result in a $300 short-term capital loss. If ABC should rise to $50, the 100 share long position could be sold, resulting in $3,000 long-term capital gain, and a $300 long-term capital loss would result under the short sale rules on the exercise of the Call and delivery of the stock to close the short position. The net long-term capital gain would be $2,700. Thus, T was able to insure a minimum long-term capital gain at a cost of $300, and, if successful, as in the example, obtain an additional economic gain of $1,700 for a total of $2,700 of long-term capital gain.

---

5 CONVERT SHORT-TERM GAIN INTO LONG-TERM GAIN

Investors owning appreciated securities or options for less than one year may wish to protect their economic gain and still maintain their position in order to have the recognized gain treated as long-term. The after-tax benefits that can be derived from converting short-term gains into long-term gains by means of the ensuing transactions are illustrated in the following chart.

Correlation between after-tax benefits of
short-term and long-term gains

Percent tax bracket of investor	Short-term	Long-term
50	$10	$6¼*
45	10	6¾
40	10	7⅛
35	10	7½
30	10	8

*A $6.25 long-term capital gain is equivalent to a $10 short-term capital gain when measured in terms of after-tax profit to the taxpayer in the 50 percent tax bracket. Thus, an investor could incur expenses or losses of more than $3 to obtain long-term capital gains and still retain more after-tax dollars than realizing a $10 short-term gain.

.01 Sale of Call on Appreciated Long Position

An investor who has owned appreciated stock for less than one year can sell a Call on the stock which will not expire until the stock has been held for more than one year. The investor will thus give the purchaser of the Call an option to acquire the investor's stock at a specific price within a specified period of time. If the stock should have a further moderate increase in value, and the Call is exercised toward the end of its term, the investor will be assured of long-term capital gain to the extent that the Call price plus the amount received on the sale of the Call exceeds the basis of the stock. If the stock has substantially increased in value, the investor could buy other shares of the stock in the open market to deliver against the Call or, if dealing in Listed Calls, buy the Call long in a closing transaction, recognize a short-term loss, and sell his long position for greater long-term gain. Due to the increased holding period requirements, the Call period may also have to be for a longer duration to ensure long-term capital gain treatment.

Example. T acquires 100 shares of ABC on 2/1/82 at $10 per share. On 12/18/82 ABC is selling at $30 per share. T sells a Listed Call in ABC at $30 due 2/19/83 for the equivalent of $2 per share ($200). If the ABC stock is selling on or about 2/18/83 at slightly above $30, the holder of the Call will exercise it and T will recognize a long-term capital gain of $22 per share ($30 plus $2 less $10). If ABC stock is selling at $40, T would buy the Listed Call to close for approximately $1,000, the equivalent of $10 per share, thus recognizing a short-term capital loss of $8 per share. He could also sell his long position with a basis of $10 for $40, recognizing a long-term gain of $30. His net economic gain is still $22, but $30 is long-term gain and $8 is short-term loss.

If the market value of the stock should fall, the investor is economically protected to the extent of the premium received on the Call, which would be taxed as a short-term gain (a lapse of a Call written before September 1, 1976, resulted in ordinary income). Under the facts in the example, an investor in the 50 percent tax bracket will realize greater economic gain after taxes by waiting for a more than one year holding period before selling, provided that ABC stock stays above $21.25 (long-term gain of at least $11.25 netting $9 plus $1 of after-tax income on $2 proceeds from the sale of the Call, is equivalent to the $20 of short-term gain which would have been realized from a sale at $30). Thus unless there is a substantial break in the market, the investor will be assured of some long-term capital gain with a hedge against a decline to the extent of the premium received on the sale of the Call.

If the Call is sold initially at a price below the market ("in the money"), the investor will increase the chances that the Call will be exercised, so that the increased premium for writing the more valuable Call will be given long-term capital gain treatment. Thus, in the example above, if a Listed Call on ABC at $20 were being traded, it probably would be selling close to its intrinsic value of $10 per share with very little additional premium, if any, for the time value. Assuming a selling price equivalent to $10 per share ($1,000), T, by writing such an "in the money" Listed Call, will be assured of exercise and long-term capital gain (on the assumption of exercise after February 1, 1983) as long as the stock remains above $20 per share.

.02 Deferred Delivery under NYSE Rule 64(3) (Seller's Option)

The investor may take advantage of the current market price and still prolong his holding period for up to 60 days. This is accomplished by selling at today's market price, and contracting that payment and delivery will take place on a specified date within 60 days following the date of contract, with all dividends to stockholders of record before the delivery date belonging to the seller. Special arrangements must be made to have the dividends accrue to the seller. Otherwise, under the normal deferred delivery transaction, dividends payable after the contract date would go to the buyer, which might affect the rule on when the sale takes place. The intent of the parties is that title passes on the delivery date. Thus, an investor who has a holding period of between 10 months and one year could convert unrealized short-term gain into long-term gain without any economic risk. It is understood that the Treasury's position in such a case is that the contract date is not regarded as controlling, and that the sale does not take place until the delivery date. A slight reduction in sales price is generally required to obtain a purchaser for deferred delivery stock.

Example. T acquired XYZ stock on February 1, 1982, at $30 per share. On December 15, 1982, the market value has risen to $64, at which time T wishes to liquidate his position and thereby protect his gain. By selling on a deferred delivery basis, for delivery on February 2, 1983, usually at a $1 to $2 discount (assuming no usual dividend record date falls in the interim), T will recognize in 1983 long-term gain of approximately $32 per share ($62 discounted selling price less $30 cost) in lieu of recognizing $34 short-term gain per share in 1982. T, who is in the 50 percent tax bracket, will earn in after-tax dollars, $24 per share under the deferred delivery sale, in lieu of $17 per share had he sold the stock in the regular way on December 15, 1982.

.03 Selling Short Against Appreciated Calls to Insure Gain

Where an investor has held a long-term Unlisted Call for less than one year, he may economically protect himself against a decline in the market by selling short a comparable number of shares of the underlying stock. If, after the one-year holding period, the Call is still appreciated, he can sell the Call, recognizing long-term gain, and close out the short sale, recognizing short-term gain or loss. In the event the market continues to rise after the short sale, a sale of the Call after the one-year holding period will result in an increased long-term capital gain and the closing of the short position would create a short-term loss. In any event, the investor has locked in his economic profit. The Call and the underlying stock are not considered substan-

tially identical so as to come within the short sale rules.[4] (See
37.04.)

Example. T acquires on March 1, 1982, a one-year, ten-day Unlisted
Call on 100 shares of ABC stock at $30 per share for a cost of $400. On
February 1, 1983, ABC stock is selling at $50. By selling short 100 shares
at $50, T is assured of economic gain of at least $1,600 ($5,000 short sale
amount less a cost of $3,000 for the stock if purchased and $400 for the
Call). Assume that on March 1, 1983, ABC stock is selling at $70. T would
sell the Call for approximately $4,000 (difference between market value of
$70 per share and the Call price of $30 per share), recognizing $3,600 of
long-term gain (after deducting cost of $400 for the Call). T would sustain
a short-term loss of $2,000 on the closing of the short sale. His economic
pretax gain is still $1,600. If the ABC stock had instead been selling at
$15 on March 1, T would realize $3,500 short-term gain on the closing of
the short sale, a long-term loss of $400 on the expiration of the Call (loss
would be short-term if the Call were sold prior to the one-year holding
period), for a net economic gain of $3,100.

---

6 CREATE SHORT-TERM CAPITAL LOSS AND 60 PERCENT LONG-TERM CAPITAL GAIN

.01 Mixed Straddles—Cash and Carry Transactions

Sophisticated investors will find interesting economic opportunities in cash and carry transactions; and, if successful, interesting tax
implications will occur. T, who is expecting gold to fall in value, purchases 100 ounces of spot gold at $450 per ounce (refer to as one
warrant) and simultaneously sells one regulated futures contract
(Futures) three months out at $470 per ounce (spread represents an
annual interest yield of 18 percent). Assume that one week later
gold has fallen by $30 per ounce, such that the spot gold (or war-
rant) is worth $420 and the Futures (taking into consideration
reduced value without any change in interest rates) is selling at $438
per ounce. By collapsing both positions, T will lose $3,000 on the
spot commodity. (Interest for the one week that had to be capitalized on the spot commodity has been disregarded for purposes of the
illustration.) Such loss will be a short-term capital loss. The repurchase of the short Futures would result in a gain of $3,200, of which
40 percent would be short-term ($1,280) and 60 percent long-term

---

[4] Rev. Rul. 58-384, C.B. 1958-2, 410.

($1,920). Thus, a net short-term loss of $1,720 and long-term capital gain of $1,920 would result from the transaction under the new mixed straddle and commodity Futures rules (see **40.03(c)**). Of course, an opposite economic and tax effect would occur if gold had risen in value (i.e., the gain on the spot gold would be short-term and the loss on the Futures would be 60 percent long-term and 40 percent short-term). NOTE: short-term trading, both on the long and short side of commodity Futures, have in the opinion of the authors become more advantageous under the new tax law.

7 CONVERT CAPITAL LOSS INTO ORDINARY DEDUCTION

An investor may have incurred a substantial capital loss and does not expect to realize offsetting capital gains in the near future. The capital loss may be offset against ordinary income, within limitations, but it may take many years before the investor could fully utilize the capital loss in this manner. He may be of advanced age and there may be a good likelihood that he will die before obtaining the full benefit of his capital loss. Any unused capital loss would expire with his demise. In addition, if the loss is long-term, it would require $2 of the long-term loss to offset $1 of ordinary income, so that the investor would in effect lose the benefit of one half his loss. A capital gain created to offset the large capital loss would result, in effect, in "tax-free income," while the ordinary deduction would offset ordinary income. (See **9** for discussion of creating capital gain and ordinary deduction.)

8 CREATE LONG-TERM GAIN AND SHORT-TERM LOSS

The ensuing transactions may create the desired short-term capital loss which will offset existing short-term capital gains, or short-term capital gains created from naked or covered option writing (see **9.02**), or other similar transactions, and simultaneously create the desired long-term capital gain.

.01 Arbitraging Securities Not Substantially Identical

Long-term capital gains can be obtained in arbitrage situations if the long position is held open for more than one year and if the securities sold short are not "substantially identical" to the long securities for purposes of the short sale rules.[5] (See **37.04**.)

---

[5] Rev. Rul. 62-153, C.B. 1962-2, 186.

> **Example.** X and Y corporations plan to merge and the stock of X corporation will be exchanged evenly for shares of Y corporation. Prior to approval by the shareholders, the two securities are not considered to be substantially identical. (See **37.04**.) X stock is selling at $20 and Y stock is selling at $22. The investor buys X stock and sells Y stock short. It is immaterial that the X stock subsequently becomes "substantially identical" to the Y stock. It should also be immaterial that after an exchange for X stock, Y stock is now held in a long position. The exchange should not be deemed an acquisition of the Y stock bringing into play the short sale rules. (See **37.03**.)
>
> The closing of the long position of the Y stock received in the exchange against the short position of Y after the requisite one-year holding period will result in long-term gain to the extent of the initial spread of $2 per share. If the value of Y stock at the time of delivery rises above $22 per share, then the Y stock received on the exchange should be sold in order to recognize long-term capital gains greater than the initial spread of $2 per share. The short position should be covered through the purchase in the open market of Y stock, resulting in the recognition of a short-term capital loss which could be utilized to offset short-term capital gains. The net economic gain will be equal to the initial spread of $2 per share, but the character of the gain and loss for tax purposes will be different.

.02 Acquisition of Shares in a Mutual Fund

An investor in a high tax bracket and having large short-term capital gains would welcome the opportunity to create short-term capital losses and long-term capital gains, and thereby convert his realized short-term capital gains into long-term capital gains. The investor should consider buying shares in a mutual fund immediately prior to a large capital gain distribution, hold the mutual fund for more than 31 days, and then liquidate his position.[6] The market value of the fund will drop approximately equivalent to the amount of the capital gain distribution if there is no other change in the value of the assets of the fund for the 31-day period. The investor will treat the capital gains distribution as long-term and the loss on the sale of the fund as short-term. However, the investor is subjected to the vagaries of the market for the 31-day period. The "loading" charges of some mutual funds would increase the loss on the sale to such an extent as to make this device uneconomic. However, shares of so-called no-load

---

[6] Code section 852(b)(4) necessitates a 31-day holding period; otherwise the loss on sales of the stock would be treated as long-term.

funds may be available. Shares of a "close-end" mutual fund could also be utilized in a similar manner; however, a commission expense will be incurred upon acquisition and subsequent sale of such shares.

Example. T purchases on November 15, 1982, 1,000 shares of ABC Fund (a no-load fund) for $20 per share. ABC Fund distributes a $2 long-term capital gain dividend. T will recognize long-term capital gains on the receipt of the $2,000 distribution even though he has held ABC stock for merely one day. The value of ABC Fund will fall to $18 per share. Assuming that there are no changes in the value of ABC Fund for the next 31 days, T would sell the 1,000 shares after December 16, 1982, and realize a $2,000 short-term capital loss (cost of $20,000 less selling amount of $18,000).

---

9 CREATE CAPITAL GAIN AND ORDINARY DEDUCTION

Certain forms of investments discussed below, by their component steps and tax treatment, had created capital gain and ordinary deduction. Many investors have avoided these types of investments because of apparent complexities and oftentimes undesired short-term capital gain results. However, sophisticated investors have realized that the pure economics (i.e., the profit potential) is overriding, and have accepted these forms of investments as the most desirable from a risk-reward viewpoint. Until the change in the law, they looked to additional types of investments, such as the commodity straddle transactions to offset the short-term capital gains and create long-term capital gains.

Sometimes the separate tax treatment of each component of these transactions can be beneficial to the taxpayer without any further transactions. For example, investors with substantial capital loss carry-overs will effectively have the short-term capital gain treated as tax-free income.

.01 Cash and Carry Commodity Transaction

Prior to the 1981 ERTA, effective June 24, 1981, a capital gain and ordinary deduction could be created by purchasing a spot commodity contract and selling a commodity future contract at a greater sales price. The investor hopes to make money in this transaction due to expectations of changes in interest rates, possible lock-in of "positive interest carry," or potential closing of the spread (or even the inversion thereof) between the spot price and the future price. (See 40.03(g) for more details.) The commodity received on the spot contract would be stored in a warehouse and the warehousing expense and interest charge incurred in borrowing to carry the commodity are deductible against ordinary income under the prior law. Upon closing the Futures contract, the investor would realize a capital gain (generally short-term, unless the commodity was held for more than one year).

Example. T purchases on May 1, 1981, 20,000 ounces of silver at $9.80 per ounce and sells four contracts of July 1982, silver at $10.22 per ounce. Based upon the assumptions used, T will have a pretax profit of $1,200 and an after-tax profit of $2,900. Several observations concerning the illustration are relevant.

1. The pretax profit will vary depending upon the relationship of the cost of financing when compared to the spread between the spot price and the Future price (i.e., $10.22 − $9.80 = $.42 spread per ounce). Note that a cash and carry transaction would not be valid for tax purposes if the interest rates are so high that the investor could not under reasonable circumstances realize an economic gain.
2. In lieu of cash, U.S. Treasury bills are accepted as original margin on the sale of July 1982 silver (minimum face amount of $10,000). Fluctuations in the price of the Futures contract will result in changes in margin requirements (variation margin).
3. A shorter-term Futures contract could have been sold, causing the locked-in spread to be treated as short-term capital gain. (The holding period of the spot silver must be more than one year to be accorded long-term capital gain treatment.) A simultaneous commodity straddle transaction in silver Futures could have been created to defer the gain into a subsequent year and convert it into long-term capital gain.
4. The investor should not enter into the spot commodity transaction in a jurisdiction where a sales tax liability might be applicable to the gross purchase amount.

While deductions can no longer be obtained for interest expense, storage, and other expenses while holding the commodity, there is still the potential of obtaining long-term capital gains. By buying the spot commodity with little or no margin, the investor is assured of long-term capital gains because of the spread between the two positions. If the short Futures contract goes up in value, an investor can realize 60 percent of the gain as long-term and 40 percent as short-term regardless of whether the Futures contract is sold before the required more-than-six-months holding period or marked-to-market at the end of the year. Any loss on sale of the commodity would be short-term and could be offset against the short-term gain realized on the Futures contract or other short-term gains. The commodity straddle rules apply if the investor elects not to include the regulated Futures contract under the marked-to-market rule. Apparently the Treasury is taking the position that the straddles rules apply even if an election is made. See discussion of mixed straddles starting on 40.03(c).

.02 Covered Option Writing

Covered option writing (i.e., writing one Call for each 100 shares of stock owned or, in the alternative, writing one Put for each 100 shares of stock sold short) may result in a reduction of risk of loss under adverse market conditions and increased economic yield on his investment position. Covered option writing on a fully margined basis will tend to further increase the economic yield under stable or positive market conditions and will create larger capital gains and larger interest expense deductions. (See 38 for detailed discussion of options.)

Example. On September 30, 1982, T purchases 1,000 shares of ABC stock at $28½ and writes 10 ABC Calls, Jan 25s, for a premium of $650 each ($6½ per share) or a total of $6,500. Thus, T is selling to an investor the right to purchase 1,000 shares of ABC stock at $25 per share any time between September 30, 1982, and January 22, 1983. The intrinsic value of the Call is $3½ per share (the difference between $28½ fair market value and $25 striking price of the Call), and the balance of the premium of the Call of $3 per share represents the time value portion. Assuming no change in price of the underlying stock, the time value generally diminishes as the Call approaches expiration. Disregarding commission expense, the maximum economic gain that T could realize, which will occur as long as ABC stock stays at or above $25 per share, is $3,000, which will be short-term capital gain in 1983, if the Call is exercised after December 23, 1982. This amount will be reduced by the interest cost on the borrowed funds of $14,250 by approximately $400, most of which will be deducted in 1982. The net cash amount invested by T is approximately $8,000 (50 percent of $28,500, less the Call premium of $6,500). T cannot incur an economic loss unless ABC stock falls below $22 per share ($28½ cost less option premium of $6½). The amount of the time value premium is a function of the volatility of the underlying stock (period of time to expiration and the relationship of intrinsic value to total premium). Generally, as the intrinsic value increases, the time premium will shrink, irrespective of time to expiration.

If the Call should expire unexercised (i.e., ABC stock is selling below $25), the $6,500 premium will be short-term capital gain in 1983. If ABC stock is also sold (e.g., sold at $24 per share), the resulting loss will be a short-term capital loss of $4,500.

If ABC should rise to $40 per share, T may wish to buy, in a closing transaction, the ABC Jan 25s for the equivalent of $15 per share ($15,000 for 10 Calls) and recognize a short-term capital loss of $8,500. T could write higher striking price and longer duration ABC Calls (e.g., Oct 35s) with a view towards obtaining additional yield and maturing his stock position for long-term capital gain potential. The short sale rules do not apply to this type of transaction.

Options written prior to September 2, 1976, were accorded ordinary income or loss treatment on a closing transaction or if the Call lapsed unexpired. The only Listed options were Calls. Thus, in the above situation, the $8,500 loss would have been ordinary loss under the prior law.

.03 Treasury Bills, Futures, and Options

Because of the restrictions placed on Listed options and tax shelters by the 1976 TRA, some investors had turned to Treasury bills and Treasury bill Futures as a means of obtaining an ordinary deduction and capital gains. Treasury bills or Treasury bill Futures acquired after June 23, 1981, can no longer be used for the purpose of obtaining an ordinary deduction. (See **41.03.**)

Example (a). T establishes a Treasury bill spread (i.e., purchases the January 10, 1981, Treasury bills and sells the February 7, 1981, short). The nature of the Treasury bills, since they are discounted paper, is that, at the expiration of a period of time, a loss will be realized in the short position with a corresponding "gain" on the long position. Accordingly, T will buy in the short position to establish an ordinary loss and resell another short position to continue the hedge. In the subsequent year both positions will be terminated. The resulting net gain will be ordinary income. The economics of the transaction are that the one-month spread between the long and short position can produce income, provided interest rates rise. In the alternative, a loss will be sustained if interest rates decline. In addition, a change in the yield curve could have significant economic effect.

> **Example (b).** In lieu of establishing a long position in Treasury bills, T could in Example (a) purchase Treasury bill Futures as his long position, which are traded on a listed exchange. However, a hedge would not be established. Instead, gain or loss on the Futures contract will depend upon changes in the yield rate. The gain sustained on the Treasury bill Futures will be capital gain (see **41.03**). Thus, if the position was held for more than six months, the gain would be long-term capital gain. A Treasury bill Future is a commodity traded on a listed exchange and, accordingly, only the six-month holding period would be required to establish long-term capital gain.
>
> Any short-term gain generated on this spread might be converted into a long-term gain by means of a commodity straddle entered into before June 24, 1981.

A simple means of deferring ordinary income can be obtained by purchasing a large quantity of Treasury bills on margin. An interest deduction can be taken in the current year and the Treasury bill income is not reportable until the bills mature in the following year. Repurchase agreements, executed on a 30-day basis, with longer-term Treasuries might be the only way to show a potential economic profit on the assumption that interest rates remain constant. However, with the current volatile interest rates, it should be easier to demonstrate a profit motive for shorter-term Treasuries.

.04   Selling Short before Ex-Dividend Date

An investor intending to establish a short position should enter into the short sale before the ex-dividend date in order to obtain an ordinary deduction for the amount paid as a dividend on the short sale and thus have the resulting equivalent amount potentially available as capital gain. (However, if the dividend is a stock dividend or liquidating dividend, the Treasury will not allow the deduction.) Generally the market value of the stock on the ex-dividend date falls in an amount equal to the dividend paid. If the investor subsequently covers his short position and there is no other variation in the value of the stock, he will realize a short-term capital gain approximately equivalent to the amount paid as a dividend on the short sale. The same possibility may exist with respect to selling short a flat bond where a significant arrearage interest will be made in the near future. A short-term gain might be desired in order to offset short-term losses that would otherwise offset long-term gains. However, it should be noted that where the sole purpose of the transaction is tax avoidance, the deductibility of the dividend paid may be questioned. (See **48.06.**)

> **Example (a).** ABC stock is scheduled to go ex-dividend a $1 dividend on December 15, 1982; T wishes to sell the stock short at $60. If he establishes the short position prior to December 15, 1982, he will have to pay $1 per share for such dividend, for which he becomes entitled to a $1 per share ordinary deduction. Assuming no other changes in market value, ABC stock should fall in price to $59 thereby creating a potential short-term gain of $1 per share. However, if T waits until December 15, 1982, he will establish his short position at a price of $59 per share, the market value on that day. T will not have any ordinary deduction, nor the built-in potential capital gain of $1 per share.

> **Example (b).** ABC 6½ percent debentures are trading flat at $86. An arrearage interest payment of 2½ years or $16.25 will be paid on December 1, 1982. T wishes to sell the debenture short on the assumption that the debenture, after the interest payment, will fall in price more than $16.25. Assuming no other changes in market value, ABC debenture should decrease in price to $69.75 thereby creating a potential short-term gain of $162.50 per $1,000 bond. T will have to pay $162.50 per $1,000 bond on the short side which should be an ordinary deduction (see **48.06**).

.05 Sale and Repurchase of Appreciated Bonds

Holders of taxable bonds which are selling at a premium and have appreciated in value, for example, because of changes in the going interest rate, should sell the bonds, and shortly thereafter repurchase an equal number of the same bonds. Gains on the sale of the bonds held for more than one year are taxed at the lower capital gains rate. The premium paid on the subsequent repurchase (not attributable to any conversion privilege) may be deducted against ordinary income through amortization usually computed to be the maturity date.[7] (See **43.02(b).**)

> **Example.** T owns $50,000 of 15 percent noncallable and nonconvertible XYZ bonds due January 1, 1988, which he acquired at par in 1981.

---

[7] Rev. Rul.55-353, C.B. 1955-1, 381.

These bonds on January 2, 1983, are selling at 105 and are therefore worth $52,500. If T sells these bonds, he will recognize a long-term capital gain of $2,500. Assuming he still wants to maintain his investment position in these bonds, he would repurchase them at 105 for $52,500. T should then elect to amortize the $2,500 premium over the remaining term of the bonds. Thus, T would be entitled to a deduction against ordinary income of $500 per year ($2,500 amortized over the period of 1983 through 1988). T, in the 50 percent tax bracket, may pay a capital gain tax of $500 in 1983, but would have available ordinary deductions each year, which might result in tax savings of $250 annually or $1,250 over the five-year period.

.06 Deep Discount Bonds

When interest rates are at high levels, many high-grade low-interest-rate bonds will be selling at substantial discounts. Investors who anticipate a decline in the interest rates are in a position to make substantial gains by purchasing these deep discount bonds on the highest margin available. The interest income on these bonds is taxable at ordinary income rates, but the spread between the purchase price and the amount received on sale or redemption is taxed at capital gain rates. The interest paid on the bank loans is deductible (see **48.05** for a discussion of limitations on investment interest expense) against ordinary income. Moreover, the higher the income tax bracket of the investor, the greater will be his after-tax gain. This type of transaction was even more attractive when the interest expense was prepaid, but a current deduction for prepayment is no longer permitted.

Example. T, in the 50 percent bracket, purchases on February 1, 1982, $100,000 of XYZ 4 percent bonds due February 1, 1987, at 65, which is financed by a bank loan for $65,000 at 16 percent interest. Assuming the bonds are redeemed at par at maturity, the following are the pretax and after-tax results:

	Pretax results		*After-tax results*	
Interest income	$20,000		$10,000	
Gain on redemption	35,000	$55,000	28,000	$38,000
Less: Interest paid	52,000		26,000	
Commissions	250	52,250	200	26,200
Net gain		$ 2,750		$11,800

.07 Nondividend Paying Stock

Long-term gain and ordinary deduction can also be obtained by purchasing on margin nondividend-paying stock of a corporation which plows all of the corporate profits back into the business. The average investor can deduct the interest paid on the margin and pay capital gains tax on sale of the stock. (See **48.05** for discussion of limitations on the deductibility of investment interest expense.)

Example. On January 2, 1982, T purchases on 50 percent margin 100 shares of ABC stock for $50,000. T pays the maximum amount of deductible interest in 1982, and deducts this amount in the year paid. On January 3, 1983, the stock has appreciated in value to $60,000 and T sells the stock and pays a capital gains tax on the $10,000 gain.

.08 Detached Bond Coupons

An investor can realize capital gains in lieu of interest income by buying detached bond coupons at a discount and selling them just before the coupons mature. The gain will be long-term if the bond coupons were held for more than one year. This investment can result in tax-free income if the investor has unused capital losses to offset the capital gain realized on the sale. The investor can also use this investment as a means of converting ordinary income into capital gain by borrowing the funds needed to purchase the bond coupons. However, the transactions may be disregarded for tax purposes if the interest expense greatly exceeds the discount on the bond coupons and there is little likelihood that the investor can realize an economic profit from the transaction before tax considerations. (See **43.09(f)** for detailed discussion of detached bond coupons.) Proposed legislation would affect this transaction.

.09 Tax Shelters

Certain types of tax shelters can also generate ordinary deductions and capital gains upon disposition. Real estate investments can still produce losses during the early years (but there are transitional rules limiting construction period deductions except for low-cost housing) and a gain on sale will be treated as capital gains after first recapturing certain depreciation in excess of straight-line depreciation. An oil and gas investment will throw off larger deductions in the first year, but under the new rules gain on a subsequent sale will be treated as ordinary income to the extent of excess intangible drilling expenses. Investing in a breeder cattle program for a period of approximately five years will also result in ordinary deductions in the early years and capital gains primarily from the sale of cattle born after commencement of the cattle breeder program. (See 67 for a more detailed discussion of tax shelters.) One of the benefits of tax shelters is that income generally will be deferred for a longer period of time than through the use of securities or commodities. The economic risks involved, the costs of entering into the transaction, and the capital requirements must also be considered before a decision is reached as to the best type of investment to accomplish the desired economic and tax goals.

10 CREATE CAPITAL GAINS–OFFSET BY CAPITAL LOSSES

.01 Forward Conversions–Listed Options

With the expansion of trading in Listed Calls and Puts in recent years and high interest rates, an interesting opportunity exists for the sophisticated investor to generate annual income of 15 to 20 percent in the form of primarily short-term capital gains. Those taxpayers who have capital losses will effectively generate tax-free income. In addition, those taxpayers who have current unrelated short-term capital gains might have an opportunity to generate short-term capital losses this year from conversion transactions and short-term capital gain in the succeeding taxable year. Thus, a net economic gain in the form of short-term capital gain, with the possibility of "timing differences," can be obtained from forward conversion investments for individual taxpayers.

> **Example.** On October 19, 1982, taxpayer purchases 1,000 shares of ABC at $51 per share, 10 Puts on ABC with an exercise price of 50 expiring January 22, 1983 (Jan 50 Puts), at a cost of $3,000 ($3 per share) and sells (writes) 10 Calls on ABC with an exercise price of 50 expiring January 22, 1983 (Jan 50 Calls), for a premium of $6,000 ($6 per share). The taxpayer will be guaranteed a net economic profit of $2,300 irrespective of the price of the stock in January 1983, resulting in an annual yield of 19¼ percent as shown below. The Put will protect him in the event of a decline in price, whereas the stock will be called away if the price of the stock rises.

Cost of 1,000 shares of ABC at $51	$51,000
Cost of 10 ABC Jan 50 Puts	3,000
Estimated total transaction costs	300
Total	$54,300
Less: Premium received–sale of 10 ABC Jan 50 Calls . . .	6,000
Net out-of-pocket cost	$48,300

Profit on close of transaction:		
Put or Call proceeds, 1,000 at $50	$50,000	
Net out-of-pocket cost	48,300	
Net profit	$ 1,700	
Estimated dividend income for quarter	600	
Total profit		$ 2,300
Effective Annual Yield		19¼%

The $2,300 net economic profit consists of $600 dividend income in 1982 or 1983 with the balance of $1,700 considered to be short-term capital gain taxable in 1983.

In the event that the price of ABC moves substantially at year end, the taxpayer might collapse the loss side of the transaction, recognizing such capital loss in 1982 and the gain side in 1983 while still earning approximately the same effective annual yield.

11 OBTAIN LONG-TERM GAINS IN A DECLINING MARKET– ACQUISITION OF A PUT IN LIEU OF SELLING SHORT

If the investor is bearish with regard to a particular stock, he should consider the purchase of a 1-year, 10-day (or longer term) Unlisted Put in lieu of selling the stock short. In the event his expectations of a falling market are realized, he may sell the Put just prior to its expiration (or after a one-year hold period), recognizing long-term gain. (See **12.01** and **38.04(b)**.) The investor's gain will be lower, as compared to a short sale of the stock (by the cost of the Put), but the gain will be taxed at substantially lower rates. On the other hand, had the investor sold the stock short, any gain on the closing of the short sale would be short-term. (See **37**.) If the stock should rise in price, the investor should sell the Put prior to the one-year holding period in order to have the loss sustained treated as short-term. (See **38.04(b)**.) His loss would be limited to the cost of the Put. However, with a short sale, his loss could be substantially greater. In view of the fact that the amount of funds necessary to acquire a Put may be substantially less than the funds necessary to margin a short sale, greater economic leverage may be obtained by acquiring a Put. The economic leverage may be further increased through the acquisition of a "discounted Put" (the option price of the stock is below the current market price) at a substantially reduced cost, but with the potential profit also reduced to the extent of the discount. The cost of acquiring a Put for more than one year in order to obtain long-term capital gain treatment is more expensive than the previous requirement of a six-month holding period. There are also additional risks that prices will increase because of the extended holding period, but, on the other hand, the investor will also have a greater period of time to fulfill his expectations and he can sell or exercise his Put, if required, before the requisite one-year holding period is met.

Example. T expects XYZ stock selling at $30 per share to fall in price. T purchases a one-year 10-day Unlisted Put for $400, which gives him the right to sell 100 shares of XYZ stock at $30 during the term of the option. Assume that at the end of one year, XYZ stock is selling for $20. T would then sell the Put for approximately $1,000, realizing a net long-term gain of $600 ($1,000 less the $400 cost of the Put). If T had sold short 100 shares of XYZ stock, he would have realized approximately $1,000 economic gain, which would be treated as short-term.

If T were in the 50 percent tax bracket, the long-term gain of $600 would produce $480 in after-tax income, while the short-term gain of $1,000 would produce $500 in after-tax income. If XYZ stock had instead risen to $50 at the end of the one-year period, T would sustain only a $400 short-term loss (assuming he had sold the Put just prior to the one-year holding period) as compared to a $2,000 short-term loss had he sold short 100 shares of XYZ stock. T's investment in the Put would be lower if he acquired a discounted Put (e.g., $300 for a Put on XYZ stock at $27 where the market value of the stock was $30 per share).

---

12 OBTAIN LONG-TERM GAINS ON APPRECIATED OPTIONS

.01 Sale of a Call or Put Held for More than One Year

Where the investor holds an Unlisted Call, which has appreciated in value, for more than one year, and he does not wish to maintain an interest in the stock, the Call should be sold in order to convert the recognized gain into a long-term gain. If the Call is exercised and the underlying stock is sold within one year, the resulting gain would constitute a short-term gain. (See 38.04(d).)

Similar action should be taken with respect to an Unlisted Put held for more than one year. Although the acquisition of a Put is considered a short sale for purposes of applying the short sale rules, under other tax provisions dealing with options the Put is treated as a capital asset in the hands of the investor and its sale results in long- or short-term capital gain or loss depending upon the holding period.

Example. An investor on June 1, 1982, purchased a one-year, 10-day Unlisted Call on 100 shares of XYZ stock at $30 per share for $400. On June 2, 1983, XYZ stock is selling at $50 per share. The investor should sell the Call in lieu of exercising it and then sell the stock. The sale of the Call will produce a long-term capital gain of approximately $1,600, while the sale of the stock received on exercise of the Call will result in approximately the same amount of short-term gain.

.02 Adjustments to Unlisted Put or Call Option Price— Dividends, Rights, Etc.

Where the option price of an Unlisted Put or Call is to be adjusted because of any dividends, and the like, the time the option is exercised may be an important consideration. For example, where an extraordinary fully taxable dividend has been declared, the exercise of the Call after the ex-dividend date would reduce the acquisition price to the investor with a possible greater capital gain upon subsequent disposition. The dividend in this instance would be taxable to the previous holder of the stock, not the investor. Similarly, an investor should exercise a Put prior to the ex-dividend date in order to produce a greater long-term capital gain (assuming the stock was held for more than one year prior to the acquisition of the Put so as to avoid the short sales rules). If the Put is exercised after the ex-dividend date, the investor receives dividend income with a corresponding downward adjustment in the selling price of the stock resulting in reduced long-term capital gain. (See discussion of Puts and Calls on **38.01** to **38.09**.)

Example. T acquires a 30-day Unlisted Call on December 1, 1982, for $200 to buy 100 shares of XYZ stock at $30 (the current market price). XYZ stock will go ex-dividend an extraordinary fully taxable dividend of $5 per share on December 15, 1982. On December 14, 1982, XYZ stock is selling at $36 per share. If T exercises the Call prior to December 15, 1982, his basis in XYZ stock will be $32 per share ($30 purchase price plus $2 per share paid for the Call). The market value of XYZ stock, assuming no further fluctuation in price, will drop to $31 per share after the stock goes ex-dividend the $5 dividend distribution. Then T will be taxed on the $5 per share dividend distribution and have a potential capital loss of $1 per share (basis of $32 less market value of $31). However, if T waited until December 15, 1982, to exercise the Call, the exercise price would be adjusted downward to $25 because of the dividend distribution. Thus T would be holding XYZ stock having a fair market value of $31 per share with a basis of $27 per share ($25 purchase price plus $2 per share paid for the Call). T would now have a potential $4 capital gain and no dividend income.

.03 Use of an Unlisted Call and a Short Sale

Investors expecting a sharp and substantial, but temporary, rise in the market value of a security should consider buying a one-year, 10-day Call on the stock and, when the expected rise occurs, selling the stock short. The investor thereby safeguards the amount of profit as of the desired moment of time and also retains the possibility of realizing such profit in the form of long-term capital gains. The cost of the Call, coupled with commissions and various other expenses, makes this method attractive only if a substantial but unstable rise in the market is expected. The Call is considered a capital asset in the hands of the investor, and, if sold after the one-year holding period at a gain, will result in a long-term capital gain.

Example. Let us assume that the investor on August 1, 1981, purchases for $5 per share ($500) a one-year, 10-day Unlisted Call on 100 shares of Z Corporation's stock at $20 per share. One month later, when the market value of Z stock has reached $30, the investor wants to insure his net economic gain of $5 per share ($30 market value of the stock less the cost of $20 and the cost of the Call of $5 per share). However, the investor would like to maximize the after-tax effect of the $5 gain by converting as much of the gain as possible into long-term capital gain. He therefore sells short 100 shares of Z stock at $30 per share. The short sale rules would not apply to any gain on the Call in this situation because a Call is not a security for this purpose. The one-year capital gain holding period requirement will adversely affect this type of transaction since the cost of the Call increases as the Call period is increased. Also note in the example below that greater economic gain can be realized if the stock substantially decreases in value after the short sale, but this is offset by the recognition of short-term gain in lieu of long-term gains.

Action on August 2, 1982 by the investor, with resulting tax effects, will depend upon the market value of the Z stock and may be summarized by the following chart (commissions and expenses of sale have been disregarded):

Market price of stock on August 2	Short-term gain (loss) per share on covering short sale		Long-term gain on sale of call (or loss on expiration)— per share		Net economic gain per share
$40	($10)	short-term loss	$15	long-term gain	$ 5
30		none	5	long-term gain	5
27	3	short-term gain	2	long-term gain	5
15	15	short-term gain	(5)	long-term loss (if Call expires)	10

13   LIMIT LOSS IN VOLATILE STOCK AND RETAIN POTENTIALITY OF LONG-TERM GAIN

.01   Acquisition of an Unlisted Put Simultaneously with the Purchase of Stock

The simultaneous purchase of an Unlisted Put and the underlying stock under certain circumstances (described in **37.03(e)**) will prevent the Put from being treated as a short sale. This exception to the short sale rules allows the investor to limit any loss in the transaction to the cost of a Put, without sacrificing the possibility of long-term gain in the event the stock increases in value. The practical use of this transaction is limited to volatile securities which may have a substantial swing in market value in either direction.

> **Example.** On May 1, 1982, T purchases 100 shares of ABC stock at $70 per share and at the same time buys a one-year, 10-day Unlisted Put on ABC stock at $70 for $1,000 ($10 per share). If the market value of the stock should fall to $30 per share, T could sell the stock for $70 by exercising the Put. Thus T's loss is limited to the cost of the Put, $1,000. (It would appear that T could sell the Put for $4,000, recognizing a gain of $3,000, which should be given long-term capital gains treatment, provided the Put was held for more than one year. The stock could be sold immediately prior to meeting the one-year holding period requirement, resulting in $4,000 short-term capital loss. (See **37.03(e)** for further discussion of this alternative.)
>
> Should the stock rise substantially, for example, to $100 per share, T

could sell his position, recognizing gain of $2,000 (cost of unexercised Put must be added to basis of stock), which would be given long-term gain treatment if the stock was held for more than one year. If T had sold the "worthless" Put prior to the one-year holding period, there is a possibility that the $1,000 paid for the Put would result in a short-term loss and that the long-term gain on the subsequent sale of the stock would be correspondingly increased.

Thus, T has limited any loss on the transaction to $1,000, the cost of the Put, and still has potential economic gain (long-term capital gain after one year) if there is a rise in the price of ABC stock.

14 OBTAIN LONG-TERM GAIN ON SALE OF APPRECIATED WHEN-ISSUED CONTRACTS

An investor who has held "when-issued" stock for more than one year should consider, where practical, the private sale of the when-issued stock (technically the sale of a contract to buy stock when and if issued) prior to settlement date, in lieu of the receipt of the new stock and the immediate sale thereof, or selling the when-issued stock through a stock exchange. Gain realized on the private sale will be long-term while the sale of the new stock received, or of the when-issued stock through a stock exchange, will cause the gain to be short-term (see discussion in 39.05). This is similar to the sale of a Call held for more than one year as compared to the exercise thereof and selling the stock. (See 38.04(d).)

Example. T bought 100 shares of ABC stock "when-issued" on November 1, 1981, at $30 per share. The when-issued stock is scheduled to "go regular" on December 15, 1982. Assume that on November 2, 1982, ABC when-issued is selling for $50 per share. If T sells the when-issued through the stock exchange, which is the usual transaction, the $2,000 gain will be considered to be recognized on the settlement date, December 15, 1982, as a short-term gain, even though the when-issued stock had been held for more than one year. If T waits until December 15, 1982, to receive the "regular" stock of ABC, and then sells the stock at $50 on the next day, his $2,000 gain will still be short-term. T should sell the *when-issued contract* on November 2, 1982, in a private sale in which case the $2,000 gain recognized will be treated as long-term.

With respect to when-issued stock sold short (technically entering into a contract to sell stock for a fixed price when and if issued), the investor should sell or assign the contract-right rather than close out the short position. However, in this instance, it is questionable whether long-term gain will result even though the contract was held for more than one year. (See **39.05.**)

15 PROTECT GAIN ON EXERCISE OF A STOCK OPTION

A corporate executive or employee must not dispose of stock received upon exercise of incentive stock option plan until the stock has been held for more than one year and two years from the date the options were granted.[8] (Under a qualified stock option plan the stock must be held for three years.)[9]

The possibility of loss during the required holding period after exercise may be eliminated by purchasing an Unlisted Put concurrently with the exercise of the option.[10] However, the cost of a Put for the required one-year holding period for incentive stock options may be so high as to preclude this method of protecting the gain.

Another possible way of locking in the profit on stock acquired under an incentive or qualified stock option plan and still meet the requisite holding period, is to sell short a comparable number of shares of the stock ("short against the box"—see **2.01**). For determining the time when gain or loss on the short sale is recognized, the stock is not deemed sold until the short sale is closed. Thus, under this rule a disqualifying disposition should not take place until the closing of the short sale. However, the Treasury has ruled that a short sale is considered a disposition of the stock for purposes of meeting the holding period requirement.[11] Another disadvantage to the use of a short sale is that the underlying stock must be held for more than one year before a short sale is made, so as to avoid the short sale rule denying long-term gain treatment (see **37.03(a)**). If shares of another corporation in the same industry have had a similar price movement, the executive may consider hedging his investment by selling short the other stock. However, additional funds required for margin purposes may cause this hedge to also be impractical.

Officers, directors, and 10 percent or more shareholders of listed corporations and other corporations required to file periodic reports

---

[8] Code: 422A as amended by 1981 ERTA: 251.

[9] Code: 422(a). Qualified stock options exercised after May 21, 1981, will be treated as nonqualified stock options unless an election is made to convert them into incentive stock options.

[10] Rev. Rul. 59-242, C.B. 1959-2, 125.

[11] Rev. Rul. 73-92, C.B. 1973-1, 208.

with the SEC are apparently forbidden by the Securities Exchange Act of 1934[12] to sell short the stock of their corporation or to go "short against the box" for more than a limited period.

16 CREATE LARGER CAPITAL GAINS–SALE OF EX-DIVIDEND STOCK "FOR CASH"

Assuming no other market fluctuations, the price of stock that goes ex-dividend is generally reduced by the amount of the dividend. The investor should sell the stock before, not after, the ex-dividend date, in order to produce greater capital gain by the amount of the dividend payment. Where the stock is sold after the ex-dividend date, but prior to the record date, the sale should be made "for cash." (See 2.04.) The dividend under these circumstances belongs to the purchaser. However, the selling price of the stock is increased by the amount of the dividend and will thus result in greater capital gains to the seller.

17 ACCELERATE INCOME

Sometimes an investor may have sustained business or capital losses, or may have incurred investment expenses or other deductions, such as medical expenses or casualty losses, which exceed his projected income for the year. Under the tax rules, many of these excess expenses cannot be carried to other years, and a failure to generate additional income will see these losses expire without tax benefit. Income can be generated by entering into a commodity forward straddle and selling the profit position in the earlier year. However, a capital loss is created in the later year rather than an ordinary loss. Entering into a regulated Futures straddle will not produce income in the earlier years because the offsetting position would have to be marked-to-market at year end. A mixed straddle could be used to accelerate gains provided the investor has elected not to use the marked-to-market rule for the offsetting regulated Futures contract.

Other possible action is a sale of bond coupons (see 43.09(f)) or of future dividends. See 46 for general discussion of assignment of income.

---

[12] Section 16 (c).

18 AVOID WASH SALE RULES

.01 Short Sale—"Short Against the Box"

In order to deduct a loss on securities for tax purposes and still maintain the same long position, a method frequently used in the past in order to avoid the wash sale rules was the simultaneous purchase and short sale of the same security, and 31 days thereafter, the covering of the short position with the original shares held. The expected results were a recognition of the loss, and maintenance of the same long position with the lower basis. The Treasury has issued regulations[13] which, if upheld by the courts, would prevent this method of obtaining a deduction for the loss. (See **36.09.**) However, a variation of this short sale transaction might still be used effectively to accomplish the same objective of deducting the loss and maintaining the same long position. (See **36.01** for discussion of wash sale rules.)

.02 Other Methods

Investors sometimes avoid the wash sale provisions by replacing securities sold with securities in another corporation in the same industry. Another method frequently utilized is "doubling up" or buying an equivalent amount of the same issue, holding both lots for 31 days, and then selling the original holding and recognizing the loss. This latter method has the disadvantage of tying up and risking additional capital. Of course the investor could sell the loss securities, wait 31 days, and repurchase them. However, he is now without any economic interest in the securities for the 31-day period. A sale of the loss securities in January may result in greater proceeds than a sale in December if the securities are expected to drop further in value, because of tax-loss selling at the end of the year, and then recover. Tax factors alone should not affect economic decisions.

.03 Sale of "In the Money" Puts

The wash sales provisions, disallowing a loss deduction, is triggered when within the 30-day period the taxpayer has acquired, or has entered into a contract or option to acquire, substantially identical

---

[13] Reg. 1.1091-1 (g).

property. The sale of the stock at a loss with a simultaneous sale of an "in the money" Put, where effective economic interest in the movement of the price of the stock (up to a certain point) remains with the investor, should not come within the technical requirements of the wash sales rules so as to disallow the loss deduction.

> **Example.** T owned 100 shares of X stock with a basis of $50 per share for more than one year. The current market value of X stock is $20 per share. T wishes to recognize a $3,000 long-term capital loss deduction without giving up his economic interest in the stock. Simultaneous with a sale of X stock for $20 per share, T could write a Put, with an expiration date of more than 30 days and with a strike price of $30. T will receive approximately $1,000 for the sale of this "in the money" Put. As long as X stock is selling at a price below $30, T will be assured that the stock will be sold to him at $30 near the expiration date of the Put. T's tax basis will be the $30 per share paid less the $10 per share premium received on the sale of the Put, or a net of $20 per share. The 30-day acquisition period rule under the wash sales provisions will not have been violated. The sale of the "in the money" Put (whether Listed or Unlisted), should not be considered as the acquisition of an option or absolute right to acquire the stock unless the option is so deep "in the money" that it is absolutely certain that the Put will be exercised. If X stock should rise in value above $30 per share during the period of the outstanding Put, T's economic interest will disappear. He will not receive back the stock because the worthless Put will be allowed to expire unexercised, resulting in a short-term gain of $1,000. Therefore, T should make sure that the intrinsic value of the Put (the amount of dollars that the Put is "in the money"), is of sufficient size to take into account the possibility of a reasonable sudden rise in the value of the stock during the Put period.
>
> Unlisted "in the money" Puts might also be used with securities (including tax-free municipals) to accomplish the above stated objective.

19 AVAILABLE TAX ELECTIONS

.01 Allocation of Basis to Stock Rights Received

Where the fair market value of stock rights received is less than 15 percent of the value of stock, no allocation of the basis of such stock to the rights is made unless the investor so elects. If the investor intends to sell only the rights, or to exercise the rights with a view toward selling the newly acquired stock within one year, or before selling the old shares, an election to allocate the basis should be made in order to reduce the amount of gain recognized on the sale of the rights or the new shares. An election should also be made if the investor intends to sell both his old and newly acquired shares in order to maximize the long-term gains on the old shares and reduce the amount of short-term gains on the new shares. If the old shares are sold at a loss, an election should be made so as to reduce the amount of long-term losses. Where the investor intends to retain the stock acquired on exercise of the rights, there may be an advantage in not making the election if such action results in creating widely different bases which permit selective gain or loss on later sales. Where stock dividends are received, part of the basis of the old stock *must always* be allocated to the stock dividends. (See **33.04** for discussion of the method of making the allocation to either dividend stock or rights.)

Example. T owns 100 shares of X stock with a basis of $100 per share. He receives 100 rights to purchase more shares. The market value of the stock, on the first day traded ex-rights, is $180 per share and the rights are then worth $20 per right (less than 15 percent of $180). If T sells the rights at $20 each and makes no election, he will recognize $2,000 of gain (long-term or short-term depending upon the length of time the 100 shares of X stock were held). However, T may elect to allocate a portion of the basis of the $100 per share of X stock to the rights. Thus $10 ($100 times $20/$200) of basis would be allocated to each right. The gain that is recognized on the sale of such rights will thus be reduced to $1,000.

.02 Obligations Issued at a Discount

An investor may elect in any taxable year to include in income annually the increase in the redemption value of certain noninterest-bearing obligations issued at a discount, such as Series E savings bonds. Otherwise the entire discount element will generally result in ordinary income treatment in the year of redemption. The election is binding and applies to all such obligations owned and later acquired. All increases in value occurring in years preceding the election must be included in taxable income in the year of election. Investors, such as minors or retired persons with little or no taxable income, may find this election to be most advantageous.

Recognition of gain on the increased value of certain U.S. Government obligations not previously recognized as income in the years earned may be further deferred by exchanging them for other similar obligations. (See 43.10.)

Example. W purchased a $100 Series E savings bond for $75 in June, 1975. In 1977, she elects to include the increased annual redemption value in her income. At the end of 1977, between 2½ and 3 years have passed since the issuance date so W will recognize approximately $9.50 of interest income, which represents the full increment in value from date of purchase to the end of the year in which the election is made. (The amount of the increment depends upon the date of issuance of the savings bond and may be affected by an increase in rates of return on such bonds.) Without such election, W would recognize $25 of interest income upon redemption of the bond at initial maturity. She could, based upon past precedents, continue holding such bond without recognizing income as Congress has not permitted any U.S. savings bonds issued since 1941 to finally mature unless the bonds have a 40-year maturity. W could exchange the Series E bond for certain Series H bonds (which pay current interest) without being required to recognize any interest income represented in the increased value of the Series E bond and not previously reported as income. The interest represented by the increment in value would have to be reported when the Series H bonds were redeemed.

.03 Amortization of Bond Premiums

Taxpayers in all tax brackets generally will find it advantageous to elect to amortize premiums paid upon the acquisition of taxable bonds. The allowable deduction for amortization operates to decrease ordinary income and to reduce the basis of the securities. The alternative is the maintenance of basis and a consequent capital loss or reduction of capital gain upon redemption or sale. (See **43.02** for method of computation and restrictions.)

Example. T purchases on January 21, 1977 a $5,000 10 percent ABC bond due January 2, 1987, for $5,500. T elects to amortize the premium of $500 over the 10-year term of the bond, thus obtaining annually a $50 ordinary deduction. Upon redemption in 1987 for $5,000, T will recognize neither gain nor loss, since the basis will have been reduced to $5,000. However, without such election, T would sustain a $500 long-term capital loss upon redemption ($5,500 cost less redemption amount of $5,000). Thus the election gives T annual deductions against ordinary income and may prevent capital loss upon subsequent sale or redemption of the bond.

.04 Elect Not to Use the Installment Sale

Under the revised installment sale rules (see **47**), any gains on payments received in year following the year of sale of securities are automatically deferred until the year of payment unless an election is made not to use the installment method. An investor may have expiring losses or credits and could only use these tax attributes if the entire gain is recognized in the year of sale. The investor may have already realized long-term gains and short-term losses and may wish to apply the short-term gain to be realized on the sale against the short-term losses rather than pay a higher tax on the short-term gain in the subsequent year. Another possible situation is that he expects to be in a much lower tax bracket in the year of sale and the tax savings would be greater than the benefits from deferring the payment of tax. Other items, such as income averaging, alternative minimum tax, and excess itemized deductions in the current year, may also make it more beneficial for the investor to elect to report the entire gain in the year of sale.

20 UNDESIRABILITY OF LONG-TERM GAIN IN CERTAIN SITUATIONS

Normally an investor would prefer to have recognized gains on securities treated as long-term and losses treated as short-term. If an investor had large capital losses in the year, it is immaterial whether he realizes long-term or short-term capital gains, since the losses will offset any capital gain on a $1 to $1 basis. Therefore, an investor need not risk his potential gain by retaining the security until long-term gains can be obtained. Similarly, if an investor has only short-term gains or long-term gains, it is immaterial whether the losses are long-term or short-term because either type of loss can be fully offset against the capital gains. In this situation an investor should realize his long-term losses and save his short-term losses, if any, for use in future years. However, if the capital losses exceed the capital gains, it is preferable to have short-term losses that can be offset against ordinary income on a $1 to $1 basis, whereas $2 of long-term losses are required to reduce $1 of ordinary income. In a case where an investor has recognized short-term gains and long-term losses, there is no benefit from realizing the long-term gains in that year. The long-term losses will merely offset the long-term gains, leaving short-term gains subject to tax at regular rates. Where possible the long-term gains should be deferred until the subsequent year, possibly by means of a short sale. (See **37.02**.) Realization of long-term capital gains, in lieu of short-term gains, is not advantageous where an investor has excess personal deductions (e.g., medical expense, charitable contributions, investment expenses) which cannot be carried to other years and the capital gains are less than the excess deductions. If the capital gains exceeds the excess deductions then it may be more advantageous to recognize long-term capital gains. There would also be no benefit in holding the securities for long-term capital gains treatment if the investor expects to compute his tax liability under the alternative minimum tax (see 58). The capital gain deduction is added back in determining the minimum tax.

Example. T has excess deductions of $10,000. His XYZ stock, which he has held for several years, has unrealized appreciation of approximately $10,000. He also owns ABC stock on which he has unrealized short-term gains of approximately $10,000. In this situation it would be preferable to sell the ABC stock since the ordinary deductions would offset the short-term gain. The long-term gain on the XYZ stock could be taken in a subsequent year. There would be no benefit in selling the XYZ stock in the loss year since the $6,000 capital gain deduction would be wasted because it cannot be carried over to another year. However, if the unrealized gain on the XYZ stock were $25,000, then the full $25,000 of long-term gain would not be subjected to tax because it would be offset by the $15,000 capital gain deduction and the $10,000 of excess ordinary deductions. The possible effects of the alternative minimum tax should be considered before completing the transaction.

---

21 STOCK TRANSFER TAXES

Investors should be aware that a state transfer tax paid on the sale of stock is properly deducted as a tax and not merely as a sales expense in computing gain or loss in the transaction. This results in larger capital gains or smaller capital losses and an ordinary deduction. Although the tax savings may be small in amount, the amount may become significant where there have been many trades resulting in long-term gains. Treating the state transfer taxes as deductions will also produce extra tax deductions where the investor has net capital losses in excess of the $3,000 maximum deduction available after 1977. However, the deduction would be lost if the investor uses the standard deduction. The tax is being phased out.

Example. T had 200 separate transactions in various stocks selling above $20 (each transaction in 100 share lots) resulting in a net long-term capital gain of $20,000, computed by deducting New York State transfer taxes from the proceeds of sale. Approximately $1,000 of such transfer taxes would be paid and would be allowed as an ordinary tax deduction. Thus $21,000 will be given long-term capital gain treatment. If T had used the standard deduction (zero bracket amount), the $1,000 transfer tax would be wasted despite the fact that the capital gains have been increased from $20,000 to $21,000. It is possible that in this type of situation T could choose to reduce the capital gains by the transfer tax. If T had instead incurred a net loss of $20,000 computed in the same manner, only $3,000 would be allowed as a deduction against ordinary income. However, T should also claim a $1,000 ordinary deduction. The remaining loss of $13,000 ($20,000 less $1,000 transfer tax less $6,000 under the rule requiring $6,000 of long-term losses to offset $3,000 of ordinary income) will be available as a capital loss carry-over into future years.

22 INTEREST ON MARGIN ACCOUNTS

Interest charged on a stock brokerage margin account is deductible by a cash-basis taxpayer in the year in which credits such as dividends, cash deposits, or proceeds from sale of securities are made to the account sufficient to absorb the interest charge.[14] Therefore, a payment should be made into the margin account towards the end of December in order to assure the deduction of interest charges of that month and prior months where there have been no recent credits to the account of adequate amounts. This may be accomplished by mailing a check before December 31, although received by the broker in January, indicating the payment is for the unpaid interest. Prior to the 1976 TRA, additional deductions could be created by prepaying the next year's interest on the margin accounts.[15] This is no longer permissible. (See **48.05**.) It should be noted that interest expense incurred on the purchase of taxable securities on margin may be partially disallowed if an investor owns or purchases tax-exempt securities for cash or through another account. Where an investor has also purchased a home, automobile, or other large personal expenditure, it is preferable for tax purposes to incur a liability for the personal expenditure rather than on the purchase of taxable securities. There would not be any disallowance of interest expense in the latter situation. Also note that the interest expense deduction may be subject to limitations, or may constitute a tax preference where certain deductions, including interest expense, exceed 60 percent of adjusted gross income. (See **57**.) In the latter situation, it

---

[14] Rev. Rul. 70-221, C.B. 1970-1, 33.   [15] Rev. Rul. 68-643, C.B. 1968-2, 76.

may be more beneficial to defer the interest expense to a subsequent year.

23 PREPAYMENT OF STATE INCOME TAXES

Where large capital gains are subject to state income tax, it may be advisable to prepay the state income tax in order to obtain the current deduction of such taxes. Otherwise, the deduction of the state income tax on the federal income tax return for the following year may produce a much smaller benefit.

24 CONTRIBUTION OF APPRECIATED SECURITIES

Contributions after 1969 to public charities and certain private foundations of appreciated long-term securities will result in a contribution deduction (subject to a 30 percent limitation with the excess carried forward for five years) equal to the fair market value of the property at the time of the gift. The appreciation in value escapes taxation. An election may be made to apply the 50 percent limitation rather than the 30 percent limitation to the contribution, but only 60 percent of the appreciation would be deductible. If a contribution is made to a private foundation, other than to an operating foundation or one which passes through all of its contributions to a qualified charity within 2½ months of the following year, only 60 percent of the appreciation is deductible (subject to a 20 percent limitation).[16] Taxpayers who normally make charitable donations each year should still consider giving appreciated securities or sell securities to the charity at a discount in lieu of giving cash. The cash can be used to purchase the same or similar stock and thereby obtain a high tax basis for the stock. Donations of short-term securities should be avoided since no charitable deduction will be allowed for the appreciation. Depreciated securities should also not be donated but sold to establish a tax loss.[17] The taxpayer would then donate the proceeds if there are no appreciated long-term securities which could be contributed.

Example. T normally makes $1,000 of charitable contributions each year. T has owned for more than one year 100 shares of ABC stock with a

---

[16] Code: 170(b)(1)(d) and (e), increasing the charitable deduction from 50 percent to 60 percent.

[17] Withers, 69 TC 900. (1978).

fair market value of $10 per share, which cost him $1 per share. T should contribute these securities to a qualified charity. In this way, $900 of appreciation would escape tax. (See below for "bargain sales" of appreciated securities.)

An investor who has received tax-free public utility stock dividends can contribute these shares to charity and obtain a charitable deduction for the full value of the shares if held more than one year prior to the contribution. However, the charitable deduction will be disallowed to the extent the investor received any tax-free stock distributions within one year of the contribution. For example, assume an investor receives 10 shares of qualified public utility stock on January 1, 1982, and on March 1, 1982. On February 1, 1983, the investor donates the 10 shares received on January 1, 1982. He will not be entitled to any charitable deduction because the March 1, 1982, shares were received within one year of the time of the donation. Note the charitable deduction will be allowed if the investor does not elect to treat the March 1, 1982, stock distribution as a tax-free dividend. (See **52.02** for discussion of public utility dividends.)

Prior to 1979, taxpayers in the top tax brackets could have realized a greater profit by contributing shares with a low tax basis to charity rather than selling the shares and keeping the after-tax proceeds. This would not be true for post-1981 taxable years, because the maximum tax rate on long-term capital gains has been reduced from 28 percent to 20 percent and the maximum rate has been reduced from 70 percent to 50 percent.

Example. T, who was in the 70 percent tax bracket in 1978, owned 100 shares with a market value of $50,000 and a basis of $100. A sale before November, 1978 would result in net proceeds of approximately $32,500, assuming an aggregate capital gains tax and minimum tax of 35 percent. By donating the shares to charity, T would receive a charitable deduction which would increase his after-tax income by $35,000. Thus, a gift to charity enabled T to realize an additional profit of $2,500. In addition, the charity of his choice received property worth $50,000. If the contribution was made in 1982, when the maximum rate on ordinary income is 50 percent, T would be entitled to a charitable deduction which would increase his after-tax income by $25,000. A sale of the property in 1982, when the maximum tax in capital gains is 20 percent, would result in net proceeds of $40,000, or $15,000 more than a contribution to charity. Thus, the reduced maximum tax on both ordinary income and capital gains will make it more expensive to make gifts of securities to charity. Any intended gift to charity should be with appreciated long-term stock that would otherwise have been sold, rather than cash, in order that the gain escape tax. This is true irrespective of the tax bracket of the taxpayer.

25 BARGAIN SALES OF APPRECIATED SECURITIES TO CHARITIES

A sale of appreciated securities to a qualified charity at their tax basis will also result in a contribution deduction (subject to percentage limitations) equal to the amount of appreciation. However, sales after December 19, 1969, are subject to tax. The amount of gain is determined by subtracting from the sales price a portion of the donor's basis, in the ratio of the sales price to the market value of the security.[18] Despite being partially taxable, a bargain sale of the security may result in greater after-tax dollars than an outright contribution of the security or a sale of the security followed by a cash contribution. Note that the effect of the bargain sales provision is to place the taxpayer in the same position as a sale of shares equal in value to the tax basis and a charitable contribution of the remaining shares. Use of the latter method, however, would result in additional transfer tax, additional sales commission (especially if there is an odd lot sale), and a possibly reduced sales price if there is a small market for this amount of shares.

Example. T owns 100 shares of XYZ stock, purchased in 1968 at $40 per share. On February 1, 1982, this stock is selling at $100 per share. T, who is in the 50 percent bracket, wishes to close out his position and make a charitable contribution of $6,000. A sale would produce a $6,000 long-term gain and a tax of $1,200. His after-tax proceeds will be $8,800 ($10,000 selling amount less $1,200 in taxes). After donating $6,000 to charity and thereby reducing his tax by $3,000, he will retain $5,800 after taxes. However, if T sells the 100 shares to a qualified charity for his cost of $4,000, he would be entitled to a $6,000 charitable deduction which would reduce his income taxes by $3,000. A $500 tax would be paid on the bargain sale (20 percent of $4,000 sales price less allocated basis of $1,600). Thus, T's after-tax proceeds would be $6,500 ($4,000 selling

---

[18] Code: 1011 (b); Reg. 1.1011-2.

amount plus $2,500 net savings of income taxes), or $700 more than if the security was first sold and $6,000 of cash was donated to charity.

26 CHARITABLE LEAD TRUST

Deductions for charitable contributions can be accelerated by creating a trust for less than 10 years, fund the trust with tax-exempt bonds, and provide for annual guaranteed payments of income to charitable organizations. See **64** for detailed discussion of charitable lead trusts and other tax benefits that can be obtained by the use of short-term trusts.

27 CAPITAL GAIN OR NONTAXABLE DIVIDENDS, AND TAX-EXEMPT INTEREST

A high-bracket investor should measure the income yield on invested capital in terms of after-tax dollars earned. Consideration should be given to investments offering tax-sheltered yields, such as securities in certain public utilities,[19] natural resources corporations, and trusts where part of the yield is considered a return of capital.

The investor should also compare his after-tax yield on savings bond interest, industrial bond interest, and other income with interest income from tax-exempt state or municipal bonds, or tax-exempt savings certificates.

The tax factors are recognized in the securities market in that variations in values do exist because of different tax treatment. For example, a U.S. Government obligation selling at a discount will sell at a price which produces a lower pre-tax yield than a U.S. Government obligation selling at par. This occurs because the discount will be treated as capital gain upon subsequent retirement.

28 TRANSFER OF APPRECIATED SECURITIES TO RELATIVES

High-bracket taxpayers may effectively avoid the income tax on sales of appreciated securities by transferring them, at cost, to relatives, such as children, in lower tax brackets. The relatives, in turn, could sell the securities at the market value, recognizing (and paying

---

[19] These tax-free dividends have been reduced in many instances after June 30, 1972. Code: 312(m).

tax on) the full appreciation. If the donor is of advanced age or there is no intent to sell the security in the immediate future, a step-up in basis could be obtained if the donor dies owning the shares. (See **33.06**.) A gift of the securities could result in gift tax liability if the amount of the gift exceeded available exemptions and credits. The basis of the securities may be increased by the payment of gift taxes.[20]

Example. T owns 100 shares of ABC stock purchased November 1, 1982, at $10 per share. On December 15, 1982, this stock is selling at $30 per share. If T, who is in the 50 percent bracket, sells such securities for full value, he will recognize $2,000 of short-term capital gain and pay a tax of $1,000. However, T could sell the 100 shares to his son for $1,000 and make a gift of the balance of the value. If there were no other gifts to his son during the year, there would be no gift tax on this transfer. Assuming the son is in the 16 percent tax bracket, he would pay only $320 of income taxes on the $2,000 short-term capital gain recognized by him upon the sale of the stock, as compared to $1,000 of tax that would have been paid by the father.

If the relative sells the securities as soon as he receives them, the Treasury may attempt to impute the gain to the high-bracket taxpayer, on the theory that the relative acted as his agent in making the sale. Therefore, it is helpful to be able to show that the relative acted as a free agent in his own behalf. This is usually easier to show in the case of an adult relative, and more difficult if the transfer is made to a minor for whom the high-bracket taxpayer is guardian.

29 TRANSFER OF INCOME FROM SECURITIES TO RELATIVES

A high-bracket investor who is currently providing for the needs of an elderly or indigent relative, or is saving for the future needs of the younger members of the family, should consider interest-free loans or setting up a 10-year support trust.[21] A taxpayer in the 50 percent tax bracket must earn $4,000 in order to give his needy relative $2,000. By placing securities in trust for at least a 10-year period with the income distributed annually, the trust income would be taxed to the trust beneficiary and not to the grantor. As a result of the beneficiary's personal exemption, zero bracket amount, or stan-

---

[20] Code: 1015(d).   [21] Code: 673(a).

dard deduction (if the beneficiary is not a dependent of the grantor or another person), and $100 dividends received deduction for 1982, at least $3,400 could be received by the beneficiary free of tax. If the beneficiary is a dependent of the grantor or another person, and, therefore, cannot utilize the standard deduction, then the amount of tax-free dividend and other income would be at least $1,100. Any additional income will be taxed at the lowest tax brackets. Alternatively, an investor can avoid the expense of creating a support trust by taking advantage of the current high yields on tax-exempt bonds. By receiving the tax-free interest and giving it to his dependent, the investor can also claim a deduction for the dependent's personal exemption and any medical expenses paid in his behalf.

Example. T, who is in the 50 percent bracket, gives his elderly mother $2,000 annually from his dividends and interest. To obtain the $2,000 after-tax amount, T must receive $4,000 of income and pay a $2,000 tax on the income. If T sets up a trust for his mother for a period of 10 years or his mother's life, whichever is shorter, with the trust principal reverting to T at the end of the period, the income would be taxed to T's mother and not to T. T's mother is entitled to a personal exemption of $2,000 (over age 65), a standard deduction of $2,300 and a dividend exclusion of $100. Instead of paying a $2,000 tax on the income, T's mother would pay no tax and would have $4,000 for her personal needs. Approximately 45 percent of the value of the securities placed in trust would be subject to gift tax, but with the greater annual gift tax exemptions ($10,000 per donee, $20,000 for joint gifts) and credits for gifts made after 1981, in most cases no gift-tax liability will arise.

---

30 GOVERNMENT OBLIGATIONS ACCEPTABLE IN PAYMENT OF FEDERAL ESTATE TAXES

Certain U.S. Treasury bonds ("flower bonds") selling at a discount are redeemable at face value in payment of federal estate taxes. With the reduced maximum estate tax rates for post-1981 years and the depressed bond market due to the high interest rates, substantial savings in estate tax can be accomplished by the purchase of these bonds by an individual with a short life expectancy. (See **43.11.**)

31 DEATHBED PLANNING

Both economic conditions and changes in the tax law have a substantial effect on "deathbed" actions. As indicated previously, individuals with a short life expectancy should consider purchasing "flower bonds." As a result of the repeal of the basis carry-over rules and the enactment of an unlimited marital deduction for post-1981 years, a taxpayer can save both income taxes and estate taxes by deferring the sale of appreciated property until after death and bequeathing all his property to the surviving spouse. The surviving spouse will obtain a higher tax basis for the securities, except for one half of the securities held in joint name (see 33.06). However, the surviving spouse may not qualify for joint return or head of the household treatment in subsequent years. Consequently, the income received by the spouse may be subject to the higher separate return rates. The unneeded assets can be bequeathed to other family members in lower tax brackets or to a discretionary trust, at least to the extent of the applicable unified estate tax credit. This could result also in income tax and estate tax savings during the life of the surviving spouse and at the time of the spouse's death. There are other tax benefits that can be obtained from deathbed planning for securities.

An investor with depreciated securities should sell the securities before death to offset any capital gains for the year and to obtain the maximum deduction for capital losses that can be offset against ordinary income ($3,000 for years after 1977). At death, the lower fair market value will become the tax basis of the securities in the hands of the decedent's estate or beneficiaries. (See 33.06.)

A conflict on whether to sell before death or to get a basis step-up at death but risk a decrease in the value of the stock can be resolved by "selling short against the box." (See 2.01.) A short sale will preserve the economic value of the stock and the gain on sale can be averted by delaying the closing of the short position until after the death of the investor. (See 37.05.) An alternative to a short sale would be an installment sale. Gain on the sale could be deferred until the sales proceeds are received by electing the installment method. (See 2.06.) Thus, if the decedent's estate or beneficiaries would be in a lower tax bracket, the deferral of the sales proceeds would result in the estate or beneficiaries paying less taxes on the gains. In addition, they would be entitled to a deduction for the estate taxes payable on the unpaid installment gain.

If an investor has capital losses or net operating losses from his business, he could realize capital gains before death to take advantage of these losses since they will expire at death even if he files a joint return with his surviving spouse. Of course, with the repeal of the basis carry-over rules, his estate or beneficiaries would also escape tax on the appreciation since the new tax basis of the inherited stock generally would be its fair market value at time of death. Again, the decedent may wish to sell the appreciated securities because he anticipates a downturn in the market. As an alternative the surviving spouse can make use of the capital losses or net operating losses by selling her appreciated securities. These sales can occur before or after the death of the investor, provided they take place in the year of death and a joint return is filed for such year.

Principles of Taxation of

Securities Transactions

¶32

32 INTRODUCTION

A general coverage of the income tax provisions applicable to transactions by an individual investor, on a cash basis, in publicly traded securities is given in this section. Also included is a summary of the tax provisions affecting other types of investors. The existence of complex tax rules necessitates a limited discussion of some types of securities transactions. A review of the 1976 Tax Reform Act (1976 TRA), the Revenue Act of 1978 (1978 RA), and the Economic Recovery Act of 1981 (1981 ERTA), provisions that may have a direct or indirect effect on securities transactions, also is included in this section.

.01 Time of Reporting Income or Deductions

A cash-basis investor generally will include dividend income, interest income, and gains on the sale of securities in his gross income in the year in which cash or other property is received.[22] Thus, dividend income is not included in income at the time the dividend is declared, or when the dividend check is issued by the distributing corporation, but when the check is received by the shareholder even if received in the following year.[23] A dividend of property other than cash, however, is valued at the date of distribution although received at a later date.[24] Gain on the sale of securities is also taxed

---

[22] Reg. 1.446-1(c)(1).
[23] Reg. 1.451-2(b); Rev. Rul. 68-126, C.B. 1968-1, 194.
[24] Reg. 1.301-1(b).

in the year the sale proceeds are received and not the day the trans-action was entered into ("regular way" sales). In the case of stock sold on an exchange, the settlement date and not the trade date is controlling.[25] Ordinarily, the settlement date will be the fifth busi-ness day following the trade date. Interest expense, transfer taxes, and other deductible investment expenses are also deductible when paid, rather than at the time incurred. Losses on the sale of securi-ties, however, are deductible on the trade date even though delivery and receipt of the proceeds occurs in the subsequent year.[26] A cash-basis investor may cause the gain to be recognized in the year of the trade by making the sale "for cash." However, gain or loss on the closing of a short sale of securities, or on the closing of a short (or written) listed option, will be reflected in the year the settlement date occurs because the controlling event is the delivery of the securities.[27]

.02 General Rules for Capital Gains and Losses

All securities held by investors, except acquisitions before June 24, 1981 of short-term U.S. or other government obligations issued at a discount, without interest, are considered capital assets.[28] Capital gains or losses are determined by taking the difference between the sales price or proceeds received and the tax basis of the security (usually cost of the security). Sales, exchanges, or redemptions of publicly traded securities will, in general, result in capital gains or losses, which are divided into two basic classifications: long-term and short-term. For taxable years beginning after 1977, a sale or exchange of a security would generally result in a long-term gain or loss if the security was owned for more than one year. A shorter holding period (see **34.01**) would result in a short-term gain or loss.[29]

In the case of binding contracts entered into in one year where part or all of the proceeds of sale are received in a subsequent year, the holding period rule for the year the gain or loss on the sale is realized—rather than the year the gain or loss is recognized or re-

---

[25] Harden F. Taylor, 43 B.T.A. 563 (1941); Rev. Rul. 72-381, C.B. 1972-2, 233.

[26] Rev. Rul. 70-344, C.B. 1970-2, 50.

[27] Code: 1233 and 1234.

[28] Code: 1221(5), repealed by 1981 ERTA: 505. A sale of securities by a trader, who is not a dealer in the secu-rities, results in capital gain or loss. H. M. Adnee, 41TC40 (1963); L. J.

Kabernat, TC Memo 1972-1320; Van Suetendall, 152 F. 2d 654. (CA-2, 1946). Even a predominant business motive cannot preclude the stock from capital gain or loss treatment, as long as there was substantial investment motive for acquiring or holding the stock. Rev. Rul. 78-94, CB 1978-1, 58.

[29] Code: 1222.

ported for tax purposes—is to be used in determining whether the amounts received are subject to long-term or short-term capital gain treatment.[30] Thus, if a security is sold at a profit at the end of 1976 but the settlement date is in 1977, the 1976 (more than six months) holding period rule governs. Similarly, if securities are sold in 1976 and the seller elects to report the gain under the installment method pursuant to Section 453, the six-month holding period rule for 1976 is to be applied in determining whether the seller will recognize long-term or short-term gain on receipt of the installment payments in subsequent years. Note, however, that if the sale is not consummated until a subsequent year, as in the case of a short sale,[31] the controlling year for determination of the applicable holding period rules will be the year the transaction is closed and gain or loss is realized, and not when the parties entered into an executory contract of sale. The six-month holding period rule remains in effect for future transactions in any commodity subject to the rules of a board of trade or commodity exchange (Futures).[32] However, this rule will have no effect on regulated Futures contracts acquired after June 23, 1981, that are subject to the mark-to-market rules. (See **40.03**.) The more-than-one-year holding period requirement will still apply to the gain or loss realized on sale of a commodity, as distinguished from regulated commodity Futures contract. If a commodity is used to close a Futures transaction, the general straddle provisions may apply to the mixed straddle[33] and adjustment must be made for gains or losses recognized under the mark-to-market rule. For example, if in July an investor buys a spot commodity contract and sells a Futures contract which requires delivery after the seventh month, the closing of the Futures contract with the spot commodity will be treated as a termination of the Futures contract with gain or loss recognized on the Futures contract based on its market value at time of termination. Sixty percent of the gain or loss will be long-term and 40 percent will be short-term. Any gain or loss on disposition of the commodity, based on the value of the commodity at the time of delivery, will be short-term. A sale of a Call, Put, or other security option will also fall under the general rules even if the option is with respect to a security that is sold over a commodity exchange. See **40.04** for a full discussion of rules applicable to commodities.

All long-term transactions are netted to produce a net long-term

---

[30] 1976 TRA: 1402(c).
[31] Reg. 1.1233-1(a)(1).
[32] Code: 1222; IR 1787 (3/30/77).

[33] Code: 1092, as amended. See **40.03(c)** for discussion of tax treatment of mixed straddles.

gain or loss. Short-term transactions are similarly netted. Net long-term gains are reduced by net short-term losses (referred to in the Internal Revenue Code as "net capital gain"); net short-term gains are reduced by net long-term losses.[34]

A deduction of 60 percent is allowed against net capital gains (net long-term gains less net short-term losses) realized on sales or exchanges after October 31, 1978, or proceeds from prior sales received after such dates.[35] Note that the capital gains deduction is a tax preference item[36] that is included in the alternative minimum tax computation and is no longer subject to the 15 percent add-on minimum tax.[37] (See 58.) Individuals can no longer use the alternative capital gains tax of 25 percent on the first $50,000 of net capital gains for post-1978 years, but a similar alternative tax is available under the transitional rules for 1981. An investor with net capital gains realized after June 9, 1981, may use an alternative tax rate of 20 percent for the qualified net capital gains, rather than compute his tax for 1981 under the regular method.[38] This will aid investors with marginal tax brackets in excess of 50 percent for 1981. An alternative tax will not be necessary for post-1981 years because the maximum effective rates in those years has been reduced from 28 percent to 20 percent (50 percent maximum rate times 40 percent of capital gains). Only net capital gains arising from sales or exchanges occurring after June 9, 1981, limited to the 1981 total net capital gains, will qualify for the transitional 20 percent alternative tax. Note that payments received on installment sales made before June 9, 1981, are not eligible for the 20 percent alternative tax. Low-bracket investors may find that their capital gains rates may in some cases be less than five percent because of the reduction in the tax rates for the years 1981-83. Net short-term gains in excess of net long-term losses are taxed as ordinary income. Income averaging may also be used for both types of capital gains if it will result in a lesser tax. (See 60.)

.03 Capital Losses and Carry-overs

Where there is a net capital loss sustained in or carried to taxable years beginning after 1977, the amount of the loss allowed as a deduction against ordinary income is limited to $3,000 or the taxable

[34] Code: 1222.
[35] Code: 1202; Rev. Rul. 79-22, C.B. 1979-1, 275. A 50 percent deduction is allowed for pre-November 1, 1978 net capital gains.
[36] Code: 57(a)(9)(A).
[37] Code: 55. The maximum alternative tax rate is 25 percent but will be reduced to 20 percent commencing with 1982, and with respect to long-term gains on sales after June 9, 1981.
[38] 1981 ERTA: 102(a).

income for the year, whichever is smaller.[39] Previously, the deductible amount was $1,000 for taxable years beginning before 1977, increased to $2,000 for years beginning in 1977.[40] Married persons filing separately can deduct only one half of the otherwise deductible amount against their ordinary income.[41] Thus, for the year 1981, each spouse could apply up to $1,500 of his or her net capital loss against ordinary income. Short-term capital losses, including short-term loss carry-overs, are to be first deducted against ordinary income up to the applicable amount for the year.[42] If there are no short-term losses or they total less than the applicable amount, then long-term losses may be deducted to the extent of the difference. For years beginning after 1969, only 50 percent of an investor's net-long term losses may be deducted from ordinary income subject to the above-mentioned applicable limitation.[43] The ratio of $2 of long-term capital loss against $1 of ordinary income has not been changed despite the fact that the net capital gains deduction has been increased to 60 percent for post-October 31, 1978, transactions. Thus, for 1981, long-term losses of $6,000 must be used to obtain a $3,000 ordinary deduction. Any amount in excess of $6,000 may be carried over to succeeding years, but the nondeductible half of the $6,000 will be lost.[44] Long-term losses arising in years before 1970 continue to be deductible in full, subject to the applicable limitation.[45] Pre-1970 long-term capital losses are first deductible against ordinary income before long-term capital losses incurred in the current year.[46] For example, if in the above example there were remaining long-term capital loss carry-overs from pre-1970 taxable years of $8,000 and the investor incurred a $4,000 long-term capital loss in 1981, $6,000 of the pre-1970 long-term losses are applied against ordinary income in 1981 and the remaining $2,000 pre-1970 long-term loss plus the $4,000 long-term loss from 1981 are carried to 1982, with the pre-1970 long-term loss having priority over any long-term losses incurred in 1982 in reducing ordinary income for 1982. Note also that long-term losses may be deducted in full against short-term gains. For this purpose long-term losses incurred in the current year would be applied first against short-term gains.

Capital loss carry-overs are now allowed for an unlimited period,

---

[39] Code: 1211(b)(2); Reg. 1.1211-1(b).

[40] Code: 1211(b).

[41] Spouses filing separately for pre-1977 taxable years could each carryover and apply $1,000 of their pre-1970 capital losses against their ordinary income. Post-1969 capital losses are limited to the $500 maximum in effect for those years. Rev. Rul. 72-105, C.B. 1972-1, 228.

[42] Code: 1211(b)(1).

[43] Code: 1211(b)(1)(c)(ii).

[44] Code: 1212(b)(2)(B).

[45] Code: 1212(b)(3).

[46] Rev. Rul. 71-195, C.B. 1971-1, 225.

but the losses retain their original character. Capital losses sustained after 1963 are carried over separately as long-term or short-term losses, depending upon the nature of the losses in the year sustained and are combined with the losses of the same category for the succeeding year as if they had been incurred in such succeeding year.[47]

Treasury regulations provide specific rules for allocating capital carry-overs between husband and wife where a joint return is filed in one year and separate returns are filed in another year.[48] Generally, spouses are treated as separate taxpayers who are permitted to combine their capital gains and losses as though they were one individual by filing a joint return. Thus, capital losses from separate returns may be carried over and applied in a joint return. Excess capital losses may be carried from one joint return to another. Where separate returns are filed in a subsequent year, however, the long-term and short-term capital losses are each separately apportioned between the spouses in accordance with the amounts of such losses each contributed. For example, if the husband had $2,000 of long-term gains and $2,000 of short-term losses, and the wife had $2,000 of long-term losses and $3,000 of short-term losses, the husband would be entitled to 40 percent ($2,000 short-term losses over $5,000 total short-term losses) of the short-term capital loss carry-over even though on a separate return basis he would have no excess capital loss for the year. Upon the death of a spouse the decedent's share of the unused capital losses in the final joint return cannot be carried over by the surviving spouse, nor by the decedent's estate or beneficiaries.[49]

.04 Futures Capital Loss Carry-back

Net capital losses incurred in regulated Futures contracts after 1980 that are subject to the mark-to-market rules may, if elected, be carried back three years and offset against net profits from Futures contracts in such years.[50] (See **40.03(b)**.)

33 BASIS OF SECURITIES

.01 In General

The investor has the burden of proof in establishing the basis of a security sold. The Treasury may be able to impose a lesser or zero

---

[47] Code: 1212(b)(1), before amendment.
[48] Reg. 1.1212-1(c).
[49] Rev. Rul. 74-175, C.B. 1974-1, 52.

[50] Code: 1212(c), as amended by 1981 ERTA: 504.

basis in the event the burden is not met.[51] Thus the importance of accurate record-keeping is self evident.

.02 Purchase

The tax basis of securities acquired by purchase is ordinarily the cost of acquisition, including the commissions paid. Interest equalization tax, if applicable for purchases before July 1, 1974 (see **54.03**), is added to the basis of the security. Securities received in exchange for other securities in a corporate reorganization or other nontaxable exchange will generally take the same basis as the securities exchanged. On the other hand, if the exchange is taxable, the fair market value at such time becomes the basis of the securities.[52] Reference to published Capital Charges services will ordinarily provide the information necessary to establish basis for any publicly held security received in an exchange or distribution.

.03 Taxable Distribution

The basis of securities received by the investor in a taxable corporate distribution is the fair market value at such time.[53]

.04 Stock Dividends and Stock Rights

The general rule is that a portion of the basis of the "old" stock is allocated to a nontaxable stock dividend (or right).[54] The allocation is based upon fair market values of the stock or rights received in relation to the fair market value of the "old" stock at the time of distribution. Where a stock distribution is taxable (e.g., is treated as a cash dividend[55] or consists of stock of another corporation), the basis of the stock will be the same as the amount of the dividend income to the shareholder. Reference to published Capital Changes services will provide the necessary percentage of allocation.

Where the fair market value of rights at the time of distribution is less than 15 percent of the value of the stock, no allocation is made and the basis of the rights is zero, unless the investor elects to make the allocation under the general rule.[56] The allocation *must always* be made where stock dividends are received, regardless of the market value of the properties.

---

[51] *Eder,* 9 TCM 98 (1950); Biggs, T. C. Memo. 1968-240; see infra for special rule when property is acquired by gift.
[52] Rev. Rul. 55-757, C.B. 1955-2, 557.

[53] Code: 301 (d); Reg. 1.301-1 (h).
[54] Code: 307; Reg. 1.307-1.
[55] Code: 305.
[56] Code: 307 (b); Reg. 1.307-2.

.05 Gift

Securities acquired by gift (after 1920) have a basis for purposes of determining gain equal to the donor's basis. For the purpose of determining loss, the fair market value of the property at the time of the gift, if less than the donor's basis, is used.[57] Thus it is possible under certain circumstances that neither gain nor loss will be recognized. Where it is impossible to determine the basis of the donor, the fair market value at the time the donor acquired the property will be the basis to the donor for purposes of determining the donee's basis.[58]

The donee's basis for securities received as a gift before 1977, as determined under the above rules, is increased by the amount of gift tax paid with respect to the gift, but not above the fair market value at the time of the gift.[59] With regard to gifts received after 1976, the donee's basis is increased only by the portion of the gift tax paid on the net appreciation in the value of the gift (i.e., the excess of fair market value at time of gift over donor's basis).[60] For example, if a gift tax of $2,000 was paid on a gift of $100,000, of which the net appreciation was $10,000, the donor's basis would be increased by $200 (10 percent of $2,000). Where the donor died before 1982 and the securities received as a gift are included in the donor's taxable estate, the basis of the securities to the donee is generally the value used for estate tax purposes.[61] For post-1981 years, these gifts generally are no longer includible in the decedent's estate, and the basis of the securities in the hands of the donee will not change because of the death of the donor.[62] (See 34.02 for effect on holding period.) If an election was made to use the carry-over basis rules for a death after 1976 (see following paragraph), the donee would retain the holding period of the donor.[63]

.06 Inheritance

Securities received by inheritance take a basis equal to the value used for estate tax purposes (fair market value at date of death or if alternate value is elected, the value six months after death[64] or at date of earlier disposition).[65] An heir, however, ordinarily is not bound by the valuation used for estate taxes and is allowed to use a

---

[57] Code: 1015(a); Reg. 1.1015-1.
[58] Reg. 1.1015-1(a)(3).
[59] Code: 1015(d).
[60] Code: Section 1015(d)(6) as amended by 1976 TRA: 2005(c).
[61] Reg. 1.1014-6.

[62] Code: 424(d), as amended 1981 ERTA: 424(a).
[63] Code: 1223(2).
[64] A one year period is used for decedents dying before 1971.
[65] Code 1014.

correct valuation unless he is prevented from using another valuation because of his involvement in the estate tax valuation.[66] Since under the 1981 ERTA only one half of the property held in joint name with the surviving spouse is includible in the decedent's estate, there will be no adjustment in the one half of the jointly owned stock deemed to be owned by the surviving spouse.[67] Property transferred by the decedent within three years of death with no restrictions is generally no longer includible in the decedent's estate and, therefore, there will be no further adjustment of the donee's basis in the property.[68] There will also be no basis adjustment for appreciated gifts to the decedent within one year of the decedent's death and transferred after death to the donor (or spouse).[69]

The complex basis carry-overs provisions, which were to apply to deaths occurring after 1979, have been repealed.[70] However, in the case of a decedent dying after December 31, 1976, and before November 7, 1978, an election can be made to use the basis carry-over rules.

.07 Qualified Employee Pension Plans

The basis of employer securities or other securities distributed by qualified employee plans, including pension plans, thrift plans, and employee stock ownership plans (ESOP) will include both the aggregate amount of the employee contributions plus any gain realized on the distribution.[71] The entire net unrealized appreciation on employer securities is not taxable if a lump sum distribution in termination of the employee's interest is made to the employee; otherwise, only the net unrealized appreciation attributable to the employer securities is excluded from tax.[72] Thus, by electing a lump sum distribution, an employee can escape tax on the entire net unrealized appreciation on employer securities. Any gain realized on a lump sum distribution is either subject to long-term capital gains treatment, with respect to pre-1974 employer contributions, or may be subject to a special 10-year averaging convention.[73] A capital gains tax will be paid on the excluded net appreciation only when the employer securities are ultimately sold.

---

[66] *Hess, Jr.,* 537 F. 2d 457 (Ct. Cls. 1976), Cert. Den.; *Ford,* 276 F. 2d 17 (Ct. Cls. 1960); Rev. Rul. 54-97, C.B. 1954-1, 113.

[67] Code: 2040(b)(2), as amended by 1981 ERTA: 402(c); Code: 1014.

[68] Code: 2035(d), as amended by 1981 ERTA: 424.

[69] Code: 1014(e), as amended by 1981 ERTA: 425.

[70] Code: 1023, repealed by P.L. 96-223.

[71] Reg. 1.402(a)-1(b).

[72] Code: 402(e)(4)(J).

[73] Code: 402(a)(2), 402(e)(4)(E).

.08 Miscellaneous

The basis of securities may require adjustment due to distributions treated as a return of capital,[74] tax-free spin-off of a subsidiary corporation,[75] partial liquidation of a corporation,[76] redemption through use of related corporations,[77] deemed dividend distribution,[78] undistributed capital gains of an investment company,[79] bond premium which the investor has elected (or has been required) to amortize[80] (see 43.02), annual adjustment for original issue discount on bonds issued after May 27, 1969[81] (see 43.03) and stock rights and stock dividends received.[82] Reference to published Capital Changes services will generally provide the necessary information regarding distributions, and so on.

34 HOLDING PERIOD

.01 Introduction

The determination of the holding period of securities is important in order to ascertain the nature of the gain or loss on their sale. With respect to post-1977 sales, securities held for more than one year will generally result in long-term capital gain or loss, while a sale of securities held for not more than one year will generally cause the gain or loss to be treated as short-term.[83] The investor has the burden of proving the length of time he has held the securities.[84]

.02 Measurement of Holding Period

(a) Acquisition by purchase. The period of ownership is measured in terms of whole months rather than in days. This period begins on the day after acquisition and ends on the day of sale. Stock acquired on the last day of a calendar month must have been held at least until the first day of the 12th succeeding month, in order to be held "long-term" for post-1977 sales.[85] For example, stock acquired on April 30, 1981, and sold on April 30, 1982, is not considered as being held for more than 12 months. However, stock acquired Feb-

---

[74] Code: 301(c); 1016(a)(4).
[75] Code: 355.
[76] Code: 346.
[77] Code: 304.
[78] Code: 305(b).
[79] Code: 852(b)(3)(D)(iii).
[80] Code: 1016(a)(5).
[81] Code: 1232(a)(3)(E).

[82] Code: 307.
[83] The holding period for long-term capital gain treatment was more than six months for pre-1972 sales and was increased to more than nine months for 1977 sales.
[84] Taylor, 76 F. 2d 904 (CA-2, 1935).
[85] Cf. Rev. Rul. 66-7, 1966-1, C.B., 188.

ruary 27, 1981, and sold on February 28, 1982, is considered as being held for more than one year.

The *trade dates* are the controlling dates. Therefore, dates of delivery of stock or securities and payment (which may be delayed by holidays) generally have no effect.[86]

In an exception to the usual rule, the holding period of stock received upon the exercise of stock rights includes the day of exercise (acquisition of the stock).[87] The holding period of stock acquired through the exercise of a call begins the day after the acquisition of the stock.[88]

The date payment is received (ordinarily the settlement date) on securities sold on a stock exchange will determine the year in which gain is to be recognized.[89] However, with the probable exception of a deferred delivery under New York Stock Exchange rule 64(3) (see 5.02), the holding period terminates on the trade date for purposes of determining whether the transaction is long-term or short-term.[90] The trade date determines the year in which a loss on a sale of a security is deductible.[91] (See 2.04 for further details.) In the case of a short sale, gain or loss is recognized in the year the transaction is closed. (See 37.03(a).)

The holding period of securities acquired as the result of the acquisition of a "when-issued" contract begins the day after the securities are actually acquired, not when the contract is purchased.[92] Where buy and sell contracts of securities trading on a when-issued basis are not sold or exchanged prior to their maturity, but are retained until settlement date, the sale and purchase of the underlying securities take place on the settlement date, resulting in short-term gain or loss.[93]

Stock scrip represents a fractional share of stock and its holding period will depend upon the manner in which it is acquired. Scrip received in payment of accrued interest or a taxable dividend is income in the year received and its holding period begins when the scrip is acquired.[94] The issuance of scrip in lieu of fractional shares as part of a stock dividend is nontaxable until sold, and it will tack on to its holding period the holding period of the underlying stock.[95]

---

[86] I.T. 3705, C.B. 1945, 174 (superseded by Rev. Rul. 70-598, C.B. 1970-2, 168); Rev. Rul. 66-97, C.B. 1966-1, 190; Rev. Rul. 70-344, C.B. 1970-2, 50.

[87] Code: 1223(6); Reg. 1.1223-1(f); Rev. Rul. 56-572, C.B. 1956-2, 182.

[88] *Weir*, 10 TC 996 (1948).

[89] Rev. Rul. 72-381, C.B. 1972-2, 233.

[90] Rev. Rul. 70-598, C.B. 1970-2, 168.

[91] G.C.M. 21503, C.B. 1939-2, 205 (superseded by Rev. Rul. 70-344, C.B. 1970-2, 50).

[92] I.T. 3721, C.B. 1945, 164.

[93] *Shanis*, 19 TC 641 (1953), aff'd per curiam 213 F. 2d 151 (CA-3, 1954).

[94] *Andrews*, 46 BTA (1942) (ACQ.); *Patterson v Anderson*, 20 F. Supp. 799 (D.Ct. N.Y., 1937).

[95] Rev. Rul. 69-202, C.B. 1969-1, 95.

Similarly, the holding period of scrip received in other nontaxable transactions, including reorganizations and reverse stock splits whereby a shareholder exchanges his shares for a smaller number of shares, will include the holding period of the shares surrendered in the tax-free exchange. Where a shareholder purchases additional scrip in order to receive a full share of stock, the basis of the additional scrip purchased will be the purchase price of the scrip and its holding period will commence the day after purchase.[96]

Losses from worthless securities are deemed to have occurred on the last day of taxable year of worthlessness.[97]

(b) Tax-free exchange. Stock acquired through the conversion of the issuing corporation's convertible bond will have a holding period beginning with the holding period of the bond. Where a cash payment is necessary in the exchange, the portion of each share of stock represented by such cash payment will receive a new holding period.[98]

(c) Illustration. Assume a convertible bond was purchased on February 1, 1981, for $100. On October 1, 1981, when the underlying stock is worth $200, the bond is converted into one share of stock with the payment of an additional $50. The conversion is tax-free, but the share of stock will have a split-holding period for purposes of determining long-term or short-term gain or loss. That part of the share attributable to the bond will have a basis of $100 and a holding period relating back to the purchase of the bond, whereas the portion of the share attributable to cash paid on conversion will have a basis of $50 and a holding period beginning with the day following the conversion date. However, since the stock on the conversion date had a value of $200, $150 or ¾ of such value is attributable to the bond and $50 or ¼ is attributable to the $50 cash payment. On any subsequent disposition of the share, ¾ of the sales price will be attributable to the bond portion for purposes of determining the amount and the character (short- or long-term) of the gain or loss. The remaining portion will be attributed to the $50 payment as shown by the following table:

1. Sales price	200	300	160	150	60
2. Amount attributable to bond	150	225	120	112.50	45
3. Gain or loss attributable to bond	50	125	20	12.50	(55)
4. Amount attributable to $50 payment	50	75	40	37.50	15
5. Gain or loss attributable to $50 payment	0	25	(10)	(12.50)	(35)

---

[96] See footnote 97, infra.
[97] Code: 165(g).

[98] Rev. Rul. 62-140, C.B. 1962-2, 181.

In general, where the investor exchanges securities in a tax-free transaction, and the basis of the securities received is determined in whole or in part with reference to the basis of the securities given up, there will be a tacking on of the holding period of the property exchanged.[99]

(d) **Taxable exchanges.**   Securities received in a taxable exchange, taxable reorganization, corporate distribution or liquidation, generally will have a new tax basis equal to its fair market value and, thus, will also receive a new holding period. The new holding period will commence from the time of the exchange, similar to a purchase of securities. However, in the case of a one-month liquidation under Section 333, the holding period of any securities received in the liquidation will include the holding period of the investor's stock in the liquidated corporation.[100]

(e) **Treasury bonds and notes.**   The date of acquisition of U.S. Treasury bonds and notes (or bills) acquired through auction is the date the Secretary of the Treasury gives notification of acceptance in a news release to the successful competitive and noncompetitive bidders. The acquisition date of Treasury notes sold through an offering on a subscription basis at a specified yield is the date the subscription is submitted.[101]

(f) **Gifts.**   A donee receiving securities as a gift may tack on to his holding period the holding period of the donor, provided that upon sale of the securities the donor's basis is required to be used, in whole or in part, in determining gain or loss on the transaction.[102] The donor's basis is always used where securities received as a gift after 1920 are sold at a gain; but if the securities are sold at a loss, the basis of the securities is the lower of the donor's basis or the fair market value at the time of the gift.[103] Where the fair market value is lower, the donee's holding period starts at the date of the gift without any tacking on of the donor's holding period.[104]

The Treasury has ruled that if stock is purchased and placed in a margin account in joint names, then there is no completed gift.[105]

---

[99] Code: 1223(1).
[100] Code: 334(c).
[101] Rev. Rul. 78-5, C.B. 1978-1, 263.
[102] Code: 1223(2). The donor's holding period is used even if the donee is required to pay the gift taxes. *Turner,* 410 F. 2d 952 (CA-6, 1969).

[103] Code: 1015(a).
[104] I.T. 3453, C.B. 1941-1, 254 (declared obsolete by Rev. Rul. 69-43, C.B. 1969-1, 310).
[105] Rev. Rul. 69-148, C.B. 1969-1, 226.

Under this questionable ruling, presumably all income is attributed to the donor. No gift occurs until the donee withdraws the stock or other funds from the account.

If a gift of security is made by a donor who died before 1982 and the value of the security is reported in the donor's estate tax return (value at date of death or alternate value) because the gift was considered to have been made in contemplation of death[106] or the donor retained certain rights in the security,[107] the holding period of the security would start at the date of the gift. There would be no tacking on of the donor's holding period because the donor's basis was not used in determining the donee's basis.[108] With respect to post-1981 deaths, however, gifts within three years of death are not includible in the donor's estate unless he retained certain interest in the gifted securities.[109] Accordingly, the basis and holding period of the securities in the hands of the donee would not change because of the death of the donor.[110] If the securities are included in the donor's gross estate because of the retention of certain interest or powers, then the basis and holding period would be the same as other property inherited from the decedent.

(g) **Death.** The holding period of securities inherited from a decedent relates back to the date of death. However, the securities are considered to have been held by the estate or heirs for more than one year even if actually held for less than one year.[111] If appreciated securities are gifted within one year of the donee's death and are returned after death to the donor, there is no basis adjustment arising from the donee's death. (See 33.06.) Accordingly, the original donor will retain the same holding period in the securities.[112]

With respect to securities purchased by the estate or testamentary trust, the holding period starts from the date of such purchase. In general, the date of distribution to the beneficiary is not significant in determining the beneficiary's holding period.[113]

(h) **Wash sales.** (See 36.01.)

(i) **Stock rights and nontaxable stock dividends.** Stock rights and stock

---

[106] Code: 2035.
[107] Code: 2036-2038.
[108] Rev. Rul. 59-86, C.B. 1959-1, 209.
[109] Code: 2035(d), as amended by 1981 ERTA: 424(a). Gifts of insurance pol-

icies would be included in the donor's estate.
[110] Code: 1014, 1223(11).
[111] Code: 1223(11).
[112] Code: 1223(2).
[113] *Brewster v. Gage*, 280 U.S. 327 (1930)

dividends received in a nontaxable distribution take the same holding period as the "old" stock.[114] Thus, when stock rights are sold, the holding period of the "old" stock is "tacked on" in determining the holding period of the rights. However, securities acquired through exercise of the rights will not take on a "tacked on" holding period. The holding period will start on the date of exercise.[115]

(j) **Short sales.** (See 37.03.)

35 IDENTIFICATION OF SECURITIES

.01 Importance of Identification

Where an investor holds various lots of securities acquired at different times or at different prices, and sells only a part of his holdings, the proper identification of which securities are sold has great significance in determining the tax effect of the sale. Because of differences in holding periods and bases, a sale may result in either short-term or long-term gain or loss, depending upon which securities are deemed sold. Adequate record-keeping on the part of the investor will enable him to control the type and amount of gain or loss to be recognized when a portion of a position is sold.

.02 Rules of the Regulations

The Treasury has provided certain guidelines, consistent with court decisions, with respect to the identification of securities sold.[116]

(a) **Securities held by brokers, banks, and the like.** Where securities are held by a broker in a cash or margin account or by a bank or other custodian or agent, an adequate identification of the securities sold is made if the investor specifies to the broker or other agent at the time of the sale, the particular securities to be sold and written confirmation is received from the broker or other agent within a reasonable time thereafter.[117] The designated securities are treated as sold even though the broker, and so on, delivers other securities to the transferee. Identification of the securities sold from the account should be by purchase date, cost or both.[118]

---

[114] Code: 1223(5); Rev. Rul. 72-71, C.B. 1972-1, 99.
[115] Code: 1223(6); Reg. 1.1223-1(f); Rev. Rul. 56-572, C.B. 1956-2, 182.
[116] Reg. 1.1012-1(c).
[117] Reg. 1.1012-1(c)(3)(i).
[118] Reg. 1.1012-1(c)(2).

(b) Securities held by investor. Where securities are held by the investor, the securities sold will be those represented by certificates actually delivered, even if the investor intended, or instructed the broker to sell securities from a different lot.[119] However, where a single certificate represents securities acquired at different times or at different prices, the investor will have made an adequate identification of the portion sold, if he specifies the particular lot to be sold by identifying the purchase date, cost or both, of the securities, and written confirmation thereof is received from the broker within a reasonable time thereafter.[120] If transfer of part of the securities represented by a single certificate is made directly to the purchaser and not to a broker, adequate identification is made where the investor maintains a written record of the particular securities which he intended to sell.[121]

(c) First-in, first-out. Where the investor cannot "identify" the lots from which the securities are sold, he is required to apply the first-in, first-out (FIFO) rule, so that the securities sold are deemed to be the earliest acquired.[122] On the other hand, if delivery is made from lots held at a particular source, then the FIFO rule applies only to securities held at that source.[123] Thus, where the investor delivers stock from lots held by broker A and other lots are held by broker B, the FIFO rule will apply only to the lots held by broker A. The FIFO rule has also been applied to the transactions in "when issued" securities.[124]

For purposes of the FIFO rule, the earliest acquisition date has been interpreted to mean the earliest beginning date of a holding period for purposes of determining gain or loss.[125] Thus, although there is some conflict in this area, the acquisition date for securities received as a gift should be the first day of the holding period and not necessarily the date of gift.[126] Nontaxable stock dividends are treated as having been acquired at the time of the original stock purchase. Stock acquired through the exercise of rights is deemed acquired when the rights were exercised. If a portion of such stock is

---

[119] Reg. 1.1012-1 (c)(2); *Davidson,* 305 U.S. 44 (1938).
[120] Rev. Rul. 61-97, C.B. 1961-1, 394; see also TIR No. 334, 8/17/61.
[121] Reg. 1.1012-1 (c)(3)(ii).
[122] Kluger Associates, Inc., 69 TC 925 (1978), aff'd 617 F. 2d 323 (CA-2, 1980).
[123] Reg. 1.1012-1 (c)(1).

[124] I.T. 3858, C.B. 1947-2, 71.
[125] *W. A. Forretser,* 32 BTA 745 (1935); *Curtis,* 101 F. 2d 40 (CA-2, 1939); *Helvering v. Campbell,* 313 U.S. 15 (1941).
[126] *Richardson v. Smith,* (DC, Conn. 1938), rev'd on other issues 102 F. 2d 697; contra *Hanes,* 1 TCM 634 (1943).

sold and there is no specific identification, the stock deemed sold is that acquired through exercise of rights received from the earliest held stock (FIFO rule).[127]

(d) **Securities held by trust or estate.** Where the securities are held by the fiduciary of a trust or estate (and not by a broker or other custodian), adequate identification is made if the fiduciary specifies in writing in the trust's or estate's records at the time of disposition the particular security to be sold, transferred or distributed. A distributee must get written notification of the particular security distributed to him. The identified security is treated as sold, transferred, or distributed even though other securities are in fact delivered.[128]

(e) **Regulated investment company stock (mutual funds).** The basis of regulated investment company stock generally is computed in the same manner as stock of a regular corporation. Additional shares acquired through reinvestment of dividends, including capital gain dividends, will have a tax basis equal to the amount of the dividend income taxed to the investor. If a regulated investment company elects to treat undistributed capital gains as having been distributed to its shareholders, the shareholders should increase the tax bases of their shares by 72 percent (70 percent for pre-1979 capital gains) of the undistributed capital gains.[129] In determining the tax basis of shares sold, an investor may use FIFO or specific identification. However, if stock of a regulated investment company purchased or acquired at different prices are left with a custodian or agent appointed by the regulated investment company for that purpose, an investor may elect an average basis in lieu of the regular methods of identification.[130] Either the double-entry method (the shares are segregated into short-term and long-term capital gains stock) or single-category method (average cost of all shares in the account) may be elected.

.03 Reorganizations and Partial Liquidations

Identification is possible where securities are exchanged in a tax-free reorganization. One arbitrary method of identification that has been accepted is the assigning of the lowest numbered new certificate

---

[127] GCM 11743, C.B. XII-2, 31; *Keeler,* 86 F. 2d 265 (CA-8, 1936), cert. den. 300 U.S. 673.

[128] Reg. 1.1012-1 (c)(4).
[129] Code: 852(b)(3)(D)(iii).
[130] Reg. 1.1012-1 (e).

to the earliest lot purchased.[131] In a partial liquidation, the shareholder may specifically identify the shares to be redeemed or exchanged for newly issued shares; identification is not negated because the designations were recorded incorrectly on the corporation's record.[132] In absence of identification, the FIFO rule will be applied in determining gain or loss of the cancelled shares and the basis of the newly issued or remaining shares.[133] The subsequently promulgated regulations relating to identification where a single certificate represents securities acquired at different times (see 35.02(b)) may also be applicable to these transactions.

Where adequate identification is not made and securities in the same corporation are received, the courts have generally held that the first-in, first-out method must be used.[134] However, where securities of another corporation are received in a tax-free reorganization and adequate identification is not made, the cost of the securities surrendered is averaged and allocated equally among the new securities received.[135]

36 WASH SALES

.01 General Rules

Where an investor sells stock or securities at a loss and within a 30-day period before or after such sale acquires substantially identical securities, the loss will be disallowed as a "wash sale."[136] It is immaterial whether the securities purchased or sold had been purchased on margin.[137] Commodity straddles entered into after June 23, 1981, will be subject to rules similar to the wash sale rules unless all of the positions consist of a regulated Futures contract subject to the mark-to-market rule.[138] See 40.03(c) for treatment of mixed straddles. (For the definition of "substantially identical" property, see the discussion in 37.04 of the short sales rules, to which the term also applies.)

---

[131] *Ford*, 33 BTA 1229 (1936)(A); Rev. Rul. 68-23, C.B. 1968-1, 144.

[132] Rule, 127 F. 2d 979 (CA-10, 1942).

[133] *Allington*, 31 BTA 421 (1934).

[134] *Kraus*, 88 F. 2d 616 (CA-2, 1937); cf. *Fuller*, 81 F. 2d 176 (CA-1, 1936); but cf. *Big Wolf Corp.*, 2 TC 751 (1943) (A).

[135] *Von Gunten*, 76 F. 2d 670 (1935); cf. *Bloch*, 148 F. 2d 452 (CA-9, 1945); and Rev. Rul. 55-355, C.B. 1955-1, 418.

[136] Code: 1091(a). Note that an individual *trader* who qualifies as being in the business of buying and selling securities is exempt from the wash sale provisions, but a corporate investor is not excluded unless it is a *dealer* in securities. Reg. 1.1091-1(a).

[137] Rev. Rul. 71-316, C.B. 1971-2, 311.

[138] Code: 1092(b), as amended by 1981 ERTA: 501.

The entering into a contract or option to acquire substantially identical securities within the 61-day period will be treated as an actual acquisition for purposes of the wash sale rules. Thus the purchase of a Call (Listed or Unlisted) will bring into play the wash sale rules. Writing an "in the money" Put should not deny an investor a loss on the prior sale of the underlying stock unless the Put is exercised within the 30-day period. A purchase of a convertible preferred stock has also been ruled to be an acquisition of an option for wash sales purposes.[139] Apparently, the purchase of a convertible debenture would be accorded similar treatment. A loss was disallowed where the shares were sold to a close friend under an oral understanding to repurchase the same shares at the same price 33 days after the original sale.[140]

Only acquisitions by purchase or in a fully taxable exchange result in disallowance.[141] Therefore, receipt of securities as a gift or in a nontaxable exchange will not be considered an acquisition.

Employer stock received as a bonus under a work incentive plan, within 30 days from the sale of other bonus stock at a loss, is treated as an acquisition of stock for purposes of the wash sale rules.[142] Presumably a receipt of stock from a qualified employees' plan (e.g., pension plan, stock bonus plan, employee stock ownership plan—(ESOP), will also be treated as an acquisition. See below for similar treatment of employee stock options.

The basis of the substantially identical securities acquired within the 61-day period will, in effect, be increased by the amount of the disallowed loss.[143] The holding period of the securities sold at a loss will be tacked on to the newly acquired position.[144] Thus, if the old securities were held for five months and the newly acquired securities were held for more than seven months, long-term gain or loss would be recognized on the sale of the new securities.

.02 Stock Rights, Warrants, and Options

The Treasury has ruled that stock warrants come within the definition of "options" to acquire, which may cause the disallowance of a loss.[145] Thus, deduction of a loss on the sale of stock, where a warrant to buy the stock is purchased within the 61-day period, will be denied because the investor has acquired an option to buy the stock.

---

[139] Rev. Rul. 77-201, C.B. 1977-1, 250.
[140] *Stein,* T.C. Memo 1977-241.
[141] Reg. 1.1091-1 (f).
[142] Rev. Rul. 73-329, C.B. 1973-2, 302.

[143] Code: 1091 (d).
[144] Code: 1223 (4).
[145] Rev. Rul. 56-406, C.B. 1956-2, 523.

However, it is unclear whether under Section 1091(d) a disallowed loss because of the purchase of a Call is added to the basis of the acquired Call. Similarly, with respect to the holding period of the stock sold at a loss, it is also unclear as to whether under Section 1223(4) such holding period is added to the holding period of the option. (See **38.06** for a complete discussion of the issues.)

With respect to stock rights, it is arguable that the receipt of a stock right on stock held, where a sale of the underlying stock occurs within 30 days of the receipt of the right, should not bring into play the wash sale provisions, provided the right is not exercised within the 30-day period, since the investor has not "entered into an option." However, the Treasury has ruled in a related situation, that where an employee is granted a stock option under a restricted or qualified stock option plan, for purposes of the wash sale rules, he will be deemed to have entered into an option to acquire stock on the date on which the option is granted to him.[146]

The sale of an option (stock right, warrant, Call, and the like) and the subsequent purchase of a substantially identical security must be distinguished from a sale of a stock or security followed by the purchase of an option. The wash sales rule only applies to a loss realized on a sale of a stock or security. Section 1091 and its underlying regulations are silent whether a warrant or other type of option constitutes a stock or security. There are conflicting rules in other tax areas whether these options are a stock or security. A right to subscribe to a security is considered a security in the tax provisions affecting security dealers[147] and exchanges pursuant to SEC orders,[148] but not for purposes of corporate reorganizations.[149] The Treasury has implicitly ruled that a warrant is a security[150] and it may take the same view with respect to other types of options (e.g., Listed Puts and Calls). The sale of a Listed option at a loss with a subsequent repurchase within 30 days of the identical Listed option will cause the wash sales rules to apply only if a Listed option is deemed to be a "security" within Section 1091. (See below about the "substantially identical" issue.) The purchase of a Listed option "to close" at a loss with a subsequent resale within 30 days of the identical Listed option is not a wash sale because you generally need two purchases and one sale to come within Section 1091 and, under these circumstances, there are two sales and only one purchase.

---

[146] Rev. Rul. 56-452, C.B. 1956-2, 525.   [149] Reg. 1.351-1 (a) (ii) and 1.354-1 (e).
[147] Reg. 1.1236-1 (c).   [150] Rev. Rul. 56-406, C.B. 1956-2, 523.
[148] Reg. 1.1083 (f).

A granting (sale) and closing out of an option has been distinguished by the Treasury in a recent private ruling from a purchase and sale of an option. A grantor of an option does not "acquire" property within the meaning of Section 1091, and, therefore, the wash sale provisions do not apply to losses on options written by the grantor.[151] It can be inferred from the private ruling that the Treasury may consider a purchase of an option to be an acquisition of property and, accordingly, a sale of the option can come within the wash sale rules if substantially identical property was acquired within the 30-day period. Thus, if an investor sold a Call at a loss and repurchased the same Call within 30 days, the Treasury may disallow the loss under the wash sale rules.

A second consideration is whether the subsequently acquired stock or security is "substantially identical" to a stock right, warrant, Call, or other option. In general, the term has the same meaning as when used for purposes of short sales.[152] A Call has been ruled not to be substantially identical to the underlying stock for purposes of the short sale rule.[153] On the other hand, a loss on sale of a warrant was disallowed on grounds that its relative value and price changes were so similar to the later acquired stock as to make the warrant a fully convertible security and therefore substantially identical.[154] This might be the case where the stock is selling above the exercise price of the warrant so that fluctuations in the stock directly affect the market value of the warrant. The ruling did not consider other factors, such as a limited life and lack of dividend rights, in deciding that a warrant was substantially identical. Bonds issued by the same governmental agency have been ruled to be not substantially identical because of different dates of issue, dates of interest payments, maturity dates, or interest rates,[155] and similar considerations should apply to warrants and other options. Stock rights more closely resemble Calls than warrants because of the substantial difference between market price and option price and the shorter time available for exercise of the option. Generally, these different forms of options should not be considered substantially identical to the underlying stock or security, but, as stated above, under certain conditions a warrant will be treated by the Treasury as substantially identical.

If Listed options are deemed to be a security for purposes of Section 1091, then the question exists as to when Listed options are

---

[151] Private Ruling Doc. 7730002.
[152] Reg. 1.1233-1(d)(1).
[153] Rev. Rul. 58-384, C.B. 1958-2, 410.
[154] Rev. Rul. 56-406, C.B. 1956-2, 523.
[155] Fn. 202 infra.

substantially identical to each other. Listed options with different striking prices and/or different expiration dates should not be substantially identical to each other.[156] However, Listed options with the same striking price and expiration date trading on different exchanges might be deemed to be substantially identical to each other.

.03 Commodity Contracts and Foreign Currency

The Treasury had resolved a dispute among the courts[157] whether a commodity Futures contract is a security for purposes of the wash sales rules by ruling that the wash sales provisions do not apply to commodity Futures transactions.[158] This ruling would apply to commodity straddles entered into before June 24, 1981.[159] Straddle positions after June 23, 1981, which are governed by Section 1092, will be subject to similar wash sales rules. Note that regulated Futures contracts, which are taxed under the mark-to-market rules,[160] are excluded from the wash sales rules. (See discussion of commodity Futures starting in **40**.)

Losses on foreign currencies are excluded from the wash sales provisions because foreign currencies also are not securities for these purposes.[161] However, straddles in foreign currency Forward contracts entered into after June 23, 1981, are taxed under the commodity straddle provisions. Accordingly, rules similar to the wash sales provision would apply to these transactions.[162]

.04 Reduction of Holdings

Losses will not be disallowed where there is a bona fide sale of securities made to reduce the investor's holdings purchased in one lot, even though the sale is made within the 30 days after the securities were purchased and even though such transaction would literally come within the statutory provisions.[163] However, the wash sale rule was held to be applicable when separate lots were purchased on the first and fifteenth day of the same month, and the last purchase was sold at a loss on the twenty-ninth day of the same month.[164] This

---

[156] See **40.03**(d) dealing with commodity futures transactions and the "substantially identical" issue.

[157] Trenton Cotton Oil, 147 F. 2d 33 (CA-6, 1945); Corn Products Refining Co., 215 F. 2d 513 (CA-4, 1954), aff'g. 16 T.C. 395 (1951), aff'd. on other issues 350 U.S. 46 (1955).

[158] Rev. Rul. 71-568, C.B. 1971-2, 312.

[159] Code: 1092(b), as amended by 1981 ERTA: 501.

[160] Code: 1256, as amended by 1981 ERTA: 503.

[161] Rev. Rul. 74-218, C.B. 1974-1, 202.

[162] Code: 1092(b), as amended.

[163] Rev. Rul. 56-602, C.B. 1956-2, 527.

[164] Rev. Rul. 71-316, C.B. 1971-2, 311.

latter ruling is inconsistent with the concept that the wash sale rule should not apply to a transaction where the taxpayer is merely reducing his holdings notwithstanding the acquisition in two separate lots.

.05 Different Lots

Where there have been multiple purchases of identical securities at different prices and the wash sale provision applies to only some of the securities sold, matching of the sales and purchases are in the order of the date of the earliest acquisition.[165] Thus, if 100 shares are purchased on February 1 for $100 and 100 shares purchased on March 1 for $50, and the 200 shares are subsequently sold on December 1 for $10, followed by a repurchase on December 15 of 100 shares, the $90 loss on the first acquisition will be disallowed, but the $40 loss on the second acquisition is deductible. However, an investor may identify which of several lots was sold, which would affect the lots that are subject to the wash sales rule. Further, if some lots are sold at a gain and one or more at a loss, no loss will be allowed for the lots sold at a loss to the extent that shares are reacquired during the 30-day period.[166]

.06 Gain Recognized

The wash sale rules are not applicable where the stock is sold at a gain and immediately repurchased. Sales of different lots at the same time are treated separately in determining gain or loss on the shares of each lot. For example, if lot A is purchased at $20 a share and lot B at $50 a share, and all the shares are sold at $45 a share, the loss on the sale of the shares of lot B may be disallowed under the wash sales rules.[167] Prior to enactment of the provision for unlimited capital loss carry-over,[168] investors would accelerate gain in order to wipe out any capital loss carry-over that was about to expire. Such action is now rarely advantageous except possibly to offset long-term losses against short-term gains.

.07 Sales to Related Parties

The wash sale provisions do not specifically deny a loss deduction

---

[165] Reg. 1.1091-1(c); Rev. Rul. 70-231; C.B. 1970-1, 171.
[166] Rev. Rul. 70-231, C.B. 1970-1, 171.
[167] Rev. Rul. 70-231, C.B. 1970-1, 171.
[168] Code: 1212(b).

where another member of the family or other related party purchases the same security within the 61-day period.[169] However, an attempt to circumvent these rules by having the investor's wife buy back securities sold by the investor at a loss has been frustrated by the Supreme Court under another section of the Internal Revenue Code,[170] on the ground that there was an indirect sale of the stock to the wife.[171] The wife had used her own funds, but the repurchase on the open market had occurred on the same day as the sale at substantially the same price.

Where the repurchase is at a different time and price so that there is not a "direct or indirect" sale between related parties, the loss should not be disallowed even though the repurchase by a related party is within the 61-day period.[172] If a wife is using her husband's funds and acting as his agent to repurchase the stock within the 61-day period, the transaction could be attacked as not being bona fide and the loss will probably be disallowed under the wash sale rules. Similarly, if there is an "understanding" that the securities will be repurchased the loss will be disallowed.[173]

.08   Effect of Short Sales

The regulations[174] treat a short sale as a true sale for purposes of the wash sale rules *if* on such date, the taxpayer owned (or had a contract or option to acquire) securities identical to those sold short *and* subsequently delivered them to close the short sale. When these conditions are not met, the short sale is deemed to occur when it is closed out by delivery of the securities. The regulations are intended to preclude the avoidance of the wash sale rules by use of the *Doyle*[175] plan ("short against the box"), which consisted of making a simultaneous short sale and purchase of the securities, waiting for just over 30 days, and then delivering the certificates representing the original holding to close out the short sale. As the regulations apply only in interpreting the wash sale rules, they do not change the rules applicable to short sales generally. Therefore, the technique of going short against the box to postpone the recognition of gain would not be affected. (See 2.01.)

---

[169] *Norton*, 250 F. 2d 902 (CA-5, 1958).

[170] Predecessor of Code section 267; the loss would be allowed to the wife (transferee) only to the extent of the recognized gain upon subsequent sale.

[171] *J. P. McWilliams*, 331 U.S. 694 (1947).

[172] *Norton*, 250 F. 2d 902 (CA-5, 1958).

[173] *Mellon*, 36 BTA 977 (1936); E. E. Hassen, 63 T.C. 175 (1974), aff'd 599 F. 2d 305 (CA-9, 1979).

[174] Reg. 1.1091-1 (g) and 1.1233-1 (a)(5).

[175] *Doyle*, 286 F. 2d 654 (CA-7, 1961).

.09 Avoidance of Wash Sale Rules

See **18** for discussion of ways of avoiding the wash sale rules. According to the Treasury, a contract for deferred delivery (see **5.02**) will not be a means of circumventing the wash sale rules.[176]

37 SHORT SALES

.01 Definition

A short sale of securities may be defined as a contract for the sale and delivery of securities the seller does not own or does not intend to make available for delivery on the sale. The securities are usually borrowed for delivery to the buyer. Such sale may be ultimately covered by the purchase of the securities in the market or by the delivery of securities already owned but not delivered to the buyer at the time of sale.[177]

.02 Taxable Event

The taxable event occurs only when the securities are delivered to close the short sale.[178] This rule is applicable whether gain or loss is realized on the sale.[179]

.03 Statutory Rules

In general, the holding period of the property delivered to close the short sale determines whether a long- or short-term gain or loss results.[180] However, statutory rules have been established with respect to "substantially identical property" in order to prevent use of short sales to convert short-term gains into long-term gains or to create artificial long-term gains and short-term losses. "Property" for this purpose includes only stock and securities including those dealt in a "when-issued" basis, and commodity futures which are capital assets in the hands of the taxpayer.[181] A purchase of a spot commodity contract and a sale of a commodity future ("cash and carry transaction") would not come within the short sale rules since only commodity futures and not the actual commodity are considered property for purposes of the short sale rules. However, if the cash and

---

[176] Rev. Rul. 59-418, C.B. 1959-2, 184.
[177] *Provost,* 269 U.S. 443 (1926); Rev. Rul. 72-478, C.B. 1972-2, 288.
[178] Reg. 1.1233-1 (a).
[179] *Hendricks,* 51 TC 235 (1968).
[180] Reg. 1.1233-1 (a)(3).
[181] Code: 1233(e)(2)(A).

carry transaction comes under the new straddle provisions,[182] then rules similar to the short sale rules will apply to any gains realized in the transaction. In addition, the one-year holding period rule ordinarily will apply to the gain or loss realized on disposition of the commodity used to cover the Futures contract after appropriate adjustment for the gain or loss realized on termination of the Futures contract under the mark-to-market rules, since the six-month provision applies only to regulated commodity futures. Again, if the new straddle provision (Section 1092) applies to the Futures contract because the mixed straddle election is made, the gain may be treated as short-term under rules similar to the short sale rules.[183] Commodity futures transactions which would ordinarily come within the short sale rules will instead be taxed under the straddle provisions, if the commodity positions are subject to the straddle rules.[184]

See a complete discussion of commodity Futures in **40**. (See **34.01** for additional details on holding period.) The meaning of "substantially identical property" is discussed infra.

The rules may be summarized as follows:

   (a) Rule 1. If property substantially identical to that sold short has been held by the taxpayer (or his spouse)[185] on the date of the short sale for not more than one year (six months and nine months for taxable years beginning before 1977 and in 1977, respectively)[186] or is acquired by him after the short sale but before the closing thereof, then

   A. any *gain* on the closing of such short sale shall be considered as a short-term gain (even if property held for more than one year is used to close the short sale);[187]

   B. the *holding period* of such substantially identical property becomes "tainted" and is considered to begin on the closing of the short sale, or on the date of a sale, gift, or other disposition of the property, if earlier.[188] The "tainting" of the holding period will apply to only an equal quantity of substantially identical property in the chronological order of its acquisition. This rule does not apply to any excess over the quantity sold short.

   (b) Rule 2. If substantially identical property has been held by the taxpayer (or his spouse) for more than one year at the time the

---

[182] Code: 1092(b), as amended by 1981 ERTA: 501.

[183] Ibid.

[184] 1981 ERTA: 501(c).

[185] Code: 1233(e)(2)(C); Reg. 1.1233-1.(d)(3).

[186] 1976 TRA: 1402(b)(1)(T).

[187] Code: 1233(b)(1); Reg. 1.1233-1(c)(2).

[188] Code: 1233(b)(2); Reg. 1.1233-1(c)(2).

short sale was made, any *loss* on closing the short sale is considered a long-term loss even if the property delivered to close the short sale was held for not more than one year.[189]

Where the taxpayer holds both short-term and long-term positions in securities substantially identical to the securities sold short, all the above rules will be applicable. Accordingly, any gain on sale would be short-term and any loss would be long-term.

(c) **Illustration.** Investor T purchases one share of X stock on February 1, 1980, for $10 and an additional share on April 1, 1980, for $20. T sells short one share of X stock on March 1, 1981, at $30. On December 1, 1981, the X stock is selling at $40. If T then delivers the one share purchased February 1, 1980, in order to close out the short sale position, the $20 gain will be treated, by application of Rule 1(A), as short-term since substantially identical property (one share of stock purchased April 1, 1980) had been held "short-term" on the date of the short sale. In addition, the holding period of the one share of X stock purchased on April 1, 1980, is "tainted" and is considered, by application of Rule 1(B), to begin on December 1, 1981, the date of the closing of the short sale. However, if the April 1, 1980, position was used to close the short sale, the gain of $10 would be short-term under Rule 1(A), but the holding period of the February 1, 1980, position would not be affected since such stock was held for more than one year at the time of the short sale. If T closed his short position by purchasing one share of X stock on December 1, 1981, at $40, the loss of $10 would be a long-term capital loss by application of Rule 2 since substantially identical property had been held at the time of the short sale for more than one year. The holding period of the April 1, 1980, position would be tainted and would be considered by application of Rule 1(B) to begin on December 1, 1981, the date the short sale was closed.

An open question would appear to be whether the holding period taint rolls over to other substantially identical stock if the tainted stock is sold. Thus, where the investor purchases 100 shares of X stock on March 1 and 100 shares of X stock on March 3 and sells short 100 shares of X stock on May 15, the holding period of only the 100 shares purchased March 1 will be tainted. If the March 1

---

[189] Code: 1233(d); Reg. 1.1233-1(c)(4). Note that if a security was held for less than one year at the time of the short sale but for more than one year at the time the short sale was closed, any loss realized on the sale would be short term. Reg. 1.1233-1(c)(2).

stock is sold, and the short position is left open, do the short sale rules result in the March 3 stock becoming tainted? No further affirmative act seems to have occurred so as to bring the short sale rules into operation once again.

(d) **Transitional rules.** The holding period of the long position at the time of the short sale will determine whether or not the short sale rules come into play. However, the normal holding period rules at the time of the closing of the short sale will determine whether the requisite holding period was met to have long-term treatment. For example, assume the stock was held for 10 months at the time of the short sale in December 1977. The holding period of the long position is not tainted and lost because the long position was held for more than nine months and, accordingly, the short sale rules do not activate. Thus, the holding period of the long position continues to run. However, if the short position is closed in January 1978 by delivery of the long position, then held for 11 months, the required more than one-year holding period in effect in 1978 is not met and any gain or loss would be short-term. Note that if stock was sold short before June 9, 1981, and the short position was closed after such date, any long-term gain on the sale would be subject to a 20 percent maximum tax because the transaction is not closed until the short sale is completed.[190] Similarly, if the short sale were closed in 1982, any short-term gain on the sale would be taxed at a maximum 50 percent rate. (See **34.02** for further details on holding periods.)

(e) **Options to sell.** The acquisition of an option to sell stock at a fixed price (referred to as a "Put") is considered as a short sale for purposes of Rule 1 above and the exercise or failure to exercise such option is considered as a closing of the short sale.[191] However, the acquisition of a Put is *not* considered a short sale for purposes of Rule 2 above and the exercise or failure to exercise such option is *not* considered as a closing of the short sale.[192]

---

[190] 1981 ERTA: 102.

[191] Code: 1233(b); Reg. 1.1233-1(c)(3); Rev. Rul. 78-182, C.B. 1978-1, 265; Special Ruling, September 7, 1973, 74-9 CCH ¶6596. This private ruling originally indicated that the sale of the previously purchased Put would retroactively reinstate the original holding period of the long stock position. A subsequent private ruling, dated April 30, 1976, retracted the IRS's original erroneous interpretation of the short sale rules. Thus, the subsequent disposition of an acquired Put will merely start the commencement of a new holding period for the stock.

[192] Code: 1233(d); Reg. 1.1233-1(c)(4).

Note, that once the Put is acquired (other than on the same day— see below), the holding period of an equivalent amount of stock, which is held less than one year, is lost and will not start over again until the Put is disposed of. This is true even though the stock is sold later at a loss. Thus, if stock is purchased in 1978 for $21 per share and 11 months later a 9-month Put is purchased with a striking price of $20, a sale of the stock 5 months thereafter at $20 will produce a short-term capital loss because the 11-month holding period would be lost due to the purchase of the Put.

In addition, Rule 1 is not applicable if a Put and the stock intended to be used in exercising the Put are acquired on the same day, provided the stock is actually so used if the Put is exercised. Where the option does not specifically identify the property intended to be used in exercising the option, the taxpayer's records must, within 15 days after the acquisition of the stock, contain such identification. If the Put is not exercised, its cost is added to the basis of the stock with which it was identified.[193]

Where the market value of the stock has fallen so that an Unlisted Put has increased in value, the Put could be sold and, if held for more than one year, the gain will be long-term.[194] This should occur since the acquisition of the Put was not considered a short sale because of the exception discussed above. The stock could be sold prior to the long-term holding period in order to have the loss sustained treated as a short-term capital loss. (See example in **13.01** and discussion in **38.04(e)**.) However, repeated sales of Puts under similar circumstances could negate the taxpayer's "intention" to exercise the Put with the designated stock. Under such circumstances, it could then be argued that the exception would not apply in the case of any Puts the taxpayer acquired. If this argument prevailed and the stock appreciated in value, the holding period would be "tainted" by Rule 1, since the acquisition of the Put would be considered as a short sale.

Note that the writing of a Put does not constitute a short sale and should not be confused with the acquisition of a Put.[195] Consequently, if a Put is written at the time when the grantor held the underlying stock for less than the one-year period for long-term gains, the writing of the Put will not affect the holding period of the underlying stock.[196]

---

[193] Code: 1233(c); Reg. 1.1233-1(c)(3).
[194] Special Ruling, September 7, 1973, 74-9 CCH ¶6596.
[195] Rev. Rul. 78-182, C.B. 1978-1, 265.
[196] Ibid.

.04 Substantially Identical Property

The short sale rules apply only when the investor holds other securities substantially identical to the securities sold short. The solution to the perplexing problem of what this term means is far from clear. Treasury regulations indicate that the term is to be applied according to the facts and circumstances in each case, and generally is to have the same meaning as when used in the wash sale provisions.[197] This discussion covers the meaning of the term applicable to both the wash sale and short sale rules. Based upon Treasury rulings and court decisions, certain guidelines have been established.

Stocks and securities of one corporation, although not ordinarily considered to be substantially identical to stocks and securities of a different corporation, may be so considered if the corporations are predecessor and successor in a reorganization where their securities are exchanged.[198]

Where two corporations have agreed to a merger, subject to approval by shareholders, their securities should not be considered substantially identical, in that too many contingencies exist, or may arise, which might prevent the merger. Even after approval by the stockholders, other contingencies, such as intervention by the federal government, may prevent the merger. However, if the market prices of the stocks are fluctuating proportionately to each other and stockholders' approval of the merger has been obtained, the Treasury might maintain that the stocks of the two corporations are substantially identical to each other.

When-issued securities of a successor corporation may be substantially identical to the securities to be exchanged for them in a reorganization.[199] However, the Treasury has ruled that where a taxpayer has made a short sale of the when-issued common stock of a corporation, and at the time of the sale holds convertible preferred stock which is not substantially identical to the common, the conversion of the preferred into the common prior to the closing of the short sale does not constitute the acquisition of substantially identical stock.[200] (See 39.03 for further discussion of the short sale rules as applicable to when-issued transactions.)

Common stock is not considered identical to other classes of nonconvertible stock or bonds in the same corporation unless there are only minor differences between them. Convertible preferred stock, convertible bonds, or warrants are treated as substantially identical

---

[197] Reg. 1.1233-1 (d)(1).
[198] Reg. 1.1233-1 (d)(1).
[199] Reg. 1.1233-1 (c)(6), example (6).
[200] Rev. Rul. 62-153, C.B. 1962-2, 186.

to the securities into which they are convertible only when their relative values and price changes have been generally similar to the underlying security.[201] Thus, for example, where the conversion price for the bond is greater than the market price of the underlying security, the price of the bond will be more dependent upon its yield and security than upon the value of its conversion feature. Note, however, should the value of the underlying stock rise above the conversion price, the value of the bond would more closely reflect its conversion right and its price would fluctuate more uniformly with the underlying security. If the fluctuations in the price of the convertible bond and its underlying security are not uniform, it is questionable whether the securities would be considered as substantially identical.

Bonds issued by the same governmental agency may not be substantially identical if there are different dates of issue, dates of interest payments, maturity dates, callable features, or interest rates.[202] In ruling that U.S. Treasury bonds were not substantially identical for wash sale purposes because of different annual interest rates, maturity dates, and their use in payment of federal estate taxes, the Treasury indicated that it may be sufficient if they are substantially different in any material feature.[203]

A Call is not substantially identical to the underlying security for purposes of the short sale rules.[204] Thus, the buying or writing of a Listed Call option would not come within the short sale provisions. This should be true even if the Listed Call, that was written, is "in the money" and is, from a practical viewpoint, expected to be exercised near the end of the option term. Thus, the taxpayer is extending his holding period on the stock position to obtain long-term capital gain treatment (see **5**).

See **40.03(d)** for a discussion of when commodity futures are considered to be "substantially identical."

.05 Short Sale Covered after Death

An unrealized gain or loss on a short sale that remains open at the date of the investor's death is not treated as income in respect of a decedent (Section 691 income).[205] The unrealized amount is not reportable until the short sale has been fully consummated by deliv-

---

[201] Reg. 1.1233-1(d)(1); Rev. Rul. 77-201, C.B. 1977-1, 250.
[202] Rev. Rul. 58-210, C.B. 1958-1, 523; Rev. Rul. 58-211, C.B. 1958-1, 529;

Rev. Rul. 59-44, C.B. 1959-1, 205.
[203] Rev. Rul. 76-346, C.B. 1976-2, 247.
[204] Rev. Rul. 58-384, C.B. 1958-2, 410.
[205] Rev. Rul. 73-524, C.B. 1973-2, 307.

ery of the underlying stock by the estate or beneficiary to close the transaction. An investor can escape gain on appreciated securities by not closing a short sale during his lifetime. Since the securities receive a new tax basis, which generally is the amount reported on the decedent's estate tax return, a potential gain could be converted into a loss by closing the short sale after death. For example, assume an investor acquired stock at $50, sold it short at a price of $100, and the value of the stock was $120 at time of death. Closing the short sale after death resulted in a loss of $20 (new tax basis of $120 less sales price of $100), whereas a $50 gain would be included in income if the short sale were closed before death. Note that for federal estate tax purposes the net asset value would be $100. The stock would be valued at $120 and the short sale contract would be shown as a liability of $120. There would also be a receivable from the broker of $100, representing the amount of the short sale.

If the basis carry-over rules were elected, the decedent's tax basis is retained by his estate or beneficiary with certain adjustments. Thus, in the above example, the estate would realize a $50 gain when it closed the short sale. (For purposes of illustrating the rules, the assumption is that the stock was purchased after December 31, 1976, so as not to bring into consideration the "Fresh Start Rule." The effect of the basis carry-over provision is to require the decedent's estate or beneficiary to report the deferred gain on the open short sale into income as if it were Section 691 income. However, because it is not treated as Section 691 income, the estate or beneficiary does not get an income tax deduction under Section 691(c) for the federal estate tax attributable to the deferred gain. However, the estate tax attributable to the appreciation would be added to basis in computing the gain, thus effectively resulting in a similar conclusion as Section 691(c), as modified.[206] In addition, the fresh start rules on marketable securities held prior to 1977 would cause the appreciation up to December 31, 1976, to escape tax.

The above rationale would also apply to a naked short sale where the investor did not own the underlying security at death. Gain or loss on the closing would depend on the cost of the stock acquired to close the short sale.

---

[206] TRA 1976, Section 2005, Code: 691. Code: 691 was amended in two ways in order to more nearly equate the treatment of 691(a) income to carry-over basis property. First, the deduction for taxes includes all federal and state estate taxes as defined in Section 1023(f)(3). Second, the average estate tax burden, rather than as in the old law, the incremental top tax burden, is the deduction allowed. This is also similar to the treatment under Section 1023.

.06 Dividends and Interest Paid on Short Sales

For a discussion of the deductibility of dividends and interest paid on a short sale, see **48.06.**

.07 Tax Savings Opportunities

The short sale transaction lends itself to use in many situations where planned tax savings can be achieved. See **2.01, 5.02, 8.01, 9.04, 12.03, 14,** and **18.01.**

38 PUTS AND CALLS—OPTIONS TO BUY AND SELL SECURITIES

.01 Introduction

In 1973 Call options started trading on the Chicago Board of Exchange (CBOE). Subsequently, trading of Calls commenced on the American, Philadelphia, Pacific, and Midwest Stock Exchanges, with the New York Stock Exchange considering the introduction of option trading. Trading in Puts on a pilot basis was introduced in June 1977 and have been substantially expanded in recent years.

The discussion that follows will concern itself primarily with the tax implications with respect to transactions in Listed options. In most cases the same rules will be applicable to Unlisted options (i.e., those options which are not traded on the various exchanges mentioned above). One important exception, however, is that Listed options, but not Unlisted options, are excluded from the commodity straddle provisions.[207] The existence of different tax rules with respect to Unlisted options will be indicated where appropriate.

.02 Definitions

(a) Call. A Listed Call is an option to buy 100 shares of a particular stock at a fixed price ("striking price") within a stated period of time (i.e., prior to expiration date). The terms of the Call are fixed, with the only variable being the premium to be paid or received. Ordinary dividends will not affect the striking price on the Listed Call. The terms of an Unlisted Call are not fixed and are determined by negotiation between the buyer and seller. In addition, the rights and obligations are between the buyer and seller and not between a party and the Options Clearing Corporation, as with Listed Calls.

---

[207] Code: 1092 (d) (2), as amended by 1981 ERTA: 501.

Furthermore, ordinary dividends will affect the striking price of the Unlisted Call. An "in the money" Call is where the Call price is less than the current market price of the underlying stock (e.g., the stock price is $40 and the Call price is $30).

(b) **Put.** A Listed Put is an option to sell 100 shares of a particular stock at a fixed price within a stated period of time. All other aspects discussed above with respect to a Call are applicable to Listed and/or Unlisted Puts. An "in the money" Put is where the exercise price of the Put is greater than the current market price of the underlying stock (e.g., the market price is $30 and the sale price is $40).

(c) **Straddle.** A straddle is a combination of a Put and Call, both exercisable at the same market price and for the same period.

(d) **Combination.** A combination, as the term is used in connection with Listed options, is similar to a straddle except that the striking price of the Put and Call elements are not the same. (The term *Spread* was previously used for Unlisted options, but such term is now used to describe two or more different Listed Calls with different striking prices and/or maturity dates—see below).

(e) **Strip/Strap.** A strip is a term used to describe a straddle with a second Put component, whereas a strap represents a Call plus a straddle. Both were used prior to the introduction of Listed options.[208]

(f) **Time spread/Calendar spread/Horizontal spread.** These terms are used for positions in options with different expiration dates and usually the same striking price (e.g., T buys one Call ABC Apr 40 at 5½ and writes (sells) one Call ABC Jan 40 at 4, or vice versa). The relationship of the market value of ABC stock to the striking price of the Calls will determine whether the spread is a Bullish or Bearish Spread.

(g) **Vertical spread/Price spread/Strike spread.** These terms are used for positions in options with the same expiration date but different striking price (e.g., T buys one Call ABC Jan 40 at 4 and sells one Call ABC Jan 45 at 1—Bullish Vertical Spread; or T buys one Call ABC Jan 45 at 1 and sells one Call ABC Jan 40 at 4—Bearish Vertical Spread).

---

[208] These combinations are referred to as "multiple options" in Reg. 1.1234-2 (b)(4). A grantor is permitted to identify which two of the options constitute a straddle. Reg. 1.1234-2(c).

(h) **Butterfly spread/Sandwich spread.** These terms are given to positions which combine the Bullish and Bearish Vertical Spreads (e.g., T buys one Call ABC Jan 40, sells two Calls ABC Jan 45s, and buys one Call ABC Jan 50 –1:2:1 –same maturity).

(i) **Domino spread.** This term is given to positions which are similar to the butterfly spread, but have different maturity dates.

(j) **Intrinsic value.** This term is used to describe the true economic value of the option on the assumption that the option is exercised immediately (e.g., a Call ABC Jan 25 is selling for a premium of $650, and ABC is selling at $28½ per share. The intrinsic value of the option is $350 or $3½ per share).

(k) **Time value.** This term is used to describe the portion of an option's price, above its intrinsic value, which represents the value of the time left before it expires (e.g., in the example immediately above, the time value is $3 per share).

(l) **Negative parity.** This term is used to describe the occasions where the intrinsic value is greater than the total premium which could cause an unwelcome exercise of the option (e.g., On October 1, ABC stock is selling at $45 per share and the premium on an ABC Call– Oct 35 is $975–$9¾ per share. Professional arbitrageurs might take advantage of the ¼ point spread).

(m) **Covered writing/One-for-one writing.** This terminology is given to a strategy of writing one Call for each 100 shares of stock owned, or in the alternative, writing one Put for each 100 shares of stock sold short.

(n) **Uncovered writing/Naked options/Short options.** This terminology is given to a strategy of writing Calls without owning the underlying stock, or, in the alternative, writing Puts without selling the stock short.

(o) **Ratio writing.** This terminology is given to the strategy of writing more than one Call for each 100 shares of stock owned, or, in the alternative, writing more than one Put for each 100 shares of stock sold short. In effect, the writer is naked or uncovered as to the number of options in excess of his long position or short position, respectively.

Warrants and purchased stock rights are generally subject to the same tax rules as Calls. For treatment of stock rights received by a shareholder as a distribution, see 52.03.

.03 Functions of Options

The most important economic functions of Puts, Calls, and so on, are either:

1. To provide a means of reducing the risk of loss where an investment or speculation in stock is concerned, or
2. To increase the leverage that can be employed.

They may be used as a vehicle for trading the underlying stock against the option or to protect a profit in a position. Certain tax considerations may favor the purchase and/or sale of each option (see 2.02, 5.01, 5.03, 11, 12, 13, 14, 15). It is important that the cost of the option, all brokerage commissions and transfer taxes (in the purchase of a Call, not applicable to a Put) be considered in any economic or tax planning.

.04 Tax Effect on the Investor Who Purchases an Option

(a) **Capital asset.** These options are considered to be capital assets in the hands of the investor[209] and tax treatment depends upon their disposition.[210] The Tax Reform Act of 1976 did not affect the tax treatment to purchasers of options, but only to writers of options (discussed below). The premium paid to acquire an option is carried as a capitalized expenditure made in an incomplete transaction.[211] The ultimate tax treatment will depend upon whether the option is sold, allowed to lapse or exercised.

(b) **Sale of option.** If the option is sold, the difference between the cost of the option and the proceeds from the sale is treated as a capital gain or loss. The period for which the investor has held the option determines whether the capital gain or loss is short-term or long-term.[212] Inasmuch as Listed options apparently will not have expiration dates beyond one year, it will be virtually impossible to obtain long-term capital gain or loss treatment on the sale of such options.

---

[209] Code: 1234 (a).
[210] See Rev. Rul. 78-182, C.B. 1978-1, 265 for detailed discussion of tax treatment of holders and writers of Puts, Calls, and straddle options.
[211] Rev. Rul. 71-521, C.B. 1971-2, 313.
[212] Reg. 1.1234-1 (a).

However, Unlisted options may exist for periods of more than one year and, accordingly, long-term treatment may be available.

(c) **Failure to exercise option.** If an option is not exercised, it is treated as having been sold on the expiration date.[213] Therefore, a Listed option which, as indicated above, will apparently have an expiration date of less than one year, will produce a short-term capital loss. An Unlisted option with an expiration date of more than one year would produce a long-term capital loss. Consideration should be given to the sale of the more than one year Unlisted option before the expiration of the one-year holding period if it is expected that the option will not be exercised. This should create a short-term (rather than a long-term) capital loss. Where a Put has been acquired on the same date as the stock which is identified to be used if the Put is exercised so as to come within the exception to the short sale rules ("marriage" of the Put to the stock), then upon expiration of the Put, the cost thereof is not treated as a capital loss, but must be added to the basis of the stock with which it has been identified.[214] (See 37.03(e)—short sales paragraph under this chapter.)

(d) **Exercise of option.** If a Put or Call is exercised, the investor will treat the cost thereof as follows: the amount paid for the Call will increase the cost of the stock acquired, while the amount paid for the Put will decrease the proceeds of sale of the stock sold.[215] Upon the exercise of a Call, the holding period of the stock so acquired does not include the holding period of the Call, but starts the day after the Call is exercised.

(e) **Short sale rules.** The acquisition of a Put is treated as a short sale for purposes of the short sale rules so as to affect the holding period of stock held for less than one year, and the exercise or failure to exercise such Put is considered as a closing of the short sale.[216] (See 37.03(e).) Note, the holding period is lost and will not start over again until the Put is disposed of. This is true even though the

---

[213] Code: 1234(a)(2).
[214] Code: 1233(c).
[215] Rev. Rul. 58-234, C.B. 1958-1, 279.
[216] Code: 1233(b); Reg. 1.1233-1(c)(3); Special ruling September 7, 1973, 74-9 CCH ¶6596. This private ruling originally indicated that the sale of the previously purchased Put, would retroactively reinstate the original holding period of the long position. A subsequent private ruling dated April 30, 1976, retracted the IRS's original erroneous interpretation of the short sale rules. Thus, the subsequent disposition of an acquired Put will merely start the commencement of the new holding period of the stock.

stock is sold later at a loss. However, if a Put and the stock intended to be used in exercising the Put are acquired on the same day, the short sale rules mentioned above are not applicable, provided the stock is actually so used if the Put is exercised (marriage of the Put to the stock) (see 37.03(e)).[217] Where an Unlisted Put which has been held for more than one year has increased in value because the market value of the stock has fallen, a sale of the Put would produce long-term capital gain (see Example in 13.01). However, a question has been raised as to the tax consequences of a sale of the identified or married Put (e.g., at a gain or even to recoup a portion of the investment in the Put). Does such a disposition dissolve the identification or marriage such that the Put, from the beginning, would be treated as a short sale causing the holding period of the stock held less than one year to be lost? The stronger position appears to be that these short sale rules are not activated. Certainly, if the Put is not exercised because the stock has increased in value, the holding period of the married stock is not tainted retroactively and such holding period would continue. A sale of the Put has the same effect as the failure to exercise the Put[218] and accordingly, the married stock should not be tainted retroactively. Only if the Put is exercised does the identified or married stock have to be delivered. If other stock is delivered, then the short sale rules would activate from the beginning and, if applicable, the holding period of the original identified stock would be lost.

As indicated in 37.03, statutory rules have been established with respect to "substantially identical property" in order to prevent the use of short sales to convert short-term gains into long-term gains or to create artificial long-term gains and short-term losses. Property for this purpose includes only stock and securities. A question has been raised whether or not options are securities for purposes of the short sale rules. (A similar question exists for purposes of the wash sales rules and for dealers in securities.) If an option is not a security under the short sale rules, it might be possible to effect a short-against-the-box position similar to stock positions (see 2.01). Thus, for example, if T purchased on October 15, 1982, an Unlisted one-

---

[217] Rev. Rul. 78-182, C.B. 1978-1, 265.

[218] In interpreting Code: 1233(b), the April 30, 1976 private ruling, referred to in the above footnote 216, stated "For purposes of Section 1233(b), the failure to exercise a Put includes, for example, the lapse of the Put or the sale of the Put." The same conclusion should be reached with respect to the "marriage" provisions of Code: 1233(c).

year 10-day Call on ABC for $700 and two months later the value of the Call is $2,000, T could write an Unlisted Call to expire on the same date as the Call he purchased for $700. He thus would create a short-against-the-box position and by keeping the position open for more than one year, mature the $1,300 locked-in gain into long-term capital gain. If an option is a security, then this conversion cannot occur.

.05 Tax Effect on the Investor Who Grants an Option

(a) **In general.** Income is not recognized on the receipt of the premium for writing an option, nor will any gain or loss be recognized until the option is exercised, expires, or is terminated by the grantor.[219]

(b) **Nonexercise of option.** Expiration of options issued on or after September 2, 1976, will result in short-term capital gain.[220] The premium received for options granted prior to September 2, 1976, is treated as ordinary income at the time the option expires unexercised.[221] Recognition of short-term gain under the current rules will enable the writer of the option to offset the gain by capital losses realized in the same taxable year or carried over from prior years. This was not possible under the prior provisions.

(c) **Exercise of option.** The stock purchased by the investor upon the exercise of a Put he granted will acquire as a basis the option price paid by him, less the premium received on the writing of the Put.[222] The holding period of such acquired stock begins on the day after the date of the exercise of the option.[223]

For purposes of determining gain or loss, the proceeds from the sale of stock pursuant to the exercise of a Call granted by the investor will be increased by the amount of premium received upon the granting of the Call. If the stock was held by the investor for more than one year, any gain or loss, after including the premium on the granting of the option as part of the proceeds of sale, will be long-term.[224]

---

[219] See Rev. Rul. 78-182, C.B. 1978-1, 265 for detailed discussion of tax treatment of holders and writers of Puts, Calls, and straddle options.
[220] Code: 1234(b)(1).
[221] Rev. Rul. 58-234, C.B. 1958-1, 279.
[222] Ibid.
[223] Cf. *Weir,* 10 TC 996 (1948).
[224] Rev. Rul. 58-234, C.B. 1958-1, 279.

(d) **Options repurchased.** With the advent of Listed options, it became common practice for owners of stock to write Listed Call options on such stock. If the price of the stock rose, he could terminate the outstanding Call by repurchasing in the open market the identical Call option in a closing transaction. Any gain or loss realized on a closing transaction with respect to options written on or after September 2, 1976, will be treated as short-term capital gain or loss.[225] Gains and losses realized on terminations of options granted prior to September 1, 1976, were accorded ordinary gain or loss treatment.[226]

The potential tax advantage of option writing (long-term capital gain and ordinary loss), that was closed by the Tax Reform Act of 1976, was available primarily when stock prices rose. Many times it resulted in a tax disadvantage in declining markets (i.e., long or short-term capital loss and ordinary income). Thus, many writers of options on a "one-to-one basis" realized a pretax reasonable rate of return on invested dollars and mitigated their loss in declining markets, but suffered adverse tax consequences in such declining markets. The new rules eliminate the adverse tax consequences in declining markets and allow a portion of the advantages in rising markets. It is still possible to create long-term capital gain on the stock purchased and short-term capital loss on the option written. To the extent the capital losses are offset against short-term capital gains or ordinary income, a writer of options can obtain the same tax benefit that was previously available before the 1976 TRA. (See 32.03.)

A loss incurred on the reacquisition of a Call is currently deductible as a short-term capital loss and is not added to the basis of the underlying stock.[227] This is consistent with the proposition that, on lapse of an option, the premium received by the writer is taxable and is not relevant in determining the amount of gain or loss on the disposition of any particular stock.[228] A prior ruling requiring the loss on reacquisition of the Call to be added to the basis of the underlying stock has been repealed except for taxpayers who relied on the prior ruling.[229]

Where the premium attributable to the time value of a short Call is very low, or where negative parity exists, there might be an unwelcome exercise of the Call. The writer of the Call should take care to

---

[225] Code: 1234(b)(1).
[226] Special Ruling, April 8, 1974, 74-9 CCH §6597.

[227] Rev. Rul. 78-181, C.B. 1978-1, 261.
[228] Rev. Rul. 63-183, C.B. 1963-2, 285.
[229] Rev. Rul. 70-205, C.B. 1970-1, 174.

repurchase, in a closing transaction, such short Call with the possible view of rewriting another Call option with a higher striking price and further maturity date. Unwelcome exercises of Calls can occur substantially prior to maturity date, such as when the underlying stock is about to go ex-dividend a significant amount or buyers of the underlying stock are interested in large acquisitions without significantly affecting the price, or for other reasons. The investor may not have owned the underlying stock for more than one year and unwelcome exercise and delivery of the underlying stock would cause any gain to be short-term capital gain. This problem may be cured by purchasing additional shares for cash and use the new shares to satisfy the exercised Calls. If newly purchased stock is used to satisfy the exercised Call, it could be argued that stock is borrowed temporarily by the broker on behalf of the investor for delivery in satisfaction of the exercised Call and that, in effect, the equivalent of a short sale for tax purposes has occurred, with the resulting loss of holding period on the long position that was held for less than one year. Such an argument appears to be far-fetched inasmuch as a conscious short sale should be required in order to activate the short sale rules and not merely a temporary borrowing in the satisfaction of an exercised Call until the newly purchased stock can be used to satisfy the exercised Call. Stock purchased "for cash" to satisfy the exercised Call prior to settlement date would solve this potential problem.

.06 Wash Sales

Where an investor sells stock or securities at a loss and within a 30-day period before or after such sale, acquires (or enters into an option to acquire) substantially identical securities, the loss will be disallowed as a wash sale.[230] Thus, the acquisition of a Call within 30 days before or after the sale of stock or securities at a loss will cause the loss to be disallowed. The authors believe that the loss and the holding period of the stock sold should be added to the basis and holding period of the option acquired (see **36.01**).[231] If the Call is subsequently exercised, the basis of the new stock would effectively include the total basis of the Call (i.e., the cost of the Call plus the disallowed loss on the original stock position). The holding period of the new stock should not include the holding period of the option nor the holding period of the original stock position because of the

---

[230] Code: 1091 (a).   [231] Reg. 1.1091-1 (a).

general rule that the total holding period of the option upon exercise is lost.[232]

If the Call expires unexercised, the loss should be equal to the tax basis of the Call (i.e., the cost of the Call plus the disallowed loss attributable to the original stock and the nature of the gain should depend upon the total holding period of the Call).

As indicated previously, it is not clear whether an option is deemed to be a security for purposes of the wash sale rules. Thus, the sale of a Listed option at a loss with a subsequent repurchase within 30 days of the identical Listed option will cause the wash sale rules to apply only if such option is deemed to be a "security" within Section 1091. Options with different maturity dates and/or different striking prices should not be substantially identical to each other so as to come within the wash sale rules.

The purchase of a Listed option "to close" at a loss with a subsequent resale within 30 days of the identical Listed option is not a wash sale, because you generally need two purchases and one sale to come within Section 1091, and under these circumstances, there are two sales and only one purchase.

If the individual investor's activities are sufficient enough such that he is considered to be a trader, he would be exempt from the wash sale provisions.[233]

A sale of a Call at a loss with a purchase of the stock within the 30-day period is not a wash sale (see 36.02).

.07   Dividends and Other Rights Paid during Period of Unlisted Options

Both Unlisted Calls and Puts usually provide that the option price will be reduced by the value of any distributions (cash dividends, stock dividends, warrants, and the like) received on the stock during the life of the option. In such cases, all dividends, to the extent taxable, are includible in the gross income of the owner of the stock

---

[232] Code: 1223(4). A literal reading of Section 1091(d) (basis provision) and Section 1223(4) (holding period provision) could lead to the conclusion that the disallowed loss and the holding period of the stock sold are not added to the basis and holding period of the option. In addition, if the option is exercised, the disallowed loss is then effectively added to the basis of the new stock, and the holding period of the old stock, but not the holding period of the option, is tacked onto the holding period of the new stock. These literal interpretations appear to be strained and contrary to legislative intent, especially where the options are not exercised.

[233] Reg. 1.1091-1(a).

when its holder receives the dividend.[234] The adjustment to the sales price affects only the tax basis of the stock acquired on the exercise of the option and has no other tax effect.[235] The option price of Listed Puts and Calls is not affected by ordinary dividends.

.08 Straddles

(a) **Listed Straddles.** Transactions on Listed Puts and Calls with the same striking price and expiration date may be considered as a transaction in straddles. The separate identifiable premiums paid for the Put and Call components of a Listed Straddle must be used in determining the respective gain or loss on disposition of each option rather than an allocation of the total premium received for the straddle.[236] However, if a single premium is received for the entire Listed Straddle and the amount attributable to the Put and Call components cannot be determined, then an allocation of the total premium should be made.[237] The allocation can be based either upon the relative market value of each component option, or 55 percent of the premium can be allocated to the Call and 45 percent to the Put. The writing of such Listed Straddles should not create an allocation problem that existed and probably still exists with respect to Unlisted Straddles, inasmuch as the separate components of the Listed Straddles will be known (i.e., the Listed Call and Listed Put are traded separately on the exchange). The new straddle provisions limiting the losses realized on straddles (see **40.03(a)**) currently do not apply to Listed options.

(b) **Unlisted Straddles.** It is expected that the Treasury will apply similar allocation rules with respect to premiums received for Unlisted Straddles. Where separate identifiable premiums have been paid for the Put and Call components, then these identified amounts must be used if the options are exercised or in determining gain or loss on disposition of the options. When a single premium is received for Put and Call options and the amount attributable to each component is not readily identifiable, the premium can be allocated under either of the two following methods. The premium received by an investor for

---

[234] Ibid.; see generally I.T. 4007, C.B. 1950-1, 11 (superseded by Rev. Rul. 74-562, C.B. 1974-2, 28); Rev. Rul. 56-153, C.B. 1956-1, 166; and Rev. Rul. 56-211, C.B. 1956-1, 155.

[235] Rev. Rul. 58-234, C.B. 1958-1, 279.
[236] Rev. Rul. 78-182, C.B. 1978-1, 265.
[237] Rev. Rul. 78-182, C.B. 1978-1, 265; Rev. Rul. 65-31 (obsolete), C.B. 1965-1, 365.

writing a straddle must be allocated based upon the market values (at the time the straddle was written) of the Unlisted Put and Unlisted Call options contained therein.[238] In lieu of determining the market values of the two options, the taxpayer may elect by a statement attached to his income tax return to allocate 55 percent of the premium to the Call option and 45 percent to the Put option, provided that these ratios (or subsequently announced ratios) are used in allocating all future premiums received in writing straddles.[239] The premium applicable to the unexpired option will be treated as short-term capital gain upon its expiration.[240] The premium allocated to the exercised portion of the straddle will reduce the cost of stock acquired or increase the proceeds of sale of the stock sold, depending upon whether the Call or the Put option was exercised. If both options lapse, the premiums would be taxed as short-term gain.[241] The new provisions limiting the use of losses realized on straddles (see 40.03(a)) apply to all Unlisted options; it is immaterial whether the option period is more or less than one year.

With respect to straddles or other combinations of Unlisted Puts and Calls acquired by the investor, theoretically the exercise of one side of the contract should not affect the status of the unexercised portion. The part of the cost of the straddle applicable to the unexercised option should be treated as a sale of that option on the expiration date. Thus, if the Call is exercised, the cost of the straddle applicable to such buy option would be added to the basis of the stock acquired, while the cost attributable to the Put would result in a capital loss upon its expiration. Many investors have in the past taken the position that the entire cost of the straddle should be allocated to the portion exercised. However, in light of the Treasury's position with respect to the writing of a straddle, a separate allocation will be

---

[238] Ibid. Similar rules are contained in Reg. 1.1234-2(d).

[239] Rev. Proc. 65-29, C.B. 1965-2, 1023.

[240] Code: 1234(c) (applicable to straddles written after January 25, 1965, and before September 2, 1976). Section 1234(c) was deleted from the Code by the 1976 TRA because grantors of options now realize short-term capital gain on lapse of options and therefore it is no longer necessary to have a special short-term capital gain provision for writers of straddles. Under the pre-1976 TRA rules the premium applicable to the unexercised portion of a spread written before September 2, 1976, or to any unexercised part of a strip or strap not identified as part of a straddle, was treated as ordinary income to the writer when the option expires. Reg. 1.1234-2(f), Example (7). Again, these gains will be short-term for multiple options written on or after September 1, 1976.

[241] Reg. 1.1234-2(f), Example (3). The Treasury reversed its prior position in Prop. Reg. 1.1234-2(a) that the lapse would be taxed as ordinary income. The final regulation corresponds more closely with the literal language of old Section 1234(c) and is the same treatment accorded under the 1976 TRA.

required.[242] The tax treatment of straddles in Unlisted options has been changed for straddles entered into after June 23, 1981. These straddles will come under the new straddle provisions which can limit the amount of loss recognized when only one position in the straddle is closed in the taxable year and can also apply the wash and short sales rules to the straddle. (See discussion of the new straddle rules starting in **40.03(d)**.)

If the Unlisted Call portion of an Unlisted Straddle is exercised, the stock so acquired will not receive a holding period until the Unlisted Put portion either is sold or expires, since the Put will be considered an open short sale and thus taint the holding period of the newly acquired long position. The holding period thus commences when the short sale is considered covered. It is therefore recommended that if the Put portion of a straddle has any time remaining before its expiration date and is of no immediate value to the investor, the Put should be disposed of in order to allow the holding period of the newly acquired stock to commence.

.09 Options on Commodity Futures (Double Options)

Trading in options on commodity Futures has been prevalent in Europe for many years and has been available in the United States in a small way. It is expected, in the near future, that such option trading will be permitted in the United States under stringent regulatory control and will become as important to commodity Future trading as Listed options is to stock trading today. (See **40.04** for further discussion of commodity Futures options.)

39 WHEN-ISSUED TRANSACTIONS

.01 Nature of Transactions

When an investor buys or sells securities when-issued, he actually contracts to purchase or sell the securities "when, as, and if issued," and for tax purposes there is no purchase or sale until the securities are issued.[243] An investor who buys and subsequently sells securities on a when-issued basis is technically acquiring two contracts. When these contracts are cleared on the settlement date, the sale and exchange of the securities is deemed to take place on such date. Thus all gains or losses realized in such matching transactions are short-

---

[242] Reg. 1.1234-2(f), Example 1.   [243] *Walker,* 35 BTA 640 (1937)(A).

term.[244] When the investor holds several blocks of "old" securities, has sold at various times the "new" securities on a when-issued basis and cannot identify sales with specific acquisitions (see 35.02(b)), the gains or losses on the transactions are measured by matching the earliest when-issued sales with the securities sold in order of their dates of acquisition.[245] Options written on when-issued securities are treated the same as options written on issued securities. See 38.04 through 38.05 for tax treatment of purchasers and writers of options.[246]

.02 Wash Sale Rules

A loss sustained as of the settlement date of the when-issued contracts will be disallowed if substantially identical securities are acquired within 30 days of that settlement date.[247] For this purpose, securities acquired under when-issued contracts are deemed to be acquired on the settlement date. (See 36.04 for further discussion of the wash sale rules and their inapplicability where sales are made in a bona fide reduction of holdings acquired within 30 days.)

.03 Short Sales

A when-issued security is considered property for purposes of the short sale rules.[248] Therefore the acquisition of a when-issued security and the short sale of the "old" security or vice versa, where both are substantially identical, will cause the short sale rules to apply. (See 37.03 for further discussion of the short sale rules.)

.04 Holding Period of Securities Originally Purchased When-issued

If the actual securities are received pursuant to the when-issued contract, the investor's holding period for the "new" securities will start from the settlement date and not when the when-issued contract was acquired.[249] Thus, a sale of the "new" securities at a gain immediately after the receipt thereof would result in short-term gain

---

[244] Shanis, 19 T.C. 641 (1953), aff'd per curiam 213 F. 2d 151 (CA-3, 1954): IT 3721, C.B. 1945, 164.
[245] Haynes, 17 T.C. 772 (1952) (Acq.).
[246] Code: 1234(b)(2)(B).
[247] IT 3858, C.B. 1947-2, 71; however,

cf. Rev. Rul. 56-602, C.B. 1956-2, 527.
[248] Reg. 1.1233-1(c)(1).
[249] IT 3721, C.B. 1945, 164; question (e) at page 173.

even if the when-issued contract had been held for more than one year.

.05 Sale of Contract

The Treasury has ruled that a sale or exchange of a when-issued contract itself is the sale or exchange of a capital asset resulting in gain or loss.[250] Thus, it is theoretically possible to sell a contract to buy when-issued stock which has been held for more than one year and have the gain treated as long-term.[251] According to the same ruling, an identical result could be achieved by selling a contract to sell securities when-issued.[252] Although the Treasury ruling apparently remains in effect, there is a possibility that the Treasury would contend that the subsequently enacted short sales rules (see 37.03) prevent the long-term capital gain treatment.[253]

(a) **Practical limitations.** An attempt to sell a contract to buy or a contract to sell securities when-issued through a stockbroker may be frustrated in that the stockbroker, applying the stock exchange rules, will consider the sale of a contract to buy when-issued as an open sale of the when-issued securities. Similarly, an attempted sale of the contract to sell securities when-issued will be considered a purchase of the when-issued securities. Thus two positions, one long, the other short, will remain open until the settlement date. It is possible that the transaction will never be consummated, thus causing all trades to

---

[250] IT 3721, C.B. 1945, 164; Rev. Rul. 57-29, C.B. 1957-1, 519.

[251] Ibid.

[252] Ibid.; see also *Stavisky,* 34 T.C. 140 (1960), aff'd 291 F. 2d 48 (CA-2, 1961).

[253] See Sen. Rep. No. 2375, 81st Con., 2nd Sess. p. 87, C.B. 1950-2, 483, 545. The Treasury's failure to reflect in the regulations this committee report indicating that the assignment of a "when-issued" contract is equivalent to the closing of a short sale, together with its virtual reaffirmation of I.T. 3721, Rev. Rul. 57-29, C.B. 1957-1, 519, would make it very difficult for the Treasury to deny long-term capital gain treatment. In *Stavisky,* 34 T.C. 140, aff'd 291 F. 2d 48, the Tax Court had an opportunity to discuss

whether or not the short sale rules apply in this situation, but avoided the issue because the transaction took place prior to the effective date of the short sale rules. Under the facts of the case, the Court ruled a loss on the transfer of a short position in the "when-issued" securities to be long-term capital loss. Subsequent cases dealing with the sale of "short" forward contracts have also treated the gain on sale as long-term. *American Home Products Corp.,* 601 F. 2d 540 (Ct. Cl., 1979); *Hoover Co.,* 72 TC 206 (1979); *Carborundum Co.,* 74 TC No. 57 (1980). The Treasury refuses to follow these cases and will treat any gain as short term under the short sale rule.

be cancelled.[254] Perhaps the only solution therefore is a private assignment of the contracts.[255]

.06 Payment for Release from When-issued Contract

In lieu of transferring all the rights under a when-issued contract, if the investor could obtain a release from and cancellation of the contract itself by a payment to the other party, it may be contended prior to enactment of Section 1234A that ordinary loss would result instead of capital loss. However, a payment to a third party to assume a when-issued contract to sell has been held to result in capital loss.[256]

.07 Worthlessness of When-issued Contracts

If the transaction contemplated in a when-issued contract, such as a reorganization, does not take place so that the when-issued contract becomes worthless, it is believed that the cost of the contract, such as commissions, may be taken as an ordinary deduction.

40 COMMODITY FUTURES

.01 Definition

A commodity Future is a contract to purchase or sell a fixed amount of a commodity at a future date for a fixed price.[257] The exchange on which the Futures are traded specifies certain essential terms of the contract. There are two types of commodity Futures contracts. A regulated Futures contract (Futures) which is subject to the rules of a board of trade or a commodity exchange (including a designated foreign exchange) and is valued daily and a Forward contract (Forward), which is not regulated by an exchange or a board of trade.[258]

.02 Types of Commodity Futures Transactions

Transactions in commodity futures generally fall into four classifications:

---

[254] See *Stavisky*, 291 F. 2d 48 (CA-2, 1961).
[255] Ibid.
[256] Ibid.

[257] *Corn Products Refining Co.*, 350 U.S. 46 (1955), fn. 1.
[258] Code: 1092(d) and 1256(b).

1. Hedge transactions used to insure against losses caused by fluctuations in price of a commodity, included in inventory or contracted for future delivery, to be used or sold in the course of business. Such transactions will invariably give rise to ordinary income or loss treatment and therefore are not further considered here.

2. Nonhedge transactions entered into for speculation or investment purposes with a view towards making a profit. Such transactions will generally generate capital gain or loss.

3. Straddle transactions, whereby a simultaneous purchase and sale of two commodity Futures contracts on the same exchange but requiring delivery in different months, with the expectation of realizing gain through the variation of the prices of the Futures contracts as a result of market conditions. Capital gain or loss will generally result from these transactions, but the new straddle provisions will prevent taking a loss on one position in the current year and a gain on the offsetting position in the following year.

4. A "cash and carry" transaction, whereby there is a simultaneous purchase of a "spot" commodity contract requiring present delivery of the commodity (or purchase of the nearest month Futures contract with the expectation of taking delivery of the contract) and a sale of a Futures contract with the expectation of realizing an overall gain due to a change in interest rates and other economic factors on the subsequent delivery of the commodity upon the closing of the Futures contract. The expenses incurred while the commodity is stored in a warehouse are now required to be capitalized and will offset any capital gain realized upon the closing of the Futures contract.

.03 Tax Consequences

(a) **In general.** Commodity Futures contracts which are not hedges are generally treated as capital assets; gain or loss therefrom will generally be accorded capital gain or loss treatment. The tax treatment of unregulated Forward contracts have not been disturbed by the 1981 ERTA except where the Forward contract is part of a straddle transaction. Major changes have been made to regulated Futures contracts whether or not part of a straddle transaction. Because of the importance of these new provisions, a discussion of the general commodity rules has been placed at the end of this section.

Prior to the 1976 TRA, an investor could realize an ordinary loss on commodity transactions by buying and selling a Call and Put in a commodity. An ordinary loss was allowed when he closed the option he had written at a loss. Before the enactment of the new straddle provisions, a similar transaction would result in a short-term loss in the year the loss leg was closed.[259]

Under the 1981 ERTA, the tax results would depend on whether the straddle consisted entirely of Futures contracts (regulated by a domestic board of trade or an exchange or similar designated foreign exchange and is valued at the end of each day), Forward contracts (unregulated contracts), options, or mixed straddles (a combination of Futures contracts, and Forward contracts, options, or physical commodities). Generally, these rules relate to actively traded personal property, including metals, other commodities, currency, Treasury bills, other debt investments, and Unlisted stock options, but not stock and Listed stock options.[260] Positions held by an investor's spouse, partnership, trust, or similar flow-through entity are aggregated for these purposes.[261]

Business hedging contracts are excepted from these provisions.[262] These rules cannot be avoided by investing in a syndicate (i.e., more than 35 percent of the losses are allocable to limited partners).[263]

(b) Futures contracts. With respect to Futures contracts acquired after June 23, 1981, gain or loss must be reported on an annual basis under a mark-to-market rule.[263a] These Futures contracts held at the end of the year are marked-to-market as if sold at year end. Any gain or loss on each contract held at year end are included with the gains and losses on such contracts closed out during the taxable year. A termination of a Futures contract by offsetting, taking, or making delivery, and so on, will be treated as a sale of the Futures contract, using the fair market value at the time of termination.[264] With respect to such gains or losses, 40 percent is treated as short-term and 60 percent as long-term (the effective tax rate in 1982 on Futures gains cannot exceed 32 percent).[265] However, if the Futures contract is not part of an identified hedging transaction and a disposition

---

[259] Code: 1234(b).

[260] Code: 1092(d), as amended by 1981 ERTA: 501.

[261] Code: 1092(d)(3), as amended. With respect to partnership positions, the better rule should be an allocation of the partner's pro rata share and not the total position.

[262] Code: 1256(e), as amended. Neither the commodity straddle rules, mark-to-market rules or capitalization of carrying charges apply to hedging transactions.

[263] Code: 1256(e)(3), as amended.

[263a] The House Technical Correction Bill of 1982 would add certain foreign currency contracts (Forwards) entered into after May 11, 1982 and cash settlement contracts (e.g., stock index futures) to the list of contracts covered by the mark-to-market rule.

[264] Code: 1256(c), as amended by 1981 ERTA: 503.

[265] Code: 1256(a), as amended by 1981 ERTA: 503.

would result in ordinary income, then ordinary income would be reported under the mark-to-market rules.[266] In determining gains or losses on the Futures contracts in subsequent years, proper adjustment must be made for gains or losses recognized in prior years under the mark-to-market rule.

To illustrate, T purchases on October 1, 1981, a December 1982 gold contract at $470. On December 31, 1981, the value of the gold futures contract is $520. T will have to report in 1981 under the mark-to-market rule a long-term gain of $30 (60 percent X $50 unrealized gain) and a short-term gain of $20 (40 percent X $50). In December 1982, gold rises to $600 and T takes delivery of the gold. In 1982 T will report long-term gain of $48 (60 percent X $80 gain) and short-term gain of $32 (40 percent X $80 gain), computed as follows:

```
Value of gold Futures contract in December 1982 . . .   $600
Contract price  . . . . . . . . . . . . . . . . . . . .    470
Gain . . . . . . . . . . . . . . . . . . . . . . . . .   $130
Less gain reported in 1981  . . . . . . . . . . . . .      50
1982 gain  . . . . . . . . . . . . . . . . . . . . . .   $ 80
```

Note that the tax basis of the gold received will be $600, consisting of the cost of $470 plus $130 total gain realized on the Futures contract.

An investor can elect to have Futures contracts, which are part of an identified mixed straddle (includes Futures contracts and Forward contracts or spot commodities), taxed under the general straddle provision rather than the mark-to-market rule.[267] He can also elect to treat all Futures contracts held on June 23, 1981, as falling under the mark-to-market rule.[268]

An investor with a net commodity Futures loss for a taxable year can elect to carry-back the net loss (40 percent is short-term and 60 percent is long-term) to the three preceding taxable years (the first preceding year is 1981) and offset the loss against the net commodity Futures gains in these years.[269] The 40/60 ratio is retained although the Futures' losses may have offset only long-term gains or short-term gains in the loss year or in prior carry-back years. However, a carry-back would not be allowed to the extent it increases or creates a net operating loss in the carry-back year. The carry-back

---

[266] Code: 1256(f), as amended.
[267] Code: 1256(d)(4) and 1092(d)(4), as amended by 1981 ERTA: 503.
[268] 1981 ERTA: 508(c). Partnerships must make separate elections with respect to its positions. I.R. 82-13.
[269] Code: 1212, as amended by 1981 ERTA: 504.

also cannot exceed the capital gain net income for the carry-back year. For example, assume T incurred a Futures loss of $50,000 in 1983. During 1983, T also had other net short-term capital gains of $10,000. The $50,000 loss is first offset against the $10,000 short-term gain and T elects to carry-back the balance of $40,000 (assuming no other taxable income) to 1981. In 1981, T had Futures gains of $20,000 and a short-term capital loss of $5,000, or net gains of $15,000. The carry-back can offset only the net gains of $15,000 and the balance of $25,000 is carried to 1982. In 1982, T had other net capital gains of $60,000. Because there were no Futures gains in 1982, the $25,000 Futures carry-back cannot be used in 1982. Instead, it can be carried over to 1984 and be offset against any capital gains realized in that year, but $10,000 of the carry-over will be short-term ($25,000 X 40 percent) and $15,000 ($25,000 X 60 percent) will be long-term.

The mark-to-market approach can result in an accumulation of commodity gains in one tax year for commodity traders who have rolled over their gains from prior years into 1981. The investor can elect with respect to the taxable year that includes June 23, 1981, to pay the tax on the rollover Futures gains in up to five equal annual installments.[269a] As a condition to making this election, the mark-to-market rule must be applied to all Futures contracts held during the taxable year, and the tax rate on the gains will be those in effect for 1982. The first installment must be paid by the due date of the 1981 return. Interest will be charged on the subsequent installments.

(c) **Mixed straddles.** Those investors with mixed straddles (combination of Futures contracts, and Forward contracts, options, or spot commodities), which are clearly identified by the close of the day of the position, must treat the entire mixed straddle under the straddle rules described below if an election was made to exclude them from the mark-to-market rule.[270] There was some uncertainty under the original ERTA provisions as to the treatment of mixed straddles if the Futures contracts components are taxed under the mark-to-market rule. The original Senate bill provided that a taxpayer could elect to treat the entire mixed straddle under either the mark-to-market rule or the general straddle provisions. The Senate bill was changed at the last moment to provide that both the Futures contracts and the offsetting positions are to be taxed under the general

---

[269a]–1981 ERTA: 509.   [270] Code: 1256(d), as amended by ERTA: 503.

straddle provisions discussed below if the taxpayer elects not to have the mark-to-market rules apply to the Futures contracts.[271] A natural inference would be that if no election is made, then all positions of the mixed straddle would not be taxed under the general straddle provisions. However, representatives of the Treasury have pointed out that this latter position would be contrary to the legislative history, to wit, preventing the possible deferral of income and converting ordinary income or short-term gains into long-term gains. In essence, the Treasury (and the Joint Tax Committee) would interpret the law as if this provision were not in the 1981 ERTA. Under the Treasury interpretation, a taxpayer would have to report any Futures gain under the mark-to-market rule, but any Futures loss would be deferred under the general straddle provisions. The House Technical Correction Bill of 1982 would provide that the general straddle provisions of Section 1092 will apply to any regulated Futures contracts and any other position making up a mixed straddle.[271a]

The following examples will illustrate the intricacies of the mixed straddle rules.

Assume that T does not elect out of Section 1256 with respect to Futures contracts that are part of mixed straddles. In October 1981, T buys spot gold for cash at $400 and sells a December 1982 gold contract at $470. The economic gain of $70 is primarily attributable to the interest factor in pricing gold for future delivery. On December 31, 1981, the value of the spot gold is $450 and the gold Futures is $520. Under the Treasury's and Joint Tax Committee's interpretation as well as under the House Technical Correction Bill of 1982, the $50 unrealized loss in the Futures Contract will not be recog-

---

[271] Code: 1092 (d) (4), as amended by ERTA: 503. The Senate version of Section 1256 (d) provided for an election to treat the entire mixed straddle under the mark-to-market rules. The final act made a significant substantive change by limiting the applicability of the election to regulated Futures contracts. It is interesting to note that comments made by members of the Senate Finance Committee, which were printed in the Congressional Record (S 8621-2, July 28, 1981), indicate that the change was intended to be technical in nature and not a substantive change.

[271]a – If Section 1092 (d) (4) were not amended by the technical amendment, the authors believe that investors could take the reasonable position that ei-ther the entire mixed straddle is taxed under the general straddle provisions if an election is made not to treat the Futures contracts components under the mark-to-market rule; or, the general straddle provisions do not apply to the entire mixed straddle if no election is made. Under this latter approach, any unrealized gain or loss on the Futures positions would be included in income under the mark-to-market rules and gain or loss on the offsetting positions would be treated as if they were not part of a straddle. Accordingly, this could result in long-term gain or loss when the Forward contract or spot commodity is sold after being held for more than one year.

nized in 1981 due to the existence of an unrealized gain of $50 in the spot gold.[271b]

On December 1, 1982, spot gold is trading at $600 and T delivers the spot gold in fulfillment of his Futures contract. This would result in a loss of $130 on termination of the Futures contract, of which $78 is long-term loss, and $52 is short-term loss, computed as follows:

Value of gold Futures contract on termination	$600
Delivery price	470
Loss	130
Less: Mark-to-market loss in 1981 ($50 less unrealized gain of $50)	*None**
1982 loss (60% long term, 40% short term)	$130

*If the $50 mark-to-market loss were deductible in 1981, the net additional loss on termination of the Futures contract would be $80, of which $48 would be long-term loss and $32 short-term loss.

On delivery of the spot gold, T would recognize a short-term capital gain of $200 (delivery of $600 less cost of $400).[271c]

It should be noted that none of the new straddle provisions would appear to allow the Treasury to apply 40/60 short-term, long-term ratios to the gain or loss on the offsetting non-Futures positions. However, some commentators have suggested that the Treasury may have the power to require such treatment by regulations under Section 1092(b).

Assume in the above example that the market value of the spot gold drops to $300 at the time of delivery in December 1982. In this event, T would recognize a long-term gain of $102 and a short-term gain of $68 on termination of the Futures contracts as follows:

Value of gold Futures contract on termination	$300
Delivery price	470
Gain	170
Plus: Mark-to-market loss 1981 ($50 less unrealized gain of $50)	*None**
1982 gain (60% long term, 40% short term)	$170

*If the $50 mark-to-market loss were deductible in 1981, the 1982 gain on termination of the Future contract would be $220, of which $132 would be long-term gain and $88 short-term gain.

[271b] – If the general straddle provision did not apply, T would report in 1981 the $50 unrealized loss in the Future contract consisting of $30 long-term loss (60% times $50 loss) and a $20 short-term loss (40% times $50 loss). There would be no similar tax consequence because of the $50 rise in the price of the spot gold.

[271c] – Even though the spot gold was held for more than one year, the gain would be short-term under rules similar to the short sale rules. This would occur under Treasury and Joint Tax Committee interpretation as well as under the proposed House Technical Bill of 1982. Otherwise, it could be argued that such gain would be long-term due to the nonapplicability of the short sale rules in a mixed straddle situation.

On delivery of the spot gold, T would recognize a short-term loss of $100 ($400 cost of spot gold less deemed delivery price of $300).[271d]

(d) Forward contracts. These unregulated contracts acquired or straddle positions established after June 23, 1981, will be governed by the new straddle provisions.[272] An election may be made to include all Futures and other positions held on June 23, 1981, under the straddle provisions.[273] Straddles consisting only of regulated Futures contracts are subject to the mark-to-market rules.

As stated previously, a proposed amendment would clarify the uncertainty as to whether mixed straddles will be governed by these general straddle provisions when the offsetting position is Futures contracts taxed under the mark-to-market rule.[274] Thus, if an investor was long a Forward contract or held the spot commodity, and short a Futures contract subject to the mark-to-market provisions, the proposed amendment would provide that the entire straddle position would be governed by the general straddle provisions. An opposite result could have been obtained by a literal reading of the Code. If there were multiple straddle positions, some of which did not include Futures contracts, then these nonoffsetting positions will be subject to these straddle provisions. Furthermore, if a taxpayer elected to apply the general straddle provisions to the entire mixed straddle, the mark-to-market rules would not apply to the Futures components even if the offsetting positions were terminated.

Under the new straddle provisions, a loss recognized in one or more positions during a taxable year will be recognized and deductible in the taxable year only to the extent it exceeds the unrealized gains with respect to the same straddle or other positions. These would include offsetting positions with respect to which the loss arose or positions acquired before the loss was realized.[275] However, gains from an identified straddle[276] are ignored in determining the

---

[271]d – See footnote 271c.
[272] Code: 1092 as amended by ERTA: 501.
[273] ERTA 508(c).
[274] Code: 1092(d)(4), as amended.
[275] Code: 1092(a)(1), as amended. The House Technical Amendment Bill of 1982 would apply the deferral rules to unrecognized gains rather than unrealized gains. This would cover year-end sales. Furthermore, still unresolved is the issue as to which realized loss is deferred where there are multi-

ple losses, some of which are long term and some of which are short-term in nature.
[276] Positions acquired on the same day and not part of a larger straddle must be clearly identified on the investor's records as an identified straddle on the day of acquisition and either all of the positions are closed on the same day or remain open during the taxable year. Code: 1092(a)(2)(B), as amended.

amount of deductible loss for the year.[277] Gains or losses on identified straddles are not recognized until the entire position is closed.[278] Any losses that are not deductible as a result of the straddle provisions are carried over and treated as sustained in the succeeding taxable year, subject to the straddle limitations for that year.[279]

To insure compliance with these new straddle provisions, an investor with a commodity loss during the taxable year will have to disclose any unrealized gains with respect to any position (whether or not a straddle) held at year end, except for inventory, hedging transactions, or identified straddles, in accordance with regulations to be issued by the Treasury.[280] A 5 percent penalty may be imposed for failure to report the unrealized year-end gains if a tax deficiency is imposed because a loss is disallowed under the straddle provisions.[281]

The wash sale rules (see 36.01)[282] and the short sale rules (see 37.03)[283] are to apply to gains or losses realized with respect to any position of a straddle. These provisions will be contained in regulations to be issued by the Treasury.[284] It appears that, in general, the test would be "offsetting positions" rather than "substantially identical" property. These rules are to be applied before the year-end deferral of loss provision. Thus, if a Forward contract is sold at a loss and a substantially identical position was acquired within 30 days of the sale, the loss would be disallowed under the wash sale rule and added to the basis of the new position.[284a] Similarly, if an investor had an offsetting position before the commodity or contract was held for the six-months to one-year or over holding period, any gain on the sale would be short-term. Presumably, a long-term loss would arise if an offsetting position was held for more than one year at the time the investor entered into the straddle position. There will also be a loss of holding period when one of the offsetting positions is terminated.

(e) **Other rules.** Futures contracts entered into before June 23, 1981, or post-June 23, 1981 and Regulated Futures Contracts which are part of a mixed straddle, but which are excluded from the mark-to-market rule, retain the six-month holding period requirement in

---

[277] Code: 1092(a)(1)(A)(iii).
[278] Code: 1092(a)(2)(A).
[279] Code: 1092(a)(1)(B).
[280] Code: 1092(a)(3)(B).
[281] Code: 6653(g), as amended.
[282] Code: 1091(a) and (d).
[283] Code: 1233(b) and (d).

[284] Code: 1092(b).
[284a] — The regulations to be issued by the Treasury may use a shorter period than 30 days, which might be considered too long a period than is appropriate for commodities.

determining the character of the gain or loss on disposition.[284b] Thus, a sale of a "long" Futures contract held for more than six months results in long-term capital gain or loss. Similarly, a sale of a "short" commodity Futures contract can result in long-term capital gains or losses.[285] The Treasury still maintains that any gain or loss on the disposition of the "short" contract would be treated as short-term.[286] The mark-to-market rules may supersede these discussions with respect to regulated Futures contracts.[287]

The longer one-year holding period rule still applies to the sale of unregulated Forward contracts or to a sale of a commodity, as distinguished from a commodity Futures contract. For positions or property acquired before June 24, 1981, the one-year rule applies even if the commodity is used to close a Futures transaction. For example, if in January 1981 an investor buys a spot commodity contract and sells a Futures contract which requires delivery after the seventh month, the closing of the Futures contract with the spot commodity will result in a short-term gain because the one-year holding rule applies to the sale of the commodity. Note that if the above transaction occurred after June 23, 1981, the termination of the Futures contract would be treated as sale of the Futures contract using the market value at the time of termination.[288] Thus, 60 percent of the gain or loss on termination of the Futures contract would be long-term and 40 percent would be short-term. Any gain or loss on disposition of the commodity would be short-term in this example because it was held less than one year.[289]

Offsetting trades through the same broker in the same agricultural commodity future (e.g., wheat, eggs, corn, and the like) in the *same market* for delivery in the *same contract period* are closed as of the moment the offsetting trade is made, pursuant to the rules of the Commodity Exchange Authority[290] and gain or loss is recognized at that time. Where the offsetting trade is made through a different

---

[284b] – The House Technical Correction Bill of 1982 would amend Section 1223 to provide that the six-month period applies to all commodity Futures contracts other than those taxed under the mark-to-market rule.

[285] American Home Products Corp., 601 F. 2d 540 (Ct. Cl., 1979); Hoover Co., 72 TC 206 (1979); Carborundum Co., 74 TC No. 57 (1980).

[286] Priv. Rul. Doc. 8016004.

[287] Code: 1256(a), as amended.

[288] Code: 1256(c), as amended.

[289] Code: 1222. The retention of the more than six-month holding period with respect to commodity Futures was intended to be limited to agricultural commodity Futures contracts. Conference Committee Report TRA 1402; Joint Committee explanation, page 508. However, the House language was adopted covering all commodity Futures. The IRS announced that all commodity Futures are covered by the six-month rule. News Release IR 1787 (3/30/77).

[290] Commodity Exchange Authority Rules, Section 1.46(a).

broker, the transaction is not closed. Therefore, "long" and "short" positions are established and gain or loss is recognized only when the positions are covered.[291] Offsetting trades in nonagricultural commodity futures (e.g., copper, zinc, and so on) may not be required to be closed by the exchange on which they are traded. Here also long and short positions are established and gain or loss is recognized only when the positions are covered unless the mark-to-market rules apply.[292]

In determining the holding period of a commodity received in satisfaction of the commodity Futures contract, the holding period of the commodity Future will be tacked on.[293]

(f) Pre-6/24/81 straddles.   As indicated above, prior to the 1981 ERTA, a purchase of a commodity Future requiring delivery in one calendar month and a simultaneous sale of a commodity Future requiring delivery in another calendar month did not fall within the short sale rules. Therefore, an investor could have availed himself of this statutory exception when entering into this transaction for profit, to realize a short-term capital loss in the current taxable year and possible long-term capital gain in the succeeding year.

However, the Treasury has ruled that the short-term capital loss generated in a silver straddle transaction is not an economic loss and is not deductible.[294] The ruling further indicates that the net economic loss, after merging two years' transactions, is not deductible. This revenue ruling has far-reaching effects. The treasury's utilization of a broad "substance over form" concept and a "lack of real economic loss" concept could cause many transactions, in addition to commodity straddles, to be challenged. There is no effective date to this ruling and accordingly, it could be applied to any commodity straddle or similar transaction as long as the tax year is still open.

---

[291] Reg. 1.1233-1 (d) (2) (iii). The Treasury had ruled, prior to the enactment of the short sale rules (Section 1233), that gain or loss must be recognized at the moment an offsetting trade is made in the same commodity Future on the same market for delivery in the same contract period, even if the offsetting trade is made through a different broker. Mim 6243, C.B. 1948-1, 44 (obsolete); Mim 6789, C.B. 1952-1, 38 (obsolete); however cf. *Joseph Maloney*, 25 T.C. 1219 (1956). These rulings apparently have no current effect in light of the applicability of the short sale rules to commodity Futures and the example given in Reg. 1.1233-1 (d) (2) (iii).

[292] Ibid.

[293] Code: 1223(8). The House Correction Bill of 1982 would amend Section 1223(8) to provide that there would not be any tacking-on of holding period where the commodity Futures contract is governed by the mark-to-market rules of Section 1256.

[294] Rev. Rul. 77-185 (C.B. 1977-1, 22).

Many straddle cases have been docketed in the Tax Court.[294a] The enactment of the 1981 ERTA should not have any effect on the outcome of these pending cases.

It is naturally essential that transactions were entered into with an expectation of realizing a profit, but for the Treasury to present the arguments it made in the ruling and expect that a fair administration of the tax law could be based on such arguments seems unrealistic. The Treasury seems to abandon the distinction between unrealized income and realization and recognition of income, and the concept that each year stands on its own, especially with respect to the proper timing of income for a cash-basis taxpayer. The conclusion of the ruling also appears to be erroneous because the Treasury has not fully considered the economics and profit potential of commodity straddle transactions. An investor, for example, in a silver straddle, who is long the near-month Futures and short the far-month Futures will realize a significant pretax profit if interest rates drop, causing the spread between the contracts to narrow. An inversion (i.e., the further-out silver Futures falling in price below the nearer-term silver Futures) will result in a substantial pretax profit in relationship to the amount of invested capital. The ability to defer income by means of commodity straddles will no longer be available under the 1981 ERTA to traders in commodities or those entering into straddles primarily for tax purposes.

(g) **Pre-6/24/81 cash and carry.** A cash and carry transaction is similar to a commodity straddle except that the investor purchases a "spot" commodity contract in lieu of a Futures contract and takes delivery of the commodity, ordinarily through a warehouse receipt. (The investor could also purchase the nearest-month Futures contract and take delivery of the commodity.) He simultaneously sells a commodity Futures requiring delivery, preferably more than one year out. The investor hopes to make money in this transaction due to expectations of changes in interest rates and other costs of carrying the spot commodity, when compared to the "locked in" spread between the cost of the spot and the selling amount of the Futures contract. Silver, gold, and other metals lend themselves to the cash and carry transactions. However, care must be taken to be sure that the proper spread exists and other economic conditions are favorable before entering into the transaction. Prior to the 1981 ERTA, the expenses

---

[294] *a* – The Tax Court in *Harry Lee Smith,* 78 T.C. No. 26 (1982), disallowed a commodity straddle loss for lack of an economic profit motive.

for storage, insurance, transportation, and interest on borrowed funds to purchase and carry the commodity would be deductible against ordinary income.[295] With respect to a spot commodity purchased or positions taken after June 23, 1981, the above-mentioned carrying charges are no longer deductible but, instead, must be capitalized and added to the cost of the commodity.[296] This will either reduce the amount of capital gains or create a capital loss on the sale of the commodity. Furthermore, under the old rules, the closing of the short position with the commodity held in storage was not a short sale,[297] and, therefore, would result in long-term capital gains if held for more than one year (the six-month holding period rule applied only to regulated Futures).[298]

If the investor now purchases a spot commodity and sells a Futures contract that is regulated by a board of trade or exchange and marked-to-market, then the transaction will constitute a mixed straddle.[299] In this event, an investor will be subject to the mark-to-market rule with respect to the regulated Futures contract unless he elected otherwise.[300] Under the House Technical Correction Bill of 1982, and consistent with the Treasury's position, the deferral rules and short sale rules would apply to all mixed straddles. See 43.03(c) for further discussion of alternate treatment of mixed straddles. The general straddle provisions would definitely apply to the cash and carry transaction if the investor elects not to apply the mark-to-market rule. In this event, a loss would not be recognized on the closing of one position and the establishment of a new offsetting position, and any gain on the closing of the transaction would probably be short-term under the rules similar to the short sale rules.[301] Note that no capitalization is required if the investor owns only the physical commodity and has not entered into a straddle or the transaction qualifies as a business hedging transaction.

(h) **Short sales.** Under the short sale rules (see 37.03) a commodity Futures requiring delivery in one calendar month is not substantially identical to another Futures in the same commodity requiring

---

[295] C. A. Higgins, 75 Fed. Supp. 252 (Ct. Cls. 1948), *Heaven Hill Distilleries, Inc.*, 476 F. 2d 1327 (Ct. Cls. 1973); not followed where storage improved whiskey, *George L. Schultz*, 50 T.C. 688 (1968), aff'd. per curiam 420 F. 2d 490 (CA-3, 1970); Rev. Rul. 70-356, C.B. 1970-2, 68.

[296] Code: 263(g), as amended by 1981 ERTA: 502.
[297] Code: 1233(e).
[298] Code: 1222.
[299] See 40.03(c).
[300] Code: 1256(d), as amended.
[301] Code: 1092(b), as amended.

delivery in a different calendar month.[302] Thus, the regulations indicate that commodity Futures in May and July wheat are not substantially identical and, therefore, the short sale rules are not applicable.[303] The short sale rules also do not apply to Futures which trade in different markets even though they are substantially identical if offsetting transactions are entered into on the same day and both are closed on the same day.[304] Whether Futures in the same commodity traded in different markets are substantially identical will depend upon the facts and circumstances. According to the regulations, historical similarity in price movements in the two markets is the primary factor to be considered.[305] An investor who has sold a commodity Futures short is precluded from enjoying any long-term capital gain upon closing the short sale by buying in the commodity Futures because of the short sale rules.[306] Note that for purposes of the short sale rule, property includes only commodity Futures, and therefore the use of a commodity to close the commodity Futures would not fall within the provinces of the short sale provisions.[307] However, the mark-to-market rules will apply to the Futures contract so that only 60 percent of the gain or loss will be long-term and 40 percent will be short-term.[308] A Futures contract that is a component of a mixed straddle will be subject to rules similar to the short sales provisions if an election is made to exclude the Futures contract from the mark-to-market rule.[309] Forward contracts were subject to short sales rules prior to the 1981 ERTA[310] and may also be subject to the new short sale rules for commodity straddles.[311]

(i) Wash sale rules. The courts are in conflict both as to whether the wash sale provisions apply to commodity Futures transactions and, if so, whether Futures contracts with different delivery dates are "substantially identical" for purposes of the wash sale rules.[312] However, the Treasury has ruled that the wash sale rules do not apply to

---

[302] Code: 1233(e)(2)(B).
[303] Reg. 1.1233-1(d)(2)(i).
[304] Code: 1233(e)(3).
[305] Reg. 1.1233-1(d)(2)(i).
[306] Code: 1233(a); Sen. Rep. No. 2375, 81st Cong. 2nd Sess. p. 87 C.B. 1950-2, 483, p. 545; cf. *Joseph Maloney,* 25 T.C. 1219 (1956).
[307] Code: 1233(e)(2)(A).
[308] Code: 1256(c), as amended.
[309] Code: 1092(b) and (d)(4), as amended. The House Technical Correction Bill of 1982, by amending Section

1092(d)(4) would subject the mixed straddle to rules similar to the short sales provisions in *all* cases.
[310] Code: 1233(e).
[311] Code: 1092(b), as amended.
[312] *Trenton Cotton Oil Co.,* 147 F. 2d 33 (CA-6, 1945), *Corn Products Refining Co.,* 16 T.C. 395, aff'd on other issues 350 U.S. 46; *Sicanoff Vegetable Oil Corp.,* 27 T.C. 1056 (1957) rev'd on other issues 251 F. 2d 764 (CA-7, 1958).

commodity Futures.[313] As mentioned previously, for purposes of the short sale rules the latter type of contracts are not "substantially identical."[314]

Rules similar to the wash sale and short sale rules will now be applicable to straddle positions in commodities taken after June 23, 1981.[315] (See **36.01** for a discussion of wash sale rules.)

.04 Commodity Options

(a) **Introduction.** While options on physical commodities ("Actuals") have been offered by a limited number of CFTC approved dealers for a number of years now, exchange (contract market) listed options on regulated commodity Futures contracts (Futures) are expected to be approved for trading in the near future covering a broad range of Futures (e.g., sugar, gold, heating oil, Treasury bonds, etc.). These options may have a life of more than one year (up to 15 or 16 months in some cases). Exchange listed options on Futures as well as on Actuals will be attractive to speculators and hedgers who wish to limit risk of loss to the premium cost of Put and Call options acquired.

(b) **Tax effect on purchases of options on Futures.** Section 1234(a) provides that the gain or loss attributable to the sale of an option to buy or sell property shall be considered gain or loss from the sale of property "which has the same character as the property to which the option relates has in the hands of the taxpayer (or would have in the hands of the taxpayer if acquired by him)." The enactment of the new commodity rules and their possible application in whole or part to these commodity options has caused much uncertainty as to the tax treatment of these options on Futures. There have been no published rulings or cases specifically dealing with the tax treatment of options on Futures.

Prior to the 1981 ERTA, sale or termination of an option resulted in long-term or short-term gain or loss depending upon the period the options were held before disposition.[316] Since the underlying Futures would have been treated as a capital asset in the hands of a trader or investor, gain or loss on the disposition of the option owned would be characterized as capital in nature. In order for gain or loss to have been treated as long-term in nature (notwithstanding the pre-ERTA

---

[313] Rev. Rul. 71-568, C.B. 1971-2, C.B. 312.
[314] Code: 1233(e)(2)(B).

[315] Code: 1092(b), as amended by 1981 ERTA: 501.
[316] Code: 1234(a).

more-than-six-month holding period requirement for Futures) a more-than-12-month statutory holding period requirement would had to have been satisfied in order for the gain or loss on disposition of an option to have been considered long term in nature.

It could be argued that options on Futures should be treated as regulated Futures contracts themselves, subject to the provisions of Section 1256. Thus, gain or loss realized on disposition would be subject to the 60-40 long-term/short-term treatment, and options held at the close of the taxable year would be subject to the mark-to-market recognition rule.[317] Under such circumstances, the general rules of Section 1234(a) would not come into play. However, these options fail to meet the definition of Futures because: 1) they are not bilateral contracts but rather options; and 2) they are not subject to a system of variation margin.[318] Accordingly, options on regulated futures contracts should not be considered Futures and not subject to the 60-40 mark-to-market rules under Section 1256.

The authors believe that Section 1234(a) should be applicable. The problem is determining what is meant by the wording of the statute dealing with "the same character" as the underlying property (i.e., Futures).[319] It is possible that "character" is meant to be what the tax results would be upon sale of the underlying Futures, including the 60-40 long-term/short-term treatment. Under such circumstances, the gain or loss attributable to the Put or Call in the Futures would be accorded the same 60-40 treatment irrespective of the holding period of the option.[320]

A more restrictive interpretation, which the Treasury may incorporate in its regulations, is that "the same character" wording of the statute deals solely with the nature of capital gain versus ordinary income and not with the special rules of Section 1256 (i.e., 60-40 treatment). Thus, gain or loss on disposition of an option will be long-term capital gain or loss if the option is held for more than 12 months. If held for a shorter period of time, then short-term capital gain or loss will result. If the option lapsed unexercised, the loss will be short-term or long-term depending upon the holding period of the option. Should the option be exercised, no gain or loss would be realized on exercise but an adjustment would be made to the basis of the acquired Futures.

---

[317] Code: 1256(a), as amended.
[318] Code: 1256(b), as amended.
[319] Code: 1234(a).
[320] If this interpretation becomes the acceptable treatment, conversion of short-term capital gain into long-term capital gain might be available through the use of straddles in options on Futures.

(c) **Tax effect on purchasers of options on physical commodities (Actuals).**
There are no uncertainties as to the tax treatment of options on
Actuals. The general rule of Section 1234 would characterize the
options as capital in nature and gain or loss would be treated as long-
term or short-term depending upon the one year holding period requirement. Should the option be exercised, no gain or loss would be
realized upon exercise, but the premium paid would be added to the
basis of the actual commodity acquired. However, there would not
be a tack-on holding period (see general rules with respect to options
on stock—38.04(d)). The tax treatment of options on Forward contracts (Futures contracts on commodities which do not meet the
definition of regulated Futures contracts) will be the same as options
on Actuals.

(d) **Tax effect on sellers of options on Futures or physical commodities
(Actuals).** The same rules dealing with options on stock would be
applicable to these options (see 38.05). Thus, gain or loss on repurchase of either a Put or a Call option on an Futures or Actual,
whether before or after the effective date of the 1981 ERTA, will be
treated as short-term capital gain or loss regardless of the length of
time the option was outstanding prior to its termination. In case of a
lapse of an option, gain will always be short-term capital gain.[321]

(e) **Other rules.** If an investor takes a straddle position solely in
Futures or commodity options or takes offsetting positions in the
commodity, Forward options, or commodity contracts, then the
commodity straddle provisions as to loss deferral and rules similar to
the short sales rules or wash rules may be applicable. (See discussion
of mixed straddles in **40.03(c)** if the offsetting position is a Futures
contract.) Even before the 1981 ERTA, if an investor held a commodity or commodity Futures for less than the required period for
long-term gains and acquired an option to sell the commodity or
contract (Put), any gain on the ultimate sale of the commodity or
contract would be short-term capital gain.[322] For purposes of the
commodity straddle rules, an investor will be considered to have
invested in a straddle if he owns offsetting positions in a commodity
or a contract or option interest in the commodity.[323] Thus, if the
investor has entered into a straddle with part or all of the offsetting
positions consisting of Futures options, then any gain or loss with

---

[321] Code: 1234(b).   [323] Code: 1092(d)(2).
[322] Code: 1233.

respect to any position of the straddle that is subject to the commodity straddle rules will also be subject to rules similar to the wash sales and short sales provisions. Accordingly, not only will a loss realized on disposition of one of the offsetting positions be allowed only to the extent it exceeds the unrealized (unrecognized) gain on the offsetting position,[324] the excess loss would be disallowed under the wash sales rules if the investor entered into another option or contract to reduce the risk of loss on the open position.[325] Similarly, any gain realized on disposition of the option or Futures, Actual, or Forward should be treated as short-term under the new short sale rules for commodity straddles if the option was held for less than 12 months at the time the investor entered into an offsetting position.[326]

41   TREASURY BILLS AND FUTURES

.01   Description

Treasury bills are obligations of the United States which are issued on a discount basis and payable without interest at a fixed maturity date not exceeding one year from the date of issue. The price of these bills are determined by weekly auctions conducted by the Federal Reserve Bank. In 1976 the Chicago Board of Trade began trading Futures contracts on Treasury bills in a manner similar to commodity futures. The Futures market is intended to provide a hedge against the volatility in interest rates for owners of substantial amount of Treasury bills or similar indebtedness. Many investors have taken simultaneous "long" and "short" positions in Treasury bill Futures (different months) in the expectation of deriving economic profit from the transaction and, for tax purposes, ordinary losses similar to the sale of Treasury bills. As discussed below, an investor can no longer obtain ordinary loss treatment by investing in Treasury bills, Treasury bill options, or Treasury bill Futures.[327]

.02   Definition

A Treasury bill Future, like a commodity Future, is a contract to purchase or sell a fixed amount of Treasury bills at a future date for

---

[324] Code: 1092(a)(1).
[325] Code: 1092(b).
[326] Ibid.
[327] Code: 1234(a). Since Treasury bills acquired after June 23, 1981, will be considered a capital asset, gain or loss on an option on Treasury bills will no longer be considered ordinary in nature. See 1981 ERTA: 505.

a fixed amount. The basic trading unit is $1 million of face value of Treasury bills maturing in 90 days up to 24 months.

.03 Tax Consequences

Prior to the 1981 ERTA, a sale of a Treasury bill would result in ordinary income or loss because it was excluded from the definition of a capital asset.[328] A sale of a Treasury bill option would have also resulted in ordinary income or loss.[329] Some investors also claimed ordinary loss treatment on sale of Treasury bill Futures contracts. The Treasury vacillated on the proper treatment, but ultimately ruled that a Treasury bill Futures contract is a capital asset, resulting in capital gain or loss on its sale.[330] Under the Treasury's capital gains or loss interpretation, an investor with a short Futures position could still obtain an ordinary loss by delivering a Treasury bill in closing the contract. An investor with a long position, who would otherwise realize a capital loss on the sale of the Futures contract, could obtain an ordinary loss by taking delivery of the Treasury bill in satisfaction of the Futures contracts and selling it at a loss.

Treasury bills acquired after June 23, 1981, are no longer excluded from the definition of a capital asset.[331] As a consequence, losses realized on sale of Treasury bills, Treasury bill options, or Treasury bill contracts will result in capital rather than ordinary losses.[332] Any gain realized on disposition of Treasury bills will be treated as ordinary income to the extent of the investor's ratable share of the acquisition discount (excess of redemption price over investor's cost).[333] Gains in excess of the discount amount are taxed as capital gains.[334] The discount income is taxed only on the sale or redemption of the Treasury bills. Since Treasury bill Futures contracts are treated similar to commodity Futures contracts, gain or loss will be determined under the rules applicable to regulated Futures contracts. (See 40.03(b).) Treasury bill options may come under the new straddle provisions.[335] (See 40.04.)

---

[328] Code: 1221(5).

[329] Code: 1234(a).

[330] Rev. Rul. 78-414, C.B. 1978-2, 313. The principles of Rev. Rul. 77-185 was held to be also applicable to Treasury bill straddles. (See 40.03(f).)

[331] Code: 1221(5), repealed by 1981 ERTA: 505(a).

[332] Code: 1234(a) and (b).

[333] Code: 1232(a)(4), as amended by 1981 ERTA: 505(b).

[334] Code: 1256, as amended by 1981 ERTA: 503.

[335] Code: 1092, as amended by 1981 ERTA: 501.

42 OTHER FUTURES CONTRACTS

In order to prevent a purchaser or seller of an option to buy or sell property from obtaining ordinary loss treatment, any gain or loss on sale or failure to exercise the option was treated the same as the sale of the underlying property.[336] One obvious flaw with respect to Treasury bills was corrected by including Treasury bills in the definition of capital assets.[337] Another technique for obtaining ordinary loss treatment was to take a straddle position with regard to forward contracts in commodities or government obligations, such as a GNMA, close out the loss position, and claim ordinary loss treatment because there was no sales or exchange of the contract.[338] This possible flaw was also corrected by treating any cancellation, lapse, or other termination by an investor of a contract right or obligation with respect to personal property (other than stock or Listed options) as a sale or exchange of a capital asset.[339]

43 BONDS

.01 General Rules

A bond, like stock, is generally considered to be a capital asset in the hands of an investor. The rules for stock are also applicable to bonds: such as basis, holding period requirements, wash sale rules, and the like. Purchase commissions and similar expenses of acquiring bonds are included as part of the cost of acquisition; however, the amount paid on account of accrued interest is not included in the basis of the bond, but must be offset against the first payment of interest income.

.02 Amortization of Bond Premiums

(a) **Wholly tax-exempt bonds.** The investor is required to amortize the premium on wholly tax-exempt bonds for the purposes of computing basis;[340] however, no deduction for such amortization is allowable.[341] For state income tax purposes many states do not

---

[336] Code: 1234.
[337] 1981 ERTA: 505(a).
[338] The Treasury has ruled privately that the loss on a GNMA straddle would not be recognized until all related positions are closed. Priv. Rul. Doc. 8117016.

[339] Code: 1234A, as amended by 1981 ERTA: 507, effective for contracts acquired after June 23, 1981.
[340] Reg. 1.1016-5(b).
[341] Code: 171(a)(2).

require the bond premium to be amortized if the interest income is subject to state tax. Front load fees charged for the purchase of shares of municipal bond funds or Massachusetts trusts taxed as corporations, should not be amortized since they are incurred in the purchase of a stock interest and not in the purchase of a direct interest in a tax-exempt bond. Therefore, the unamortized amount should be taken into account in reporting gain or loss on a subsequent disposition. A similar treatment may not be applicable to front load fees charged in acquiring municipal bond trust interests. The purchaser is treated for tax purposes as the owner of the property and must report income and deductions as if the grantor owned the property directly. Accordingly, fees incurred in acquiring tax exempts would have to be amortized over the life of the bonds, and the amortization would not be deductible since attributable to tax exempt income. Any unamortized fees would be taken into account in determining gain or loss on a premature disposition of the trust interest.

(b) Other bonds. Investors who elect to amortize bond premiums paid in acquiring fully taxable bonds will be allowed an amortization deduction in computing taxable income (and must make a corresponding negative basis adjustment to the tax basis of the bonds), provided the optional tax tables or the standard deduction are not used in that year.[342] However, an amortization deduction will be deemed to have been taken in the standard deduction year for purposes of computing the adjusted tax basis of the bonds.[343] The binding election applies to all such bonds owned in the year of the election and to such bonds acquired in subsequent years. It is made by claiming the deduction in the return for the taxable year in question.[344] A separate election may be made by the estate or donee if the investor desires to make a lifetime gift.[345] If the decedent dies before the accrued interest is received, the decedent may still take an amortization deduction on the final tax return, although the interest income will be reported by his estate or beneficiaries.[346] An investor who has not received any interest in the taxable year is permitted but not required to deduct the amortization.[347]

The total premium to be amortized with respect to any fully taxable bond acquired after 1957 is the excess of the basis of the bond for determining loss on a sale or exchange over the amount payable

---

[342] Code: 171(a)(1).
[343] Reg. 1.171-1(b)(5).
[344] Reg. 1.171-3.

[345] Code: 171(c).
[346] Reg. 1.171-(c).
[347] Reg. 1.171-2(e).

at maturity or any earlier Call date, whichever produces the lower tax deduction.[348] See 33.03 for determination of basis. Where a premium exists as the result of the addition to the basis of the interest equalization tax paid (see 54.03) such premium is amortizable.[349] Special rules apply to premiums on bonds acquired before 1958.[350] The amortizable premium on a bond does not include that part of the premium which is attributable to the conversion features of the bond, determined as of the time of acquisition.[351] Thus, if an investor purchased $100 Eurodollar bonds which were either convertible into stock of the issuer or callable at $115 at the end of five years, there would be no amortizable bond premium before the Call at $115 is exercised assuming the value of the conversion privilege is at least $115 at the time the bond is issued.[352] The premium attributable to the period prior to the beginning of amortization may not be amortized, but remains part of the basis of the bond to be taken into account in determining gain or loss on disposition. Where the bond is called before maturity and a portion of the premium has not been amortized, the remaining premium may be deducted in the year the bond is called.[353] Note, however, on a sale of the bond, the unamortized premium remains part of the adjusted tax basis in computing gain or loss on the disposition. In the case where the bonds are not called on the Call date and the premium has not been fully amortized, the remaining premium is adjusted over the period to the next Call date or maturity date.[354]

.03 Amortization of Bond Discount

Investors owning noninterest-bearing obligations issued at a discount and redeemable for fixed amounts increasing at stated intervals, such as Series E U.S. savings bonds, may elect to report each year the annual increment in value as income received.[355] Without the election, the investor would report the bunched amount of in-

---

[348] Code: 171 (b) (1) (B) – The premium on callable tax-exempt bonds must be amortized to the "earlier" call date determined under Reg. 1.171-2(b).

[349] See Senate Finance Committee report, P.L. 88-563, section .05(c)(3).

[350] Code: 171(b)(1)(B); Reg. 1.171-2(a) (2).

[351] Code: 171(b)(1); Reg. 1.171-2(c).

[352] Reg. 1.61-12(c)(5), Example.

[353] Reg. 1.171-2(a)(2)(iii).

[354] Reg. 1.171-2(b)(2).

[355] Code: 454(a). This election is not available with respect to savings certificates issued by banks, savings and loans associations, and similar organizations. Interest (or "dividends") on such certificates is held to be taxable when there is a right to withdraw it even if the principal must be withdrawn at the same time. (Rev. Rul. 66-44, C.B. 1966-1, 94; Rev. Rul. 66-45, C.B. 1966-1, 95). See also footnote 357, infra.

come when the bond is redeemed. The election is binding as to all
such obligations owned or thereafter acquired and for all subsequent
years. In the year of election, all increases in redemption value as of
the beginning of the year must also be included in income. An execu-
tor may elect to include all of the unrealized interest on the U.S.
savings bonds in the final return of the deceased investor.[356] In the
case of all other types of obligations, other than corporate obligations issued after May 27, 1969, bond discount is not given any tax
effect until the obligation is redeemed or otherwise disposed of. For
corporate obligations issued after May 27, 1969, the original issue
discount must be included in the investor's income on a ratable
monthly basis over the life of the obligation.[357] A subsequent holder
is required to amortize the remaining discount, less any amount paid
for the obligation over the original issue price as increased by prior
amortized discount. The basis of the obligation is increased by the
bond discount included in income.[358] If the obligation is redeemed
prior to maturity and there was no plan or agreement for the premature redemption, any unearned original issue discount or premium
paid on redemption will be treated as gain from the sale of the
bond.[359] The earned portion of the original issue discount (pro rata
amount of the original issue discount up to date of redemption) will
be taxed as interest income. When the bond is issued as part of an
economic unit (also includes a warrant, or other option or property)
each component of the economic unit must be valued at the time the
economic unit is acquired by the first purchaser in order to determine the amount of original issue discount with respect to the
bond.[360] If there are a series of obligations that mature serially, or
there is a single obligation with sinking fund provisions, each series
or installment payment is treated as a separate obligation for purposes of allocating the total original issue discount.[361]

.04 Accrued Interest on Purchase or Sale

The amount paid for a bond purchased between interest payment
dates will generally include the interest earned to the date of pur-

---

[356] Priv. Rul. Doc. 7907120.
[357] Code: 1232(a)(3). "Other evidence of
indebtedness" includes certificates of
deposits, time deposits, bonus plans,
and other deposit arrangements with
banks. Reg. 1.1232-1(d).
[358] Code: 1232(a)(3)(E).
[359] Bolnick, 44 TC 245 (1965) (Acq.).

[360] Code: 1232(b); Reg. 1.1232-3(b)(2)
(ii)(a). In the case of a private place-
ment, an assumed price for the obligation may be agreed to between the issuer and the purchaser. Reg. 1.1232-
3(b)(2)(ii)(b).
[361] Reg. 1.1232-3(b)(2)(iv).

chase. The investor will reduce his first interest received by this amount.[362] When the bonds are sold, the portion of the proceeds attributable to interest earned to the date of the sale will be reported as interest income.[363] In practice, settlement dates are used in determining the amount of accrued interest.

.05 Interest Income

Interest income may be classified in two types: fully taxable and fully tax-exempt (partially tax-exempt bonds are no longer in existence). Most interest income from corporate bonds and federal bonds falls within the first classification. Interest on obligations of a state or other local authority, the District of Columbia, or a territory or possession of the United States generally is fully exempt from federal tax.[364] Tax-exempt interest may also be received from partnerships or trusts and in taxable years beginning after 1975 from municipal bond funds.[365] An investor who lends his tax-exempts to a broker for delivery to a purchaser under a short sale arrangement will not be permitted to treat the amounts received from the broker as tax-exempt income.[366] Interest on tax-free covenant bonds issued before 1934 by certain corporations is fully taxable, but a credit against tax liability of 2 percent of the interest is allowed to the taxpayer.[367] In determining which type of obligation gives the largest return, the comparison should be based on receipts after taxes.

.06 Tax-exempt Savings Certificates

Investors may purchase tax-exempt savings certificates (all savers' certificates) from qualified institutions that participate in real estate or agricultural loans.[368] These one-year certificates are available only during the period October 1, 1981, through December 31, 1982, and will have a yield of 70 percent of the yield on one-year Treasury bills. A lifetime exclusion of $1,000 of interest ($2,000 for taxpayers filing joint returns) will be allowed, but the entire interest (after penalty) will be taxable at the time any certificates are redeemed before maturity. Investment in the certificates also can result in a

---

[362] *Thompson Scenic Railway,* 9 BTA 1203 (1928); Sol. Op. 46, 3 C.B. 90 (obsolete).

[363] Reg. 1.61-7(d).

[364] Code: 103. Certain "industrial development" bonds issued after May 1, 1968, and "arbitrage" bonds issued after October 9, 1969, are no longer tax-exempt. Code: 103(c) and (d).

[365] Code: 852(b)(5).

[366] Rev. Rul. 80-135, C.B. 1980-1, 18.

[367] Code: 32(2).

[368] Code: 128, as amended by 1981 ERTA: 301.

disallowance of investment expense, including interest expense. Only investors with marginal tax brackets in excess of 30 percent should consider investing in these certificates.

.07 Net Interest Exclusion

Commencing in 1985, an investor may exclude from tax 15 percent of the first $3,000 of net interest income (15 percent of $6,000 for joint returns) after reduction for consumer interest expense.[369]

.08 Flat Bonds

Many bonds which are in default of interest or principal are traded "flat." The quoted price covers not only the principal, but gives the purchaser the right to unpaid accrued interest without any additional or separate charge. Payments of interest accrued prior to the date of purchase are treated as recovery of cost,[370] while payments attributable to interest earned after such date constitute interest income. If the payment of prepurchase date interest exceeds the basis of the bonds to the investor, the excess is taxed as proceeds of redemption usually capital gain.[371] Where bonds are sold flat, the portion of the proceeds attributable to the interest accrued after the date of purchase to the date of sale will be treated as interest income, not as giving rise to capital gain or loss.[372]

Where bonds, which are trading flat, are sold short, a question is raised about the treatment to the short seller of the payments in lieu of interest that are subsequently made by him. The rule should be similar to payments in lieu of dividends on short sales (see **48.06**) (i.e., deductible as a nonbusiness expense).[373] However, a profit motive must exist in order for the deduction to be sustained.[374] The repurchase of the short position immediately subsequent to the payment of the "flat" interest will result generally in a short-term capital gain equal to the reduction in value of the flat bond.

---

[369] Code: 128, as amended by 1981 ERTA: 302.

[370] Reg. 1.61-7(c).

[371] *Rickaby,* 27 T.C. 886 (Acq.) (1958); Rev. Rul. 60-284, C.B. 1960-2, 464.

[372] *Jaglom,* 303 F. 2d 847 (CA-2, 1962); *Langston,* 308 F. 2d 729 (CA-5, 1962).

[373] Rev. Rul. 72-521, C.B. 1972-2, 178 (replacing I.T. 3989, C.B. 1950-1, 34). The earlier ruling, specifically dealing with dividends paid on short sales, has been cited as applicable to interest paid on borrowing of securities, although the interest was disallowed on grounds of sham. J. G. Gold, 41 T.C. 419, 426, (1963).

[374] Hart, 41 T.C. 131 (1963), aff'd. 338 F. 2d 410 (CA-2, 1964). (See footnote 491.)

.09 Retirement Redemption, and Disposition of Bonds

(a) **General rule.** The retirement of a bond will be considered as the sale or exchange of that bond resulting generally in capital gain or loss treatment. Bonds issued prior to 1955 must be with interest coupons or in registered form in order to qualify for this treatment.[375]

(b) **Bonds originally issued at a discount.** Gain on the sale or retirement of bonds held by the investor for more than one year and which were originally issued (after 1954) at a discount of more than ¼ percent a year is given special treatment.[376] That portion of the gain which represents the original discount element is treated as ordinary income, with excess gain, if any, given capital gain treatment.[377] Brokerage commissions are disregarded in computing original issue discount.[378] A tax-free exchange of bonds for other bonds or preferred stock will not give rise to original issue discount.[379] In the case of convertible bonds, the issue price is not reduced by the value of the conversion feature in determining original issue discount.[380] Where bonds are issued with detachable warrants, however, a portion of the issue price must be allocated to the warrants, and thus original issue discount may result.[381] Allocation of each element of the investment unit is made on the basis of relative market values. A failure to exercise warrants issued as part of the investment unit will not affect the amount of original issue discount determined at the time the bonds were issued.[382] If a loss is realized on disposition of the bond, it is treated as a capital loss. For the treatment of original issue discount on obligations issued after May 27, 1969, see 43.03. The original discount rule generally does not apply to tax-exempt bonds or bonds purchased at a premium. However, gain on sale of tax-exempt bonds attributable to original issue discount is treated as tax-exempt interest, while the gain attributable to market discount is taxed as capital gain.[383] Similarly accrued interest income and original issue discount received on redemption of tax-exempt bonds prior to maturity represent tax-exempt income.[384] Any unearned original issue discount on premiums received on an early redemption will be taxed as gain from

---

[375] Code: 1232(b)(2).
[376] Code: 1232(a)(2).
[377] Rev. Rul. 75-117, C.B. 1975-1, 273.
[378] National Can Corp., 1981-1 USTC 9551 (DC Ill., 1981).
[379] Rev. Rul. 77-415, C.B. 1977-2, 311.

[380] Reg. 1.1232-3(b)(2).
[381] Code: 1232(b)(2); Reg. 1.1232-3(b)(2).
[382] Rev. Rul. 72-46, C.B. 1972-1, 50.
[383] Rev. Rul. 60-210, C.B. 1960-1, 38.
[384] Rev. Rul. 72-587, C.B. 1972-2, 74.

exchange of the bonds.[385] Because of the reversal of its prior position the Treasury will treat unearned original issue discount received on redemption of tax exempts issued before June 9, 1980, as tax-exempt income. Where dealers acquire a series of bonds from a governmental unit at par and sell some of the bonds to the public at a discount, the Treasury has ruled that the discount is not tax-exempt.[386]

The discount on noninterest-bearing federal or municipal obligations, which are payable within one year of the date of issue, will be considered as being received when the obligation is disposed of or redeemed.[387] The excess of proceeds over basis is taxed as ordinary income in the case of federal obligations.[388] In the case of municipal obligations, the gain attributable to original issue discount is tax-exempt, while gain attributable to market discount is taxable as capital gains.[389] For a discussion of Treasury bill Futures, see **41**.

(c) **Bonds convertible into commodities.** With the surge in the value of many commodities, corporations found that they could obtain better financial terms and defer paying tax on commodities by issuing bonds at a low interest rate with the bondholder receiving cash or a stated amount of commodities at maturity. Such commodities as silver or oil have been used, with the investor being entitled to either a stated quantity of the commodity or its cash equivalent at maturity. There should be neither an original issue discount nor a bond premium at issuance since the investor may receive the face value of the bond at maturity, and it is impossible at this time to reasonably compute the value of the commodity at the time the bond matures. Accordingly, the bondholder should be entitled to capital gains treatment if the commodity or cash received upon redemption of the bond exceeds his cost of acquiring the bond. If the investor is entitled to a stated amount of a commodity, a subsequent sale will result in capital gain or loss treatment depending upon the amount received for the commodity, as compared with its value when received by the investor and the period the commodity was held before sale.

(d) **Sale and repurchase.** A common practice for owners of tax-exempt or other securities is to agree to sell the securities to a broker

---

[385] Rev. Rul. 80-143, C.B. 1980-1, 19, modifying Rev. Rul. 72-587, C.B. 1972-2, 74.

[386] Rev. Rul. 57-49, C.B. 1957-1, 62; Rev. Rul. 60-210, C.B. 1960-1, 38,

modified by Rev. Rul. 60-376, C.B. 1960-2, 38.

[387] Code: 454(b).

[388] Code: 1221(5).

[389] Rev. Rul. 60-210, C.B. 1960-1, 38; Code: 1221(5).

or bank at a fixed price and then repurchase the same amount of securities at the same price plus interest (a "reverse Repo"). This type of transaction was treated as a secured loan, with the investor entitled to the tax-exempt interest income.[390] Any interest deduction would probably be disallowed if the loan was secured by tax-exempts. (See **48.05.**) It is understood that the Treasury may be reconsidering its position. Under consideration is a new approach whereby the sale would be treated as a taxable sale unless identical securities are returned to the seller. While gain would be taxable on the sale, any loss would be disallowed under the wash sale provision. Future private rulings will not be issued on this point until the matter is resolved. Rev. Rul. 74-27 has been distinguished by the Treasury on the grounds that identical securities were returned. A change of position may open up new avenues for tax planning, including artificially recognizing gain on the transaction where advisable or enabling the broker or bank to receive tax-exempt income and in exchange the investor may obtain better terms for the loan.

Holding that the transaction is taxable merely because the identical securities are not returned to the investor is inconsistent with other rules dealing with securities held by brokers on behalf of investors. In the latter situation, no taxable exchange results merely because the original certificates are not returned to the investor. In a sale and repurchase transaction, the securities are merely collateral for a loan and economic ownership does not pass. A sale does *not* take place (the terminology "sale and repurchase" is misleading). It should not matter that the same securities are not returned or whether or not tax-exempt securities are involved.

A variation of the sale and repurchase is where an investor purchases Treasury bills or bonds due in the succeeding year and borrows funds from the brokerage firm to finance the purchase ("a Repo"). The purchase may be financed by the purchaser selling the obligations back to the broker and repurchasing them at a higher amount equivalent to an interest charge.[391] In this manner an inves-

---

[390] Rev. Rul. 74-27, C.B. 1974-1, 24; *First National Bank in Wichita,* 57 F. 2d 7 (CA-10, 1932), Cert. den. 287 U.S. 636; *American National Bank of Austin,* 421 F. 2d 442 (CA-5, 1970), Cert. den. 400 U.S. 819; but see *Bank of California, National Ass'n.,* 80 F. 2d 389 (CA-9, 1935); *Citizens National Bank of Waco,* 551 F. 2d 832 (Ct. Cl., 1977); and *American National Bank of Austin,* 573 F. 2d 120 (Ct. Cl., 1978); to the contrary where the securities were not always repurchased.

[391] In Priv. Rul. Doc. 8011067, the Treasury inexplicably refused to rule that the "Repo financing," which was incurred for valid business reasons, would result in interest deductions and long-term capital gains on sale of the bonds.

tor can defer the payment of taxes by obtaining interest deductions in the current year (subject to investment interest limitations) and interest income (or capital gains if a sale of discounted bonds) in the succeeding year. This transaction can be questioned by the Treasury unless the investor can prove that he entered into the transaction with profit motives (e.g., the investor anticipated a drop in the interest rates, which would lower his interest expense while his interest income or bond discount is fixed). With the current fluctuations in interest rates, an investor can readily establish that he entered into the transaction to make a profit. Note: an investor can sustain a substantial economic loss if the interest rates were to rise.

(e) Bonds with coupons detached.   Gain realized on sale of bonds purchased after 1957 with coupons detached will be given ordinary income treatment to the extent of the market value of the detached coupons at the time of purchase.[392] Thus, if the bond with coupons attached had a value of $900 but were sold for $800 without the coupons, the first $100 of gain on subsequent sale of the bonds would be ordinary income. Note that this provision does not affect the original seller of the bonds without the coupons. Under the general rules he would apparently realize a capital gain or loss on sale of bonds (without the coupons) and will report the interest on the detached coupons in gross income when received.

(f) Detached bond coupons.   Proceeds from the sale of detached bond coupons are taxed as ordinary income rather than capital gains since the coupons are not capital assets.[393] No portion of the basis of the bond is allocated to the detached coupons.[394] Once the bond coupons are sold, they lose their character as interest income and become capital assets.[395] Therefore, a purchaser of detached bond coupons will realize capital gain or loss on the sale of the unmatured coupons.[396] Any gain from the sale of matured bond coupons is taxed as ordinary income.[397]

---

[392] Code: 1232(c); Reg. 1.1232-4; Priv. Rul. Doc. 7934003.

[393] R. H. Shafer, 204 F. Supp. 473 (DC Ohio, 1962), aff'd per curiam 312 F. 2d 747 (CA-6, 1963).

[394] Priv. Rul. Doc. 8108108.

[395] Sol. Op. 46, C.B. 3, 90, declared obsolete by Rev. Rul. 68-575, C.B. 1968-2, 603.

[396] Rev. Rul. 54-251, C.B. 1954-2, 172.

[397] Ibid. Proposed legislation would change tax treatment of items in 43.09(e),(f). The tax advantages of bond stripping have been eliminated by the 1982 Tax Act.

.10 Exchange of Bonds—Deferral of Gain or Loss

Ordinarily an exchange of bonds for other securities, stock or property is a taxable exchange.[398] An exchange of bonds of the same debtor will also be taxable when there are material changes in the terms of the securities. Differences in the fair market value of the bonds is not a controlling factor.[399] Capital gain or loss results from an exchange of a note, secured by a real estate mortgage, for a corporate bond of the same par value but with a different market value. Unpaid interest on the note is not taxed to the noteholder because the value of the property received in exchange is less than the face value of the note.[400] Similarly, an exchange of New York City bonds for "Big MAC" bonds constitutes a taxable exchange since the bonds are not considered substantially identical. The difference between par value and the market value of the Big MAC bonds represents original issue discount and is exempt from tax on a subsequent sale or redemption.[401]

Special rules, however, permit tax-free exchanges of bonds for other bonds, securities or stock, bonds in the same or a lesser principal amount (interest rates may vary), or stock in connection with a tax-free reorganization.[402] Conversion of bonds by their terms into stock of the debtor corporation also constitutes a tax-free exchange,[403] but not a conversion into stock of another corporation.[404] For corporate acquisitions contracted after May 27, 1969, marketable bonds or bonds payable on demand will be treated as cash for purposes of computing the amount of deferred gain under the installment method. Prior to the change in the installment sale rules, marketable or demand obligations could disqualify a seller from meeting the 30 percent of sale price test.[405] The receipt of nonmarketable convertible debentures on sale of property could qualify for installment treatment since the conversion feature is considered part of the debenture and is not valued separately.[406] Where convertible debentures are received as part of the sales proceeds, the Treasury has questionably ruled that the amount of gain taxed at the time the

---

[398] Code: 1301(a).

[399] Rev. Rul. 81-169, I.R.B. 1981-25, 17. Differences in the interest rates, maturity dates, and sinking fund provisions were sufficient to cause the exchange to be taxable.

[400] Rev. Rul. 73-328, C.B. 1973-2, 296.

[401] Priv. Rul. Doc. 7902002.

[402] Code: 354, 368, 371.

[403] Rev. Rul. 72-265, C.B. 1972-1, 222.

[404] Timken, 47 B.T.A. 494 (1942); Rev. Rul. 72-265, C.B. 1972-1, 222; Rev. Rul. 69-135, C.B. 1969-1, 198.

[405] Code: 453(f); Rev. Rul. 75-117, C.B. 1975-1, 273.

[406] Rev. Rul. 71-420, C.B. 1971-2, 220.

convertible bonds are converted into stock would be based upon the value of the stock received in the exchange and would not be limited to the deferred gain. An identical position was taken that a gift of the convertible debenture would also result in tax to the grantor to the extent that the fair market value of the convertible debentures exceeded basis.[407] Certain exchanges of U.S. obligations are also nontaxable.[408] The most common types of exchanges are the exchange of Series E bonds for other government obligations, resulting in deferment of accrued interest until ultimate redemption, and exchanges of one type of long-term government obligation for another pursuant to a special announcement. Owners of Series E bonds held for more than 40 years should either exchange the bonds for other government bonds or cash them and report all of the deferred interest income because the bonds cease paying interest after 40 years. A conversion of Series E bonds to a trust in which the investor is treated as the owner for tax purposes will not be treated as a disposition causing the deferred interest income to be taxed.[409] Published Capital Changes services generally provide the necessary information regarding exchanges of publicly held securities.

.11 Flower Bonds

Certain U.S. Treasury bonds ("flower bonds") may be used after death in payment of the investor's estate tax liability at their par value. Due to the low interest yields on these bonds, they generally sell at a discount and therefore in the past a benefit could be obtained by acquiring these bonds at a discount and redeeming them at face value in payment of estate taxes. However, because the bonds are redeemable at face value, this value must be used in valuing the assets of the deceased investor's estate in computing both federal and state estate or inheritance taxes. Excess flower bonds that were sold at market value after the estate tax return was filed, and accordingly unavailable to pay a subsequent estate tax deficiency, must also be included in the estate at par value.[410] Inclusion at face value would

---

[407] Rev. Rul. 72-264, C.B. 1972-1, 131. This harsh interpretation of Section 453(d) would result in an investor realizing a greater amount of income by electing the installment method than if he reported the full amount of gain at the time of the exchange. The intent of the installment sale provision was to alleviate a hardship caused by requiring a taxpayer to pay a tax on the entire gain realized on the sale although he received little or no cash in the year of sale, and not to impose a penalty for making the election. This point has not yet been litigated.

[408] Code: 1037.

[409] Priv. Rul. Doc. 7729003.

[410] Estate of Simmie, 69 TC No. 75 (1978), aff'd 632 F. 2d 93 (CA-9 (1980).

therefore reduce the benefits of these flower bonds to the extent of the estate tax rates. Thus, if the estate tax rate were 70 percent, the benefit of utilizing flower bonds would be reduced to 30 percent of the discount. Naturally, the lower the estate tax rate, the greater the benefits from flower bonds. The recent changes made by the 1981 ERTA, including the gradual reduction of the maximum tax rate to 50 percent, should increase the benefits derived from flower bonds. No gain will be recognized on redemption of these bonds because the basis to the estate would be their face value reported in the estate tax return. Note that the number of these bonds is diminishing since the Treasury is not authorized to issue these bonds after March 3, 1971.[411]

44 WORTHLESS SECURITIES

If a security becomes completely worthless during the taxable year, its cost (tax basis) is deductible as a loss from the sale or exchange of a capital asset taking place on the last day of the taxable year.[412] No deduction is allowed for partial worthlessness or decline in market value until the security is sold or exchanged in a closed transaction. Mere bankruptcy is not sufficient to claim worthless stock loss if a shareholder may receive shares of the reorganized corporation.[413] Nor can a shareholder claim a theft loss where the bankruptcy was caused by the corporate management's fraudulent actions and statements if the shares were purchased in the open market.[414] However, an ordinary theft loss deduction may be claimed when the shareholders were induced to vote for merger because of misleading financial statements unless there is a reasonable prospect of recovery of the investment through the bankruptcy reorganization.[415] If a shareholder sells his stock before the recovery prospects materialize, it is understood that the Treasury will permit the unrecovered cost to be deductible as an ordinary theft loss rather than a capital loss.

Usually the deduction for a worthless stock loss is allowed in the year in which there is an identifiable event demonstrating worthlessness, such as bankruptcy of the corporation, reorganization with no provision for stockholders, cessation of business, and so on. Merely showing that the corporation had no liquidation value and was incurring losses each year was not sufficient reason for claiming a worthless loss deduction before the year it ceased doing business.[416]

---

[411] Code: 6312, repealed by P.L. 92-5.
[412] Code: 165(g).
[413] Rev. Rul. 77-17, C.B. 1977-1, 44.
[414] Ibid.
[415] Rev. Rul. 77-18, C.B. 1977-1, 46.
[416] Thun, T.C. Memo 1977-372.

The Treasury frequently will insist that the loss was sustained in a later or earlier year than the one in which the loss was claimed on the return. A special seven-year statute of limitations for refund claims accords some additional protection to the taxpayer who reported the loss in the wrong year.[417] However, as one court has suggested, the only safe practice is to claim a loss for worthlessness in the earliest year possible and to renew the claim in subsequent years if there is any chance of its being applicable to the income for those later years.[418]

45 LOSS ON FAILURE TO DELIVER

A loss suffered by an investor arising from the failure of his broker to deliver stock which was fully paid was held to be an ordinary loss and not a nonbusiness bad debt (a short-term loss).[419] The investor had rescinded the purchase agreement, but because of the insolvent condition of his broker he agreed to settle for an amount less than the original purchase price. An ordinary loss was allowed because there was no sale or exchange and a creditor-debtor relationship did not exist between the investor and his broker. However, a loss realized on the sale of an investor's margin stock by the trustee of an insolvent brokerage firm in the course of liquidating its business resulted in a capital loss to the investor.[420]

Losses realized on subordination agreements with stock brokerage firms were originally held to be ordinary losses.[421] Subsequent court decisions have found the losses to be capital losses unless the loss arose from a bailment arrangement with the brokerage firm.[422]

46 ASSIGNMENT OF INCOME

Ordinarily, a shareholder or bondholder cannot validly assign part or all of the dividends or interest payable on the security and still retain ownership of the security.[423] The assigned income will be taxed to the assignor when paid. (See statutory exception for short-term trust on **64**). However, an assignment of future income for con-

---

[417]Code: 6511(d).
[418]*Young,* 123 F. 2d 597 (CA-2, 1941).
[419]Meyer, T.C. Memo 1975-349, aff'd per curiam 547 F. 2d 943 (CA-5, 1977).
[420]Rev. Rul. 74-293, C.B. 1974-1, 54.
[421]Stahl, 441 F. 2d 999 (CA-DC, 1970); Michtom, 573 F. 2d 58 (Ct. Cl., 1978).

[422]Michtom, 80-2 USTC 9531 (Ct. Cl., 1980), vacating its prior decision; Lorch, 70 TC 674 (1978), aff'd 605 F. 2d 657 (CA-2, 1979), cert. den. 100 S. Ct. 1024 (1980).
[423]*Lucas* v. *Earl,* 281 U.S. 111 (1930); *Helvering* v. *Horst,* 311 U.S. 112 (1948).

sideration in a bona fide commercial transaction generally will result in ordinary income in the year of receipt.[424] A trust beneficiary who assigned his trust interest to a charity was held taxable on dividend income payable to the trust because the assignment was after the dividend declaration date.[425] In this ruling the date of declaration was the same as the record date, but the record date is usually controlling with respect to which shareholders are entitled to the dividend. On the other hand, an assignment of future dividend income to the shareholder's son for adequate consideration to enable the shareholder to utilize large interest deductions in the current year was upheld on the grounds that the transaction was not a sham.[426] The payment of adequate consideration, the dividend was from a publicly held corporation not controlled by the assignor, and the fact that the assignor was not required to perform future services in order to fulfill his obligations are important factors in determining whether the assignment will be recognized for tax purposes. This type of assignment is distinguishable from a sale of future rents, future manufacturing profits or future pipeline revenues where the purchasers had to look solely to the sellers to produce the future income.[427] Amounts received on a sale of detached bond coupons would also be included in income in the year received.[428] No portion of the basis of the bond should be allocated to the bond coupons.

Note that a sale of a production payment (i.e., a right to a specified amount of future receipts from mineral property), by the owner of the property to an investor or financial institution is treated as a loan rather than a sale of property.[429]

47 INSTALLMENT SALES

An investor will recognize gain when he receives cash or other property in exchange for his stock, securities, or other investment property.[430] Part or all of the gain can be deferred by receiving cash in the following years or by accepting notes, with one or more payments due after the year of sale.[431] Thus, if an investor receives a note with equal payments over five years, the gain on the sale will be reported proportionately as the payments are received. Receipt of a

---

[424] P. G. Lake, Inc. 356 U.S. 260 (1958).
[425] Rev. Rul. 74-562, C.B. 1974-2, 28.
[426] Stranahan Est. 472 F. 2d 867 (CA-6, 1973), rev'g. T.C. Memo 1971-250.
[427] Mapco Inc., 556 F. 2d 1107 (Ct. Cl., 1977).

[428] Priv. Rul. Doc. 8108108.
[429] Code: 636.
[430] Code: 1001.
[431] Code: 453(b).

purchaser's obligation that is payable on demand or is readily marketable (traded on an established exchange or market) will be treated as the receipt of cash.[432] The installment sales rules apply even if more than 30 percent of the sales price is received in the year of sale or the total sales price is less than $1,000.[433] Installment notes received on sales of property after adoption of a plan of liquidation under Section 337 (one-year liquidation) can now qualify for the installment method.[434] In certain cases an investor will want to report the full gain on sale (e.g., expiring net operating losses or investment credits), or the investor wants to offset the short-term gains realized on sale against long-term losses. In this event he can timely elect not to apply the installment method to this particular sale.[435] (See 50 for discussion of sales to related persons.) An installment note will qualify even if the note is guaranteed by a third party,[436] but not if the installment sale is secured by placing funds in escrow.[437]

48 EXPENSES OF THE INVESTOR

.01 In General

Ordinary and necessary expenses paid or incurred by an investor for the production or collection of income or for the management or conservation of his investments are deductible.[438]

.02 Types of Deductible Expenses

Items of investor's expenses which have been held deductible include investment counsel fees, statistical services, safe-deposit box rental, custodian fees, legal and accounting advisory services, office expenses, and secretary's salary.[439] However, for post-1975 years an investor cannot deduct a portion of the expense of his residence used for investment activities unless he qualifies as a trader and meets other tests, including that the portion of the dwelling be used exclusively and on a regular basis for business purposes.[440]

Carfare to visit broker for consultation is deductible,[441] but not

---

[432] Code: 453(f).
[433] Code: 453(b)(1)(B) and 453(b)(2)(B), repealed.
[434] Code: 453(h).
[435] Code: 453(d).
[436] Code: 453(f)(3).

[437] Pozzi, 49 T.C. 119 (1967).
[438] Code: 212.
[439] Reg. 1.212-1(g).
[440] Code: 280A.
[441] *Henderson,* T.C. Memo. 1968-22.

trips to a broker's office to watch the "ticker tapes."[442] Expenses incurred in searching for new investments have been disallowed.[443] Travel expenses incurred by an investor while making planned systematic investigations of publicly held corporations in which he held substantial interests were deductible because it was not a disguised personal trip.[444]

The Treasury has ruled that expenses incurred by stockholders in attending stockholders' meetings for the purposes of securing information on which to base future investment decisions are not deductible.[445] This questionable ruling is based on the theory that the expenses were not sufficiently related to the shareholder's investment activity so as to be deductible for income tax purposes. However, where the investor incurs reasonable expenses which are directly related to *present* investment interests, as, for example, the attendance at a stockholders' meeting in which the value of the investor's stock or the amount of the dividends payable may be affected, the deduction of such expenses should be allowed.[446] Expenses incurred in stockholders' proxy fights have been held to be deductible.[447] The expenses are deductible although the anticipated proxy contest never materializes.[448]

.03 Effect of Receipt of Tax-exempt Income

No deduction is allowed for expenses incurred which are allocable to tax-exempt income.[449] Custodial fees are disallowed to the extent attributed to services performed for tax-exempt securities.[450] Expenses that are not clearly allocable to either taxable or tax-exempt income are generally apportioned on the basis of the ratio of each to the total gross income.[451] Inclusion of capital gains, before deduction of capital losses, in gross income for purposes of allocating indirect expenses between taxable and nontaxable income is acceptable to the Treasury because there is no material distortion of income.[452] Similar rules apply to tax-exempts held in trust.[453]

---

[442] *Walters,* T.C. Memo. 1969-5.

[443] *Weinstein,* 420 F. 2d 700 (Ct. Cl. 1970).

[444] W. R. Kenney, 66 T.C. 122 (1976).

[445] Rev. Rul. 56-511, C.B. 1956-2, 170; however, see *Godson,* 5 TCM 648 (1946); *Goldner,* 27 T.C. 455 (1956).

[446] Cf. Milner Est., 1 TCM 513 (1943).

[447] *Surasky,* 325 F. 2d 181 (CA-5, 1963); *Graham,* 326 F. 2d 878 (CA-4, 1964); followed by Treasury if cost of proxy fight connected with production of income, Rev. Rul. 64-236, C.B. 1964-2, 64; however, see *Dyer,* 352 F. 2d 948 (CA-8, 1965).

[448] Nidetch, T.C. Memo 1978-313.

[449] Code: 265(1).

[450] *Alt,* 28 TCM 1501 (1969).

[451] Rev. Rul. 63-27, C.B. 1963-1, 57.

[452] Rev. Rul. 73-565, C.B. 1973-2, 90.

[453] Rev. Rul. 61-86, C.B. 1961-1, 41.

.04 Transfer Taxes

State and local transfer taxes paid on the sale of securities may be deducted against ordinary income if the taxpayer itemizes his deductions and, therefore, should not also be deducted from the selling price in computing gain or loss on the sale.[454] See 21 for an example of the tax saving which can be achieved.

.05 Interest

Limitations have been imposed on the deductibility of investment interest expense. Since 1969 the investment interest expense has been exposed to three separate treatments. Beginning in 1976 the amount of deductible investment interest expense is $10,000 ($5,000 for a married individual filing separately), plus net investment income (dividends, interest, rents, royalties, short-term gains, and gains on sale of investment property that is taxed as ordinary income, less other investment expense).[455] Any disallowed investment interest expense is carried over for an unlimited period to succeeding years subject to the interest expense limitation for that year.[456] Carryovers from pre-1976 years and interest from certain pre-September 11, 1975, debts are still subject to the limitations in effect for 1975 (see below.)[457] Proration of the net investment income is required if the investment interest expense is subject to both the old and the new limitations.[458] For example, if the net investment income is $50,000 and the investment interest expense is $100,000 of which $60,000 is attributable to pre-September 11, 1975, debt, $30,000 (60 percent of net investment income) of the net income is applied to determining the limitation for the pre-September 11, 1975, interest and the remaining $20,000 will be included in computing the post-1975 limitation. Thus, the post-1975 limitation is $30,000 ($10,000 + $20,000 net investment income) resulting in an excess investment interest of $10,000 ($40,000 interest less $30,000 limitation). The 1975 limitation is $57,500 ($25,000 + $30,000 net investment income + ½ of $5,000 excess), resulting in excess interest expense of $2,500 ($60,000 interest less $57,500 limitation). The result is allowable interest expense of $87,500, a carry-over of post-1975 disallowed interest expense of $10,000 and a carry-over of pre-1976 disallowed interest expense of $2,500.

---

[454] Code: 164(a), Reg. 1.164-1(a); Rev. Rul. 65-313, C.B. 1965-2, 47.
[455] Code: 163(d)(1).
[456] Code: 163(d)(2).
[457] 1976 TRA: 209(b).
[458] Code: 163(d)(3)(A).

If in the above example there was also interest from certain pre-December 19, 1969, debt, such interest would be deductible without limitation.[459] Starting in 1976 this provision is applied on an allocation basis rather than a specific item basis.

For years beginning after 1971 and before 1976, the allowable amount of investment interest expense is $25,000 plus net investment income (including long-term capital gains), plus one half of the investment interest expense in excess of the previously determined allowable amount.[460] Note that under the post-1975 limitations, long-term capital gains are not includible in net investment income. Capital gain distributions from regulated investment companies are treated as capital gains and not as dividend income for purposes of computing allowable interest expense.[461] On the other hand, for pre-1976 years, the 50 percent long-term capital gain deduction may not be taken to the extent the investment interest expense is allocated to the long-term capital gains. Any disallowed interest will be carried over to subsequent years, subject to the interest expense limitation for such year. As explained above, the carry-overs retain their character as pre-1976 disallowed interest expense when carried over to post-1975 years.

There was no limitation in effect for the years 1970 and 1971, but the excess interest expense (in excess of passive investment income, such as interest, dividends, rents, royalties, and short-term gains less other investment expense) is treated as a tax-preference item for purposes of the 10 percent minimum tax in effect for those years.[462]

Interest incurred for personal reasons, such as a mortgage on the family home or installment obligations to purchase appliances, are not subject to the limitations. Nor are loans incurred for business purposes subject to limitations. Indebtedness incurred to purchase a real estate syndicate interest or similar tax shelter will perhaps be treated by the Treasury as an investment borrowing and it will therefore limit the deduction of any interest incurred with respect to such investment. Interest expense paid by a partnership to purchase a controlling interest in a bank was held to be investment interest expense.[463] Borrowings by the partnership itself for business purposes should not be subject to any limitations. Whether the real

---

[459] Code: 163(d)(5).
[460] Code: 163(d)(1).
[461] Kocueck, 456 F. Supp. 740 (W.D. Texas, 1978), aff'd 628 F. 2d 906 (CA-5, 1978).
[462] Code: 57(a)(1). Note that interest expense and other investment expenses may be treated as tax preferences to the extent certain nonbusiness deductions exceed 60 percent of adjusted gross income. Code: 57(b).
[463] Miller, 70 TC 448 (1978).

estate partnership is actively engaged in a trade or business will depend upon its activity. If it is in the business of renting real property, or operating a motel or hotel, then it is engaged in a trade or business. However, if it is merely holding vacant land for appreciation, it would not be considered engaged in a trade or business,[464] and, accordingly, any interest expense incurred would be subject to limitations. Property subject to a net lease will be treated as investment property rather than business property if (a) the deductions allowed under Section 162 is less than 15 percent of the rental income from the property, or (b) the lessor is either guaranteed a specified return on his investment or is guaranteed in whole or in part against loss of income.[465] Note that the investment interest limitation is increased by any excess deductions incurred on property subject to a net lease.[466]

Interest on a margin account is deductible by a cash-basis investor in the year in which credits are made to the account sufficient to absorb the interest charge.[467] No deduction is allowed for interest paid on indebtedness incurred or continued to carry tax-exempt bonds (including all savers' certificates), interests in a unit trust or partnership, or shares in a municipal bond fund.[468] This would include a purchase of tax-exempts for cash in one brokerage account and a purchase by the same investor of taxable securities on margin in another account.[469] It is not necessary to trace the loan to the tax-exempts, but merely to show a "sufficiently direct relationship."[470] Interest expense incurred on loans for business purposes, or personal purposes, such as to purchase a home, automobile, or home appliances do not have a sufficiently direct relationship.[471] Note that refinancing an existing mortgage in order to purchase tax-exempts will result in a disallowance of the mortgage interest expenses.[472] Disallowance will result from borrowings to acquire nonbusiness portfolio investments, such as stock and securities (other than substantial ownership interest, such as 80 percent control), real estate investments, or limited partnership interests in real estate, farm, or gas and oil syndications, or similar tax shelters.[473] Once a direct relationship is shown, the interest expense will be disallowed even if it exceeds

---

[464] Prop. Reg. 1.57-2(b)(2)(i).
[465] Code: 163(d)(4).
[466] Code: 163(d)(1)(B).
[467] Rev. Rul. 70-221, C.B. 1970-1, 33.
[468] Code: 265(2) and (4); *Illinois Terminal Railroad Co.*, 375 F. 2d 1016 (Ct. Cl., 1967); *Wisconsin Cheeseman, Inc.*, 388 F. 2d 420 (CA-7, 1968).
[469] *B. H. Jacobson*, 28 TC 579 (1957) (Acq.); Bernard P. McDonough, T.C.

Memo. 1977-50.
[470] *Wisconsin Cheeseman, Inc.*, supra; *Ball*, 54 T.C. 1200 (1970).
[471] Rev. Proc. 72-18, Section 4.02, C.B. 1972-1, 740.
[472] Amedeo Louis Mariorenzi, T.C. Memo. 1973-141, aff'd. 490 F. 2d 92 (C.A. 1, 1974).
[473] Rev. Proc. 72-18, Section 4.04, C.B. 1972-1, 740.

the tax-exempt income.[474] Generally, where an individual's investment in tax-exempts is insubstantial (i.e., average adjusted basis of tax-exempts does not exceed 2 percent of average adjusted basis of investment portfolio) and there is no direct relationship between the borrowings and the tax-exempts, including the use of tax-exempts as collateral, there will be no disallowance.[475] Nor should there be a disallowance where the spouses file a joint return and one spouse purchases tax-exempts with his or her funds and the other spouse incurred investment interest expense.[476] However, interest will be disallowed on funds borrowed by one spouse and used by the other spouse to purchase tax-exempts.[477] Similarly, there should be no disallowance where an estate or trust owns tax-exempts, and a nongrantor beneficiary has incurred investment interest expense. Where an investor is also a partner in an investment partnership, however, his average investment in tax-exempts and total investments must be aggregated with his pro rata share of the partnership's average investment in tax-exempts and total assets in computing the amount of disallowance of investment interest expense for both the investor and his partnership.[478] Note that the disallowance applies only to interest expense and investment expenses deductible under Section 212. Other items, such as taxes, deductible under Section 164, are fully deductible even though the activity is described in Section 212.[479] An officer-stockholder did not constructively receive income on an interest-free loan from his corporation to pay estimated tax although the taxpayer had investments in tax-exempts.[480]

Interest paid on genuine indebtedness without collusion between the investor and the creditor to avoid income taxes will be allowed as a deduction.[481] There should be some economic substance to the transaction apart from income tax effect.[482] Interest deductions

---

[474] J. S. Wynn, Jr., 411 F. 2d 614 (CA-3, 1969), Cert. Den. 396 U.S. 1008 1970).

[475] Rev. Proc. 72-18, Section 3.05, C.B. 1972-1, 740.

[476] Levitt, 368 F. Supp. 644 (1974), rev'd. on other issues, 517 F. 2d 1339 (1975); Bernard P. McDonough, T.C. Memo. 1977-50, aff'd 577 F. 2d 234 (CA-4, 1978).

[477] Rev. Rul. 79-272, C.B. 1979-2, 124.

[478] Bernard P. McDonough, T.C. Memo. 1977-50, aff'd 577 F. 2d 234 (CA-4, 1978).

[479] Rev. Rul. 78-81, C.B. 1978-1.

[480] Baker, 75 TC 166 (1980).

[481] *L. L. Stanton,* 34 T.C. 1 (1960).

[482] *E. D. Goodstein,* 267 F. 2d 127 (CA-

1, 1959); *Knetsch,* 364 U.S. 361 (1960); *Barnett,* 44 T.C. 261 (1965), aff'd 364 F. 2d 742 (CA-2, 1966); *Goldstein,* 364 F. 2d 734 (CA-2, 1966), Cert. den. This latter case denies deduction of prepaid interest on a "valid" indebtedness where there is no purpose for the transaction other than to obtain a tax deduction. See also *Gilbert,* 248 F. 2d 399, 411 (CA-2, 1957). Under the current volatile interest conditions, it would be more difficult for the Treasury to establish that interest paid on a loan to purchase discount bonds or Treasury instruments was not incurred for valid economic purposes.

were denied where the court found that the transaction was not a "sham" but lacked a business purpose.[483] An interest deduction was also denied if the debtor obtained the funds from the lender.[484] In addition, the Treasury had reversed its prior position and would allow a deduction for interest prepaid for only a 12-month period after the end of the taxable year, provided there was no distortion of income. Any remaining prepaid interest had to be deferred and deducted over the term of the loan.[485] Commencing in 1976, prepaid interest must be capitalized and deducted over the period of the loan as if the investor were on the accrued basis.[486] Thus, if an investor prepaid interest of $130 for one month in 1981 and the entire year of 1982, only $10 would be deductible in 1981 and the balance of $120 in 1982. The current provision will not apply to prepayments made before 1977 pursuant to a binding loan or contract in effect on September 16, 1975.[487] Presumably, the Treasury's one-year prepayment rule would apply to these prepayments.

.06 Dividends and Interest Paid on Short Sales

Amounts paid by investors as premiums for the use of stock borrowed to effectuate short sales of stock or to reimburse the lender of the stock for ordinary cash dividends paid on the borrowed stock are deductible as nonbusiness expenses.[488] Although never specifically enunciated by the Treasury, the same should be applicable to interest paid on short sales of debentures.[489] These payments do not constitute investment interest expense but are deductible in computing net investment income. (See 48.05 for limitations on investment interest expense.)

The Treasury has ruled that amounts paid with respect to stock dividends or liquidating dividends on stock borrowed incident to a short sale are capital expenditures and are not deductible.[489a] How-

[483] Rothschild, 407 F. 2d 404 (Ct. Cl., 1969).
[484] Battlestein, 80-1 USTC 9225 (CA-5, 1980).
[485] Rev. Rul. 68-643, C.B. 1968-2, 76, modified by Rev. Rul. 69-582, C.B. 1969-2, 29.
[486] Code: 461(g).
[487] 1976 TRA: 208(b)(2).
[488] Rev. Rul. 72-521, C.B. 1972-2, 178; Rev. Rul. 62-42, C.B. 1962-1, 133; Dart, 74 F. 2d 845 (CA-4, 1935); Wiesler, 161 F. 2d 997 (CA-6, 1947); contra, Levis Estate, 127 F. 2d 796 (CA-2, 1942).

[489] I.T. 3989, C.B. 1950-1, 34 (replaced by Rev. Rul. 72-521, C.B. 1972-2, 178) has been cited for such proposition (although interest was disallowed on grounds of sham). J. G. Gold, 41 T.C. 419, 426 (1963). "It is, of course, true that one who borrows securities in order to make a short sale may deduct the amount of interest or dividends which he pays to the lender in order to reimburse him for the interest or dividends that the lender would have received during the period of the loan."
[489]a—Rev. Rul. 72-521, C.B. 1972-2, 178.

ever, an argument can be made for treating the payment of all short dividends, including stock and liquidating dividends, as an ordinary deduction, since they are merely contractual expenses incurred as a necessary cost of obtaining the borrowed stock.[490]

Where the sole purpose for entering into a short sale transaction is tax avoidance without any expectation of financial gain, the short dividends paid will not be allowed as a deduction on the grounds that they are not ordinary and necessary expenses paid or incurred for the production of income.[491] However, where there is a possibility of economic gain, even though the primary purpose is tax savings through the creation of capital gain and ordinary deductions, a strong argument could be made for the deductibility of the dividends paid on the short sale.

49 TAX-FREE EXCHANGES

.01 Reorganizations

Recognizing that normal commercial activities would be impeded if every exchange or securities were subjected to income tax, despite the lack of any substantial change in the security holder's financial position, Congress has enacted through the years many special tax provisions exempting certain transactions from tax. An exchange of common or preferred stock for stock of another corporation in a statutory merger or consolidation,[492] or the exchange of common or preferred stock for other common or preferred stock of the same corporation in a recapitalization[493] falls within this class. The receipt of preferred stock in a reorganization may be treated similar to a dividend of preferred stock and, therefore, may result in ordinary income on its sale or redemption.[494] Other exempted transactions include an exchange by a corporation of its voting stock for stock of another corporation which it controls after exchange,[495] a "triangular merger" using stock of the parent of one of the merged corporations,[496] and exchange of bonds for bonds (not in excess of the

---

[490] *Main Line Distributors, Inc.,* 321 F. 2d 562 (CA-6, 1963)–disallowed deduction on other grounds. Cf. *1955 Production Exposition Inc.,* 41 T.C. 85 (1963).

[491] *Hart,* 41 T.C. 131 (1963) aff'd 338 F. 2d 410 (CA-2, 1964); cf. *Carl Schapiro,* 40 T.C. 34 (1963), 39. In the *Hart* case, the transactions were mere "bookkeeping" entries with no

borrowing of securities, no payment of margin, lack of investment interest, price adjustments to prevent economic substance, and no delivery of stock to cover the sale.

[492] Code: 368(a)(1)(A).
[493] Code: 368(a)(1)(E) and 1036.
[494] Code: 306(c)(1)(B).
[495] Code: 368(a)(1)(B).
[496] Code: 368(a)(2)(D), (E).

principal amount surrendered) or stock of the same corporation,[497] the conversion of convertible bonds into stock of the same corporation,[498] and, in appropriate cases, the receipt of stock upon division of a corporation.[499] Notwithstanding the tax-free treatment accorded exchanges of stock, an exchange of warrants for warrants of another party to the reorganization has been ruled by the Treasury to be a taxable exchange.[500] Published Capital Changes services generally contain the information the investor needs to determine the proper tax treatment of exchanges of publicly held securities.

With respect to the basis and holding period of the securities acquired in the exchange, see **33.04** and **34.02(d)**.

.02 Involuntary Conversions–Governmental Orders

Special provisions deferring the recognition of gain or loss are applicable to investors who were compelled to surrender their securities or receive distributions from their corporations pursuant to an order issued by the FCC,[501] SEC,[502] or the Board of Governors of the Federal Reserve System.[503] Pro rata distributions of stocks and securities to shareholders of qualified bank holding companies required to divest their interests pursuant to the Bank Holding Company Act are also nontaxable.[504] Published Capital Changes services generally describe the proper tax treatment in these situations.

.03 Exchange Funds

Holders of appreciated marketable securities formerly were able to diversify their holdings without recognition of gain by exchanging these securities for stock of a mutual fund which was specifically organized for this purpose. As a result of a change in the law, such exchanges will be treated as taxable exchanges.[505] Similar legislation was enacted to deny tax-free treatment on transfer of appreciated assets to an unincorporated investment company (partnership, trust, common trust fund), or where an undiversified investment company (more than 25 percent of its assets invested in one corporation or more than 50 percent invested in up to five corporations) enters into a reorganization with one or more investment companies.[506]

---

[497] Code: 354, 368.
[498] Rev. Rul. 72-265, C.B. 1972-1, 222.
[499] Code: 355, 368(a)(1)(D).
[500] Rev. Rul. 78-408, C.B. 1978-2, 203;
    Priv. Rul. Doc. 7949056.
[501] Code: 1071.

[502] Code: 1081.
[503] Code: 1101.
[504] Ibid.
[505] Code: 351(a), (d).
[506] Code: 368(a)(1)(F).

.04 Other Types

For discussion of tax-free exchanges of government bonds, see 2.08 and 43.10.

50 SALES TO RELATED PERSONS

Sales between related parties are viewed with suspicion by the Treasury and are strictly regulated by the Internal Revenue Code.[507] Gains realized in such transactions are generally recognized for tax purposes. Losses incurred will be disallowed for tax purposes if a member of the investor's family (spouse, descendant, ancestor, or sibling) buys the securities directly from the investor or buys them indirectly on an exchange on or about the same date and at approximately the same price.[508] The losses are not offset by gains realized on other sales.[509] The disallowed loss may be used by the purchaser to the extent the purchaser sells the security at a gain.[510] Whether the wash sale provisions can be avoided by having a related person reacquire the security is discussed in 36.07.

Interfamily sales of securities can qualify for installment sales treatment, but both the Internal Revenue Service and the judiciary will closely scrutinize the transaction. An installment sale of securities to the seller's husband was approved by the court where the husband sold the securities after holding them for five months and used the proceeds to satisfy contractual obligations.[511] However, the Tax Court in a subsequent case upheld the Treasury's contention that the sale lacked substance because of the absence of a business or personal purpose other than tax avoidance where the wife sold the securities on the same day and reinvested the proceeds in mutual funds.[512] An installment sale to the taxpayer's son was invalidated because the son was found to be acting as an agent for his father.[513] Prior to these cases, the Fifth Circuit approved an installment sale to trusts created for the benefit of the seller's children of stock of a corporation which was to be liquidated.[514] This case was followed by a rash of cases that approved, distinguished, and disagreed with the *Rushing* case. As a consequence, the installment sale rules were amended with respect to sales or dispositions to related parties.[515] If an investor

---

[507] Code: 267.

[508] *J. P. McWilliams,* 331 U.S. 694 (1946).

[509] *Reddington,* 131 F. 2d 1014 (CA-2, 1942); *Englehart,* 30 TC 1013 (1958).

[510] Code: 267(d).

[511] *Nye v U.S.,* 407 F. Supp. 1345 (D.C. N.C., 1975).

[512] Philip W. Wrenn, 67 TC No. 41 (1976).

[513] Lustgarten, 71 TC 303 (1978).

[514] Rushing, 441 F. 2d 593 (CA-5, 1971).

[515] Code: 453(e). Related parties includes the taxpayer's spouse, children, grandchildren, and parents.

sells marketable securities to a related party who then sells the securities before paying the entire amount due on the first sale, then the investor will be deemed to have received the remaining sales proceeds at the time of the second sale.[516] With respect to an intrafamily sale of nonmarketable securities, the investor will be treated as having received the remaining sales proceeds at the time of the sale unless the second sale is more than two years after the original sale.[517] The two-year holding period cannot be avoided by acquiring a Put, selling the property short, giving a right to a third party to acquire the property, or any similar transactions.[518] However, these intrafamily sales provisions will not apply if the investor can show that neither the first nor second sale was done for tax avoidance purposes.[519]

51 SMALL BUSINESS INVESTMENT COMPANY STOCK

A magic formula of capital gains and ordinary losses applies to sales of small business investment company stock.[520] Losses are fully deductible by any stockholder without limitation and, if in excess of the current year's income, may be carried back or forward as a business loss. Transactions with regard to SBIC stock do not have to be "netted" with one another.[521] Therefore, if a taxpayer had gains and losses in the same year on SBIC stock, the gains would be accorded capital gain treatment, while the losses would be deductible as ordinary losses. The Treasury has ruled that a loss sustained on the closing of a short sale of stock of a small business investment company is treated as a short-term loss and not as an ordinary loss.[522] The beneficial tax treatment will be denied unless there is strict compliance with the tax provisions.[523]

52 CURRENT DISTRIBUTIONS ON STOCK

.01 Dividend Income

Dividend income is not limited to periodic distributions of cash or property. Also included in the definition are stock redemptions, which have the effect of dividends;[524] certain sales or redemptions of

---

[516] Code: 453(e)(1).
[517] Code: 453(e)(2).
[518] Code: 453(e)(2)(B).
[519] Code: 453(e)(7).
[520] Code: 1242.

[521] Rev. Rul. 65-291, C.B. 1965-2, 290.
[522] Rev. Rul. 63-65, C.B. 1963-1, 142.
[523] *Childs,* 408 F. 2d 531 (CA-3, 1969).
[524] Code: 302.

shares of preferred stock, which were received as stock dividends on common stock;[525] stock distributions received in lieu of cash dividends;[526] sale of stock to a related corporation;[527] distributions of stock in a corporation other than the distributing corporation;[528] cash or other property received in a reorganization that has the effect of a dividend[529] and, according to the Treasury, cash paid in lieu of fractional stock dividends unless shareholders approve sale of fractional shares on their behalf.[530] However, a distribution is a taxable dividend only to the extent it is paid out of either accumulated or current earnings and profits.[531] Distributions received from a regulated investment company can qualify as a dividend, nonqualifying dividend, capital gain dividend, a distribution of tax-exempt interest, or as a return of capital.[532] Capital gain distributions in a year the regulated investment company had capital loss carry-overs are treated as regular dividends.[533] Distributions from a real estate investment trust may qualify as nonqualifying dividends, capital gain dividends, or return of capital.[534]

Published Dividend Records indicate the tax status as well as the total amount of dividends paid annually by publicly held corporations. The same information, with greater detail regarding distributions in property, is available in published Capital Changes services.

Prior to 1981, the first $100 of dividends received from most domestic corporations in a taxable year was exempt from tax.[535] (The exemption was increased to $200 if a joint return was filed and the spouse also had at least $100 of dividend income.) This exclusion was expanded for the year 1981 to $200 of dividends or interest income ($400 for a joint return, even if the entire interest or dividend income is earned by one spouse).[536] In order to avoid dis-

---

[525] Code: 306. The ordinary income taint can no longer be eliminated because of the death of a shareholder after 1976. Code: 306(c)(1)(C).

[526] Code: 305.

[527] Code: 304.

[528] Cheley, 131 F. 2d 1018 (CA-10, 1942).

[529] Code: 356.

[530] Rev. Rul. 69-15, C.B. 1969-1, 95. Cash distributed in lieu of fractional shares resulting from stock dividends, stock splits, corporate reorganizations, and the like, will be treated as received on the sale of the fractional shares if undertaken solely to save the expense and consequence of issuing and transferring fractional shares and is not separately bargained for consideration. Rev. Proc. 77-41, C.B. 1977-2, 574.

[531] Code: 316.

[532] Code: 852. A foreign tax credit may be allowed the shareholder with respect to the nonqualifying dividends. Code: 853.

[533] Rev. Rul. 76-299, C.B. 1976-2, 211.

[534] Code: 857(b) and (c).

[535] Code: 116.

[536] Code: 116 as amended by P.L. 96-223: 404(a). The exclusion originally was for the years 1981 and 1982, but the 1981 ERTA limited the exclusion only to 1981.

allowance of investment expenses, including interest expense, the investor should first apply the exclusion to dividend income and then interest income. The $100 dividend exclusion ($200 for joint returns) will be reinstated for post-1981 years, except that a $200 exclusion will be allowed for joint returns, even if all the dividend income is earned by one spouse. The dividend received credit provisions are no longer in effect, but dividends received by investors who have attained age 65 are eligible for the credit for the elderly.[537]

Distributions in excess of the current and accumulated earnings and profits of the distributing corporation are treated as a return of capital, reducing the basis of the stock, and, after the investor has fully recovered his cost, any excess distributions are generally taxed as capital gains.[538]

During the period 1982-84, investors in common or preferred shares of qualified public utilities may elect to exclude from income up to $750 ($1,500 for joint returns) of qualified common stock dividends received in lieu of cash dividends.[539] Since the stock dividends will have a zero basis, the entire proceeds received on a subsequent sale will be taxed at capital gains rates. However, if the investor sells or otherwise disposes of the shares within one year from the time of any stock distribution, the proceeds will be taxed as ordinary income to the extent of the stock distributions made within one year of the disposition.[540] This election is available only to shareholders owning less than 5 percent of the voting stock (or value) of the public utility.

.02 Stock Dividends

A distribution of stock of the issuing corporation is generally not taxed to the stockholders. Distributions will be taxed as ordinary dividends if the stockholders have an option to receive cash or property in place of the stock dividend; or the distribution is made in discharge of preference dividends for the current year or the preceding year.[541] With respect to stock distributions in place of cash dividends, the Tax Reform Act of 1969 has expanded these provisions to include (a) disproportionate distributions among the holders of various classes of common stock, (b) constructive distributions where one class of common stock receives cash dividends and another class

---

[537] Code: 116, as amended by 1981 ERTA: 302.
[538] Code: 301(c).
[539] Code: 305(e), as amended by 1981 ERTA: 321.
[540] Code: 305(e)(9), as amended.
[541] Code: 305.

obtains an increased interest in the corporate assets and earnings and profits or an increase or decrease in the ratio in which one class of securities may be converted into another class of stock, or (c) a disproportionate distribution of convertible preferred stock.[542] Cash received in lieu of fractional stock dividends will be treated as ordinary income.[543] However, if the investor is given an option either to buy or to sell fractions, and the fractional dividends are sold, capital gain or loss treatment will follow.[544] The issuance of cash for fractional shares for convenience of the distributing corporation will not cause the stock distributions to be taxable under the Section 305 rules.[545] Distributions of stock of other corporations generally are taxable as ordinary dividends. Certain distributions of stock of other corporations may qualify as tax-free "spin-offs."[546] (For discussion of tax basis and holding period of stock received as a stock dividend, see **33.04** and **34.02(i)**.)

.03 Stock Rights

The receipt of stock rights in the issuing corporation, by itself, is not a taxable event.[547] However, distributions of stock rights will be taxed as ordinary income if the stockholders have an option to receive cash or property in place of stock rights.[548]

The issuance of rights to subscribe to the issuing companies' convertible bonds is also a nontaxable distribution.[549] No income would be realized either on the acquisition or exercise of the convertible bonds.[550] The Treasury has ruled that the receipt of rights to purchase the issuing company's nonconvertible bonds is taxable.[551] A distribution of short-term transferable rights, convertible into two long-term warrants and a $100 debenture upon payment of $100, is not a taxable distribution.[552] The warrants are treated as stock for purposes of Section 305,[553] and the $100 is in payment for the de-

---

[542] Code: 305(b)(2)(5) and (c). The rules are complex with various transitional dates but generally will not apply before 1991 to distributions on stock outstanding on January 10, 1969.

[543] Special Ruling, Dec. 21, 1960.

[544] Rev. Rul. 69-15, C.B. 1969-1, 95.

[545] Reg. 1.305-3(c).

[546] Code: 355.

[547] Code: 305.

[548] Code: 305(b).

[549] *Powel*, 27 BTA 55 (1932) (Acq.).

[550] G.C.M. 13275, C.B. XIII-2, 121.

[551] G.C.M. 13414, C.B. XIII-2, 124. Note that in a private ruling concerning the issuance of A.T.&T. rights to acquire a unit consisting of warrants and debenture bonds of the issuing corporation, the issuance and exercise were held to be nontaxable. The ruling permitted the entire option price to be attributed to the purchase of the bond with the warrant receiving the same basis as the right.

[552] Rev. Rul. 72-71, C.B. 1972-1, 99.

[553] Code: 305(d).

bentures. Thus, this ruling is compatible with the prior ruling concerning rights convertible into debentures.

Sale of a nontaxable stock right results in capital gain or loss. In determining such gain or loss or the basis of stock acquired upon exercise of a stock right, the basis of the "old" stock is allocated to the nontaxable right based upon the fair market value of the rights received in relation to the fair market value of the stock (including the rights) at the time of distribution.[554] Reference to a published Capital Changes service will provide the necessary percentages of allocation. However, where the fair market value of the rights at the time of distribution is less than 15 percent of the value of the stock, no allocation is made, and the basis of the rights is zero, unless the investor elects to make the allocation.[555] (See **33.04**.)

Stock rights received in a nontaxable distribution take on the same holding period as the stock held.[556] Thus, when the rights are sold, the holding period of the stock is "tacked-on" in determining the holding period of the rights. However, securities acquired through the exercise of the rights will not take on a tacked-on holding period. The holding period will start on the date of exercise.[557]

Generally, no loss is recognized as a result of the failure to exercise nontaxable rights, unless the rights were acquired for a valuable consideration (e.g., acquired by purchase). No adjustment is made to the basis of the stock with respect to which the expired rights were distributed.[558]

Distributions by a corporation of rights to acquire stock of another corporation have been held under the pre-1954 law to be taxable at the time of exercise or sale and not at the time of issuance.[559] The amount that was taxable as a dividend could not exceed the lower of the spreads between option price and fair market value of the stock purchased at the time the rights were issued and at time of exercise.[560] It would appear that the amount received upon sale of the right, in excess of the spreads, should be taxable as capital gains,[561] but the Treasury's position was that such amount was taxable as ordinary income.[562] The Tax Court rejected the Treasury's

---

[554] Code: 307(a), Reg. 1.307-1.
[555] Code: 307(a), Reg. 1.307-2.
[556] Code: 1223(5).
[557] Code: 1223(5); Reg. 1.1223-1(f); Rev. Rul. 56-572, C.B. 1956-2, 182.
[558] Reg. 1.307-1; Special Ruling, Dec. 4, 1946.
[559] *Palmer*, 302 U.S. 63 (1937); *Choate*,

129 F. 2d 684 (CA-2, 1942); Baan, 451 F. 2d 198 (CA-9, 1971).
[560] Ibid.
[561] *Gibson*, 133 F. 2d 308 (CA-2, 1943).
[562] GCM 25063, C.B. 1947-1, 45 (declared obsolete by Rev. Rul. 71-498, C.B. 1971-2, 434).

contention that the proceeds of sale constitute ordinary and not dividend income.[563]

With the change of the statutory language in the 1954 Code, the Treasury and the Seventh Circuit have questioned the validity of the old cases. The Treasury has ruled that, under the 1954 Code, the issuance of rights to acquire stock of another company is taxable as a dividend at the time of issuance.[564] This ruling has been followed by the Seventh Circuit.[565] Similarly, the issuance of stock rights by a wholly owned subsidiary to shareholders of the parent company was ruled to be a tax-free transfer of the rights to the parent company followed by a taxable distribution to the parent company's shareholders.[566] Pursuant to these rulings, noncorporate shareholders would realize dividend income at the time of receipt to the extent of fair market value (corporate shareholders realize no income), and this amount would also increase the shareholder's basis in the rights. Upon exercise, no gain or loss would be realized by the shareholders, and the basis of the acquired stock would be the option price plus the tax basis of the stock rights. A sale or lapse of the rights would result in capital gain or loss. The distributing corporation will realize gain or loss on the exercise of the rights, depending upon whether the option price is more or less than its tax basis.

The courts are split as to whether a distribution of rights to stock of another corporation may qualify as a tax-free spin-off [567] resulting in no gain or loss or dividend income when the rights are exercised. In the most recent case a distribution of rights to acquire stock of a wholly owned subsidiary was held to be a tax-free spin-off by the Tax Court, but it was reversed on appeal.[568] Consequently, the distribution of the stock rights was held to be taxable to the parent company's shareholders at the time of the distribution. (See above discussion.) If the distribution of the stock rights were held to be tax-free, dividend income may result upon the sale of such rights.[569]

---

[563] *Tobacco Products Export Corporation*, 21 TC 625 (1954); *Baan*, 45 TC 71 (1965), rev'd on other grounds 382 F. 2d 485 (CA-9, 1967).

[564] Rev. Rul. 70-521, C.B. 1970-2, 72.

[565] *Redding*, 80-2 USTC 9637 (CA-7, 1980), rev'g. 71 TC 597 (1979). The Tax Court discussed the Palmer doctrine but refused to give an opinion as to its current validity. In *Baumer*, 580 F. 2d 863 (CA-5, 1978), the Fifth Circuit limited the Palmer decision to its own set of facts (i.e., no spread exists on the date of issuance and the option period is so short that there is no expected appreciation in the stock before the options must be exercised).

[566] Rev. Rul. 80-292, C.B. 1980-2, 104.

[567] Code: 355; see *Gordon*, 382 F. 2d 499 (CA-2, 1967), rev'd 391 U.S. 83 (1968) and *Baan*, 382 F. 2d 485 (CA-9, 1967), aff'd 391 U.S. 83 (1968). The Supreme Court did not resolve this point.

[568] *Redding*, 71 TC 597 (1979), rev'd 80-2 USTC 9637.

[569] See *Baan* and *Gordon*, supra.

53 LIQUIDATIONS

Upon complete liquidation of a corporation, a shareholder will realize capital gain or loss depending upon the value of the liquidating distributions and the tax basis of the shareholder's stock.[570] The capital gain or loss treatment also applies to a one-year liquidation, although the corporation may escape tax on sales of property during the liquidation period.[571] Installment obligation received by the shareholders as part of the liquidation distribution will qualify for installment sale treatment if the obligations were received on sale of property during the one-year liquidation period.[572] Where the one-month liquidation provision is elected, any gain realized by an individual shareholder will be taxed as dividend income to the extent of his ratable share of the corporation's earnings and profits, and any remaining gain will be taxed as capital gain to the extent the cash and marketable securities (acquired after 1953) received on liquidation exceed the ratable share of earnings and profits.[573] In the case of a partial liquidation, capital gain or loss will be realized depending upon the value of the liquidating distribution and the tax basis of the stock surrendered or deemed surrendered in the exchange.[574] While ordinarily not applicable to a publicly held corporation, capital gain treatment upon sale or liquidation will be denied if the corporation is a "collapsible corporation."[575] A liquidation of a foreign investment company or foreign controlled corporation may result in part or all of the gain being treated as dividend income.[576] (See 54.02.)

54 FOREIGN SECURITIES AND FOREIGN CURRENCY

.01 Foreign Income Tax Withheld

An investor may at his option claim foreign income tax withheld on income received from a foreign investment as a deduction, or as a credit against the federal income tax.[577] The latter is normally more

---

[570] Code: 331(a). The installment method of reporting gain is not available.

[571] Code: 337.

[572] Code: 453(h).

[573] Code: 333. This election is made only when the corporation has little or no earnings and profits and thus enables a shareholder to defer reporting gain on liquidation. He is also eligible to elect the installment method on sale of the property.

[574] Code: 331(b), 346; Rev. Rul. 57-334, C.B. 1957-2, 240.

[575] Code: 341(a)(2).

[576] Code: 1246 and 1248.

[577] Code: 164(a); 33; 901 et seq.

advantageous. In either case, the full amount of the dividend before withholding must be included in income.

.02 Foreign Investment Companies

Long-term gain from the sale of a foreign investment company stock is treated as ordinary income to the extent of the investor's ratable share of the company's undistributed earnings and profits after 1962.[578] The gain will be treated as capital gain if the foreign investment company elects to distribute its income currently.[579]

.03 Interest Equalization Tax

Certain acquisitions before July 1, 1974, by United States citizens or residents, or their agents, of foreign securities or indebtedness were subject to an interest equalization tax of up to 22½ percent.[580] The rates were subject to modification by Presidential executive order. The tax was not imposed on foreign securities acquired by the U.S. investor from a U.S. person. This exemption was available only if the seller applied for and obtained a validation certificate from the Treasury.[581] Other exemptions from this tax include investments in certain new Canadian issues and investments in less developed country corporations. The tax could not be avoided merely by acquiring the foreign securities through a foreign broker.

.04 Foreign Currency Transactions

Investors in foreign currencies will realize capital gains or losses upon culmination of the transaction.[582] Foreign currency held for investment is considered a capital asset and generally is subject to the same tax rules as securities.[583] Losses on sales of foreign currencies are not subject to the wash sales rules (see **36.03**).[584] However, if the foreign currencies come under the new straddle rules, they may be subject to rules similar to the wash sales rules.[585] Similarly, the short

---

[578] Code: 1246. Similar rules apply to gains realized by an investor who owns at least 10 percent of a foreign corporation's stock. Code: 1248.

[579] Code: 1247.

[580] Code: 4911 to 4931, expired June 30, 1974.

[581] TIR 918, July 22, 1967.

[582] Rev. Rul. 74-7, C.B. 1974-2, 198; Rev. Rul. 75-479, C.B. 1975-2, 44.

[583] Cf. *Frank C. LaGrange*, 26 T.C. 191 (1956).

[584] Rev. Rul. 74-218, C.B. 1974-1, 202.

[585] Code: 1092(b) and (c), as amended by 1981 ERTA: 501.

sale rules may also apply when there are offsetting positions in foreign currencies.[586] The short sale rules will not apply if the taxpayer has sold a foreign currency Forward contract but does not own the underlying commodity. A sale of the short Forward contract can result in a long-term capital gain.[587] In a subsequent private ruling, the Treasury refused to follow these decisions and has ruled that a sale of the short Forward contract would be treated as a short-term gain.[588] Gain on retirement of foreign debt was held to be ordinary income.[589] However, exchange of Mexican gold coins for Austrian gold coins, whose values were based on gold content and were not used as currency, qualified as a tax-free exchange under Section 1031.[590] An exchange of silver bullion for gold bullion is also tax-free.[591] On the other hand, an exchange of U.S. $20 gold coins (numismatic-type coins) for South African Krugerrand gold coins (bullion-type coins) was ruled to be a taxable exchange.[592] Losses incurred in foreign Futures transactions were disallowed for lack of substantiation.[593] Trading has commenced in foreign currency Futures. The rules applicable to these transactions are identical to the general rules of commodity Futures and are covered in 40.03.

55 INSIDER'S SHORT-SWING PROFITS

An officer, director, or 10 percent (or greater) stockholder of a listed corporation or other corporation required to file annual reports with the SEC may be required to turn over to the corporation the gains realized on the sale of its stock if he sells and purchases (or purchases and sells) the stock of the corporation within a six-month period.[594] Ordinarily, the executive will realize a capital loss on repayment.[595] Tax Court decisions allowing an ordinary deduction where the payment was made solely to protect the executive's reputation have been reversed on appeal.[596] The problem is particularly likely to arise where the executive is in need of funds to exercise a stock option.[597] Instead of selling his stock, he should borrow the

---

[586] Ibid.

[587] American Home Products Corp., 601 F. 2d 540 (Ct. Cl., 1979); Hoover Co., 72 TC 206 (1979); Carborundum Co., 74 TC No. 57 (1980).

[588] Priv. Rul. Doc. 8016004.

[589] Gillin, 423 F. 2d 309 (Ct. Cl., 1970).

[590] Rev. Rul. 76-214, C.B. 1976-1, 218.

[591] Priv. Rul. Doc. 8020107.

[592] Rev. Rul. 79-143, C.B. 1979-1, 264.

[593] Rev. Rul. 80-324, C.B. 1980-2, 340.

[594] Section 16(b) of the Securities Exchange Act of 1934.

[595] Rev. Rul. 61-115, C.B. 1961-1, 46.

[596] Mitchell, 428 F. 2d 259 (CA-6, 1970), rev'g. 52 T.C. 170 (Cert. Den. 401 U.S. 909 (1971); Brown, 529 F. 2d 609 (CA-10, 1976).

[597] Cf. Greene v. Dietz, 247 F. 2d 689 (1957); Babbitt Inc. v. Lachner, S.D. N.Y. 12/13/63.

funds, with his stock as collateral, and sell the stock after the six-month period expires. Many employee stock option plans now permit an employee to pay the amount due on exercise of the options by surrendering stock of the employer that the employee currently owns. Apparently, this is permissible under the short-swing provisions, and for tax purposes it was not treated as a sale of the surrendered stock. A voluntary conversion of convertible bonds or preferred stock into common stock followed by a sale of the common stock within six months of the conversion date also comes within the short-swing profits provisions.[598] Advice of counsel should be obtained in all doubtful cases.

56 VALUATION OF STOCK AND SECURITIES

Determining the market value of a stock or security is important not only for estate and gift tax purposes but in determining the amount of gain or loss in a taxable sale or exchange. These values are readily obtainable with respect to stock or securities sold over an exchange or over-the-counter market. A transfer of a restricted security (e.g., not registered with the SEC or subject to SEC sales restrictions), cannot be equated with the transfer of the same security that is not subject to "an investment letter" or similar SEC restriction. There is no automatic or mechanical solution. Rather, all material facts and circumstances must be considered in determining the fair market value of such restricted securities.[599]

57 ADD-ON MINIMUM TAX

In addition to the regular income tax, individual taxpayers are required to pay a minimum tax on their tax preference items that result in tax benefits. Beginning in 1976, the minimum tax was increased to 15 percent on tax preferences in excess of $10,000 ($5,000 for spouses filing separately), or, if higher, one half the regular federal income tax.[600] In 1978, an alternative minimum tax was established, and the tax preferences for the capital gain deduction and excess itemized deductions were removed from the list of prefer-

---

[598] *Park & Tilford, Inc. v. Schulte,* 160 F. 2d 984 (1947); *Heli-Coil Corp. v. Webster,* 222 F. Supp. 831 (1963).
[599] Rev. Rul. 77-287, C.B. 1977-2, 319.
[600] Code: 56. The prior minimum tax rate was 10 percent and a $30,000 deduction was allowed ($15,000 for spouses filing separately) plus the current year's federal income tax and unused tax carry-overs from prior years. For post-1982 years, the add-on minimum tax will be combined with alternative minimum tax.

ences subject to the 15 percent minimum tax and, instead, became subject to the alternative minimum tax (see below). Included in the list of tax preferences for post-1980 years are:[601]

1. Excess accelerated (ACRS) depreciation on real property.
2. Excess accelerated (ACRS) depreciation on leased property.
3. Excess amortization on pollution control facilities.
4. Excess amortization on railroad rolling stock.
5. Excess of depletion deduction over adjusted cost.
6. Excess oil and gas intangible drilling expenses in excess of net oil income.
7. Unrecognized gain on exercise of qualified stock options before May 21, 1981.[602]

With the elimination of the capital gains deduction as a tax preference, the minimum tax will apply principally to investors who participate in tax shelters.

58 ALTERNATIVE MINIMUM TAX

To insure that all taxpayers with substantial income pay some taxes, a separate alternative minimum tax was imposed for taxable years beginning after 1978.[603] This tax will be payable only if it exceeds the regular income tax (including the 15 percent add-on minimum tax). Only the foreign tax credit and certain refundable credits could be offset against the alternative minimum tax. As a consequence, taxpayers with large investment tax credits, but with little or no tax preferences, became liable for the alternative minimum tax. Investment credit, WIN credit, and new employee credit can now be offset against the alternative minimum tax if attributable to an individual's active trade or business as contrasted to a tax shelter investment. The available credit is limited, however, and cannot be applied against the alternative minimum tax attributable to the capital gain deduction or the excess itemized deductions.[604] For net capital gains realized on sales after June 9, 1981, and for post-1981 years, a maximum 20 percent rate will be in effect for all income in excess of

---

[601] Code: 57. Beginning in 1978, the tax preferences for the capital gain deduction and itemized deductions (except medical and casualty losses) in excess of 60 percent of adjusted gross income were no longer subject to the 15 percent minimum tax. Capital gain on sale of a principal residence after July 26, 1978, was also removed from the list of tax preferences.

[602] Unrecognized gains on exercise of incentive stock options will not be a tax preference.

[603] Code: 55.

[604] Code: 55(c), effective for years beginning after 1979.

$60,000.[605] The alternative minimum tax rate for pre-1982 years (other than post-June 29, 1981, qualified net capital gains) is as follows:

Income	*Rate*
0 to $20,000	exempt
$20,000 to $60,000	10%
$60,000 to $100,000	20%
Over $100,000	25%

In computing the alternate minimum taxable income, an investor's gross income is reduced by (1) total deductions allowed for the year and (2) accumulated trust income includible under Section 667; and is increased by (1) the net capital gains deduction (60 percent) and (2) itemized deductions (except medical, casualty losses, state and local taxes and Section 691(c) deductions) in excess of 60 percent of adjusted gross income (reduced by medical, casualty losses, state and local taxes, and Section 691(c) deductions). All the includible excess deductions must be added back to gross income even if the deductions exceeded adjusted gross income.[606] The tax benefit rule[607] applies only to the add-on minimum tax.

This alternative minimum tax is expected to affect only those limited taxpayers who have paid little or no tax in prior years because of the capital gains deduction or the use of itemized deductions, such as interest expense or charitable deductions. Therefore, most investors can ignore this provision in their tax planning.

59 MAXIMUM TAX ON PERSONAL SERVICE INCOME

The maximum rate for both personal service income and unearned income has been reduced to 50 percent for post-1981 years. Consequently, the provision dealing with the maximum tax on personal service income has been repealed for post-1981 years.[608] The maximum tax provision, which had been in effect since 1972, provided for a 50 percent maximum rate for income from personal service (formerly referred to as earned income). Personal service income includes salaries, wages, professional fees, commissions, qualifying partnership income, deferred compensation (without the prior one-year restriction), and pension income (other than lump sum distributions and penalty distributions from individual retirement accounts). The

---

[605] Code: 55(a), as amended by 1981 ERTA: 101(d) and 102(b).
[606] Priv. Rul. Doc. 8115020.

[607] Code: 58(h).
[608] Code: 1348, repealed by 1981 ERTA: 101(c).

maximum rate applies to only a portion of the personal service income, in the same ratio as taxable income bears to the adjusted gross income. Tax preferences (see section on minimum tax) will still reduce the eligible personal service income dollar for dollar for 1981. With the repeal of the maximum tax provision, one of the major disincentives to investing in tax shelters that generate tax preferences has been removed. Also note that post-October 31, 1978, capital gains no longer constitute a tax preference for these purposes. For pre-1982 years, some investors may find it more advantageous to use the income averaging alternative. (See 60.) Any disqualified personal service income, plus other unearned income, such as investment income, can be taxed at rates above 50 percent for pre-1982 taxable years.

60 INCOME AVERAGING FOR CAPITAL GAINS

Investors who have substantial net capital gains in the current taxable year may realize considerable savings in income tax by electing the income averaging provisions and thereby compute their tax as though the bunched income was earned over a five-year period. Income averaging is also available with respect to most types of ordinary income.[609] However, taxpayers using income averaging cannot use the capital gains alternative tax computation for pre-1979 years (see 32.02) or the maximum tax on personal service income for pre-1982 years. (See 59.)

61 "SHAM" TRANSACTIONS

An investor may make his investments in any legitimate manner in order to obtain the maximum tax savings, and he will not be punished for choosing the avenue that produces the lesser tax.[610] This rule does not give tax effect to mere paper transactions where, in lieu of actual purchases and sales, the alleged transactions are merely entries on the broker's books.[611] Nor can an investor have recognized for tax purposes a transaction he enters into solely for tax reasons (e.g., to obtain interest deductions in the current year) with no expectation of ever realizing a profit on the transaction.[612] Through

---

[609] Code: 1301-1305.
[610] Gregory v. Helvering, 293 U.S. 465 (1935); Karl F. Knetsch, 364 U.S. 361 (1960).
[611] Eli D. Goodstein, 267 F. 2d 127 (CA-1, 1959); George G. Lynch, 273 F. 2d 867 (CA-2, 1960).

[612] See Kapel Goldstein, 364 F. 2d 734 (CA-2, 1966); Michael J. Ippolito, 364 F. 2d 744 (CA-2, 1966) (Cert. Den. 385 U.S. 1005); Rothschild, 407 F. 2d 404 (Ct. Cl., 1969); Rev. Rul. 77-185, C.B. 1977-1, 22.

proper planning, an investor can obtain maximum tax savings without resort to "sham" transactions.

62 PARTNERSHIPS

A partnership can take the form of a general business partnership, an investment club, a hedge fund, or a limited partnership with a general partner making the investment decisions. It is not a taxable entity,[613] but a conduit through which dividends, capital gains, tax exempt income, and other items of income and deductions are passed through and allocated among the partners in accordance with the partnership agreement.[614] Capital gains on sales made by a partnership after June 9, 1981, should be aggregated with a partner's other post-June 8, 1981, net capital gains in computing the 20 percent alternative tax for that period.[615] The income of a partnership can be allocated among the partners based upon a partner's pro rata share of the partnership total income for the period the investor was a partner or the actual income of the partnership (including cash basis accounting method) during the period the investor was a partner.[616] Thus, losses incurred for periods before the investor became a partner cannot be allocated to the partner unless the expenses were paid while the investor was a partner. An election may be made by all the members not to be treated as a partnership if the separate income and deduction can be adequately determined without the computation of partnership income.[617] It is important that the partnership avoid falling within the classification of an association which is taxed as a corporation.[618]

The Treasury has ruled that the investment activities of an investment club do not constitute business activities and therefore, the expenses of such partnership are deductible on a pro rata basis as itemized deductions by each partner on his personal income tax return.[619] This questionable position is contrary to the general rule that partnership expenses are effectively deductible by the partners in arriving at adjusted gross income.

63 CORPORATIONS

A corporate investor generally is subject to the same rules as an individual with respect to tax basis, holding period for long-term

---

[613] Code: 701.
[614] Code: 702.
[615] 1981 ERTA: 102(d).
[616] Richardson, 76 TC No. 45 (1981).

[617] Code: 761.
[618] Reg. 1.761-1(a)(2)(i); Code 7701(a) (3); Reg. 301.7701-2.
[619] Rev. Rul. 75-523, C.B. 1975-2, 257.

capital gains, wash sales, and short sales.[619a] The total amount of cash dividends are included in gross income, but dividends paid in property to U.S. corporate shareholders are included in gross income at the lesser of market value or the adjusted tax basis in the hands of the distributing corporation.[620]

In lieu of a $100 exclusion for dividends, a corporate shareholder is entitled to an 85 percent dividends received dividend.[621] Covered option writing for a corporation has a special attraction especially in high-dividend-paying stocks, since 85 percent of the dividend income received may be tax-free. A corporation must be the owner on the record date and not the X-dividend date in order for the dividend to qualify for the 85 percent deduction.[622] In general, common and preferred stock must be held for more than 15 days, and preferred stock with dividends in arrears for more than 366 days must be held for more than 90 days, in order for the particular dividends to qualify for the 85 percent dividends received deduction.[623] The required holding period is suspended during the time the corporation owns a Put or sells the stock short.[624] Thus, the simultaneous purchase of a preferred stock and acquisition of a Put will prevent the commencement of the 15- or 90-day holding period, thereby preventing the dividend received from qualifying for the 85 percent dividends received deduction. The required holding period is also suspended for any period in which the corporation "is under a contractual obligation to sell the stock."[625] However, the writing of a Call is not the equivalent of a short sale, nor is it a contractual obligation to sell since the buyer is under no obligation to purchase the shares. Accordingly, it will not affect the holding period requirement of Section 246(c) unless the Call is exercised by the holder.[626] Nevertheless, the Treasury has indicated that the holding period may be suspended if the corporation writes an "in-the-money" Call (Call price is less than the market value of the underlying stock).[627] The authors believe that there is little justification to deviate from the general rule unless the Call is so "deep-in-the-money" that it must be exercised under all possible conditions.

Dividends received from affiliated members may qualify for an 100 percent dividends received deduction or are excluded from gross

---

[619a]–A nondealer corporation was not allowed a deduction for dividends paid on a short sale. See footnote 490.

[620] Code: 301(d)(2).

[621] Code: 243(a)(1).

[622] Priv. Rul. Doc. 7840002.

[623] Code: 246(c)(1), (2).

[624] Code: 246(c)(3).

[625] Ibid.

[626] Priv. Rul. Doc. 7836066.

[627] Rev. Rul. 80-238, C.B. 1980-2, 96.

income if both corporations join in a consolidated return.[628] Thus, ordinarily, a corporation in 1982 would prefer to realize dividends rather than long-term gains because the maximum tax rate on dividends is 6.9 percent (15 percent of 46 percent corporate rate), whereas long-term capital gains are taxed at 28 percent. The Treasury has ruled that dividends received by a corporate investor, who had loaned stock to be used to close a short sale, do not qualify for the dividends paid deduction.[629] Until this position is litigated, corporations should consider whether to lend their shares to effectuate short sales. Dividends received by a corporation from a regulated investment company may qualify, in part or in whole, for the 85 percent dividends received deduction. This should be true even though the regulated investment company engages primarily in covered writing.[630] However, the Treasury has ignored the literal language of the Code and will treat short-term gains from unexercised options as ordinary income in making the 75 percent test.[631] Dividends received deductions are not allowed on distributions from "money market" funds whose gross income consists principally of interest income.

Net long-term capital gains received in post-1981 years can either be taxed at regular corporate tax rates[632] (17 percent first $25,000 of taxable income, 20 percent next $25,000, 30 percent next $25,000, 40 percent next $25,000 and 46 percent over $100,000) similar to short-term capital gains, or be taxed at a rate of 28 percent by means of the alternative tax computation.[633] The 60 percent long-term capital gain deduction is not available to corporations. Unused capital losses cannot be offset against ordinary income but can be carried back three years and carried forward for five years as short-term capital losses.[634] However, a capital loss cannot be carried back if it will create or increase a net operating loss for the taxable years to which the loss is being carried. Note that a capital loss must be car-

---

[628] Code: 243(a)(3); Reg. 1.1502-14(a).

[629] Rev. Rul. 60-177, C.B. 1960-1, 9.

[630] The Regulated Investment Company must meet the 75 percent test of Section 854(b)(1)(B). The short-term gain recognized under Section 1234(b) does not constitute gross income for purposes of the 75 percent test. Code: 854(b)(3)(A). Note, however, that a regulated investment company will be disqualified if more than 30 percent of its gross income consists of gains on sale of securities held for less than three months (Code: 851(b)(3)).

[631] Priv. Rul. Doc. 7813075.

[632] Code: 11.

[633] Code: 1201(a). The tax rate on the first $25,000 of taxable income will be reduced from 17 percent to 16 percent for 1982 and to 15 percent for succeeding years. The rate for the next $25,000 of taxable income will be similarly reduced from 20 percent, to 19 percent, and then to 18 percent. There are no changes in the tax rates above $50,000. While the maximum capital gains rate for individuals has been reduced to 20 percent, for net capital gains after June 9, 1981, the corporate capital gains rate remains at 28 percent. 1981 ERTA: 101 and 102.

[634] Code: 1212(a).

ried back to a year in which the capital gains could be offset by net operating losses from other years.[635] Accordingly, a corporation with expiring net operating losses in 1982 should not use a commodity straddle (i.e., close out the profitable position in the year the net operating losses will expire and establish a short-term loss by closing out the loss position in the subsequent year), because any unused capital losses in the three subsequent years must be carried back and applied against the capital gain created in the expiring year before the net operating loss carry-over can be offset against the capital gain. A corporation can not enter into straddle positions after June 23, 1981, in order to create capital losses for carry-back purposes.[636]

The add-on minimum tax provisions also apply to all corporations, but personal holding companies and Subchapter S corporations are treated as individuals for this purpose.[637] While the list of tax preferences may differ somewhat from those applicable to individuals (see 57), approximately 39 percent ($^{18}/_{46}$) of long-term capital gains constitute a tax preference if the alternative tax method is utilized.[638] Beginning in 1977, the add-on minimum tax rate is 15 percent and the allowable deduction in computing the tax is the greater of $10,000 or regular federal income tax for the current year.[639]

Interest received from tax-exempt securities is excluded from the corporation's taxable income.[640] However, it is includible in earnings and profits of a corporation and constitutes a taxable dividend when distributed to shareholders.[641] Despite this detriment, investment in tax-exempts may be advisable for corporations that may be liable for tax on unreasonable accumulation of earnings,[642] or the personal holding company tax.[643] Tax-exempt income is excluded in calculating the amounts subject to tax. Corporations investing in tax-exempts suffer the risk that some of their interest expense and investment expense allocable to the tax-exempt income will be disallowed, thereby reducing the tax benefits of this type of investment. Nevertheless, interest will not be disallowed if not directly attributable to the tax-exempts or the tax-exempts constitute not more than 2 percent of the average adjusted basis of the total business assets.[644]

Publicly held corporations can now enter into personal property leasing arrangements with other corporations under liberalized terms,

---

[635] Reg. 1.1212-1(a)(3)(iv), Example (6).
[636] Code: 1092 and 1256 as amended by 1981 ERTA: 501, 503.
[637] Code: 58(i).
[638] Code: 57(a)(9)(B).
[639] Code: 56(a) and (c).
[640] Code: 103.
[641] Reg. 1.312-6(b).
[642] Code: 531.
[643] Code: 541.
[644] Rev. Proc. 72-18, C.B. 1972-1, 740.

including a minimum investment of only 10 percent of the basis of the property, that will permit them to obtain both investment credit and increased depreciation deduction on the qualified leased property.[645] Note that the "at risk rules" which limit the amount of losses a closely held corporation can deduct has been expanded to include investment tax credit.[646]

Closely held corporations, with five or less individuals directly or indirectly owning at least 50 percent of the value of the outstanding stock and whose personal holding company income (dividends, interest, royalties, and the like) constitute at least 60 percent of its adjusted ordinary gross income, may be subject to a personal holding company tax of 70 percent (50 percent for post-1981 years) on its undistributed personal holding company income. All capital gains are excluded in making the 60 percent test.[647] Net long-term gains, after adjustment for capital gains tax, are deducted in computing the personal holding company tax.[648] Personal holding company tax can be avoided by distributing all of the personal holding company income or by electing consent dividends.[649] The use of a personal holding company as a vehicle to hold the family's investments is recommended for estate planning since a large discount from the value of the underlying assets may be taken for gifts of minority interests to other family members or where the shareholder, including the original grantor, owns a minority interest at time of death.

A corporation (Subchapter S corporation) may elect to be treated similar to a partnership, whereby the shareholders report on their tax returns their share of the undistributed ordinary income, long-term capital gains, or net operating losses.[650] This election is ineffective if its passive investment income (dividends, interest, rents, gains from sale of securities, and so on) exceeds 20 percent of its gross receipts.[651] Care should be taken to limit its passive income to 20 percent. Investment in tax-exempts may be ideal for this purpose.

64 ESTATES AND TRUSTS

Estates and trusts compute their taxable income in a manner similar to individuals and pay a tax on undistributed income using the tables of an unmarried individual.[652] The investment interest expense

---

[645] Code: 168(f)(8) as amended by 1981 ERTA: 201.
[646] Code: 46(c)(8) as amended by 1981 ERTA: 211(f).
[647] Code: 543(b).
[648] Code: 545(b).
[649] Code: 565.
[650] Code: 1371-1375.
[651] Code: 1372(e)(5).
[652] Code: 641.

limitation is applicable, but trusts are not entitled to the $10,000 minimum deduction.[653] A deduction is allowed for distributions to beneficiaries, who must report the income in the year the estate's or trust's taxable year ends.[654] The character of the income will be the same as in the hands of the estate or trust.[655] Thus tax-exempt income received by an estate or trust will retain its exempt status when received by the beneficiary.

Ordinarily, the estate or trust will pay a tax based on its income on any capital gains realized unless the governing instrument provides for distribution of capital gains.[656] However, a sale of appreciated property that was transferred within two years from the date of sale will be taxed to the trust at the same rates as if the transferor had sold the property and reported the gain realized on the sale, but not in excess of the appreciation at the time transferred to the trust.[657] The two-year period cannot be avoided by a short sale of the property ("short against the box").

A capital gains tax can be avoided on discretionary distribution of appreciated property to a beneficiary where there is no obligation to make the distribution either in a specific dollar amount or in other property.[658] For example, if a fiduciary has the discretionary power to accumulate or distribute the income, a distribution of appreciated stock or securities will not be taxed to the estate or trust and the beneficiary will report income based on the value of the property received, in a similar manner as a distribution in cash, and the market value will also be the beneficiary's tax basis for the property.

A tax-planning device that was not affected by the various tax acts is a 10-year reversionary trust.[659] Under this arrangement a high-tax-bracket individual places assets in a trust, with the income to be distributed to a dependent parent or other family members who pays little or no tax on the income because of the allowable deductions, exemptions, and low tax bracket of the dependent. With the increase in the annual gift tax exclusion for gifts made in 1982 from $3,000 to $10,000 per donee ($6,000 to $20,000 for joint gifts) a grantor can contribute over $40,000 to a short-term trust without being exposed to gift taxes.[660] In the case of a minor child it is recommended that the income be accumulated in a custodian account with the grantor's spouse as the custodian. Any capital gains realized by the

[653] Code: 163(d)(1).
[654] Code: 651 and 662.
[655] Code: 652 and 663.
[656] Code: 643(a)(3).
[657] Code: 644(a)(1).

[658] Reg. 1.661(a)-(2)(f).
[659] Code: 673.
[660] Code: 2503(a) as amended by 1981 ERTA: 441.

trust will be taxed currently to the grantor although not received until termination of the trust unless the trust instrument provides that capital gains are to be distributed to a beneficiary other than the grantor or his spouse.[661] Upon termination of the trust, the trust principal, including any unrealized appreciation, reverts back to the grantor. Instead of making support payments or accumulating funds for the future needs of his children with after-tax dollars, through this arrangement the same needs are met with half the outlay due to the savings of tax. For example, if an individual in the 50 percent tax bracket makes yearly support payments of $3,000 to his dependent parents, he will have to earn $6,000 of before-tax income in order to make the payments. By distributing to a short-term trust sufficient funds to earn $3,000, the trust distributions are not taxed to the grantor and the beneficiaries escape tax by means of their exemptions and deductions. Therefore, the grantor saves $3,000 of tax annually or $30,000 over a 10-year period.

A U.S. grantor could defer tax until expiration of the trust by creating a foreign trust, preferably with a situs in a tax-haven country, invest the funds in foreign securities, and provide for income to be accumulated and paid to U.S. beneficiaries upon expiration of the trust.[662] The advantage of creating a foreign trust is that income could be earned on the funds which otherwise would have been used to pay taxes by a U.S. trust. Foreign trusts created before May 22, 1974, do not come within the new grantor trust provisions discussed below, but a U.S. beneficiary will be liable, on receipt of the accumulated income, for a nondeductible interest charge of 6 percent per annum for the year the distributed income was accumulated.[663] Foreign trusts created by a U.S. grantor after May 21, 1974, with at least one U.S. beneficiary will be treated as a grantor's trust for post-1975 years.[664] The grantor is treated as the owner of the property and must include the income earned by the foreign trust in his tax return in the year earned. Income from a foreign trust still will be excluded from U.S. tax if there are no U.S. beneficiaries. An excise tax of 35 percent of unrealized gain will be imposed on any appreciated property transferred by a U.S. person to a foreign trust, foreign corporation, or foreign partnership unless the transferor treats the contribution as a taxable exchange.[665]

An investor can accelerate his charitable deductions by creating

---

[661] Code: 677.
[662] Code: 655(c).
[663] Code: 667(a) and 668.
[664] Code: 679.
[665] Code: 1491 and 1057.

and transferring funds to a less than 10-year charitable lead trust, with the income payable to charitable beneficiaries in the form of guaranteed annuities and the securities held by the trusts reverting to the grantor at the end of the trust term.[666] By having the trust invest in tax-exempts, the grantor avoids paying a tax on the trust income. The charitable deduction should not exceed 20 percent of his adjusted gross income for the year the charitable trust is created.[667] The grantor must also limit the amount of his investment interest expense to prevent a partial disallowance because of the tax-exempt income from the trust that he is deemed to have received.[668]

65 TAX-EXEMPT ORGANIZATIONS

Qualified pension, profit sharing, and stock bonus plans, and religious, educational, charitable, and other tax-exempt organizations are not taxed on their investment income.[669] An exempt private foundation is subject to a two percent excise tax on its net investment income consisting of dividends, interest, rents, royalties, and net capital gains less applicable investment expense.[670] Note that capital losses are deductible only against capital gains and any excess capital losses cannot be carried to another year. Tax-exempt income is also exempt from the two percent excise tax. Notwithstanding their tax-exempt status, any unrelated business income is subject to a regular corporate or unincorporated tax depending upon whether the exempt organization is a corporate or unincorporated charity.[671] Investment income normally is not considered unrelated business income unless derived from debt-financed property.[672] Thus, if securities are purchased on margin, the income from the securities is taxed to the extent of the percentage of the property that is debt financed, less a deduction for a similar percentage of related investment expense. Income from lapse of options regularly written by a tax-exempt organization was held by the Treasury to constitute unrelated business income,[673] but this has been rectified by recent legislation.[674] Organizations which were hesitant to write "covered" Calls (Calls in which they own the underlying stock) are now free to utilize Calls as an investment technique to maximize income on their

[666] Code: 170(f)(2).
[667] Code: 170(b)(1)(B).
[668] Code: 265.
[669] Code: 501.
[670] Code: 4940.
[671] Code: 511.

[672] Code: 512(b)(1) and (4), and 514.
[673] Rev. Rul. 66-47, C.B. 1966-1, 149. Many authorities have questioned the accuracy of this ruling, feeling its conclusion is erroneous.
[674] Code: 512(b)(5).

investments. However, income on lapse of options now constitutes short-term gains and is subject to the two percent excise tax when earned by private foundations.[675] Income derived from temporary loans of stock to a brokerage house to cover short sales also does not constitute unrelated business income.[676]

66 NONRESIDENT ALIENS

A nonresident alien investor may be subject to U.S. tax only on certain types of income from U.S. sources. The ensuing general discussion may be superseded by a treaty between the United States and the investor's country.

In general, a 30 percent tax will be withheld on fixed income received from U.S. sources, including dividends, rental income, and interest.[677] There is no withholding tax on U.S. Treasury bills unless held by a foreign investor for more than six months.[678] Original issue discount on bonds held for not more than six months are excluded from income.[679] Original issue discount on bonds is generally taxed when the bonds are sold or redeemed, but original issue discount is taxed currently on bonds issued after March 31, 1972, with a maturity of more than six months.[680] Interest income from deposits with banks[681] or from corporations who derive less than 20 percent of its income from U.S. sources[682] are not taxable. Generally the 30 percent tax is computed without deductions, such as interest on margin account, or personal exemptions.

Capital gains are not taxed unless the foreign investor is personally present in the United States for at least 183 days or the gain is in connection with a trade or business carried on in the United States.[683] Merely buying or selling securities or commodities through a broker or agent in the United States is not considered doing business in the United States. However, a nonresident alien, who was a limited partner in a partnership doing business in the United States that carried on the business of its corporate predecessor, was taxable on the gain realized on liquidation of the corporation and on other sales of stock during the taxable year.[684] The tax treatment of income derived from writing options was not clear prior to TRA 1976. Options written after September 1, 1976, will be accorded short-term gain or loss

---

[675] Code: 1234(b).
[676] Rev. Rul. 78-88, C.B. 1978-1, 163.
[677] Code: 871 and 1441.
[678] Priv. Rul. Doc. 7838070.
[679] Code: 871(a)(1)(C).

[680] Code: 871(a)(1)(C).
[681] Code: 861(c).
[682] Code: 861(a)(1)(B).
[683] Code: 871(a)(2).
[684] Vitale, 72 TC 386 (1979).

treatment upon expiration or upon closing of the transaction, and, accordingly, will be generally exempt from U.S. taxation. If the capital gain is taxable, the 30 percent tax is imposed on the entire net capital gain, after taking into account any capital losses realized in the taxable year but without any 60 percent capital gain deduction.[685] A foreign investor who is present in the United States for only a short period of time can escape U.S. tax by selling on the installment basis and receiving the income after he has left the United States.[686] If an investor owns real property in the United States, he may be able to reduce his U.S. tax by electing to treat the real property income as being connected with a United States business.[687] A disposition of an investment in U.S. real property is now subject to U.S. tax.[688]

A 30 percent tax will also be imposed on fixed income from U.S. sources received by a foreign corporation not connected with a United States business.[689] The rules are similar to those discussed above for nonresident alien investors.

67 TAX SHELTERS

The types of tax shelters are varied. Included among the principal tax shelters are real estate, including commercial, residential, and subsidized housing, oil and gas, coal royalties, cattle feeder and breeder programs, other agricultural products, motion picture film, and leased personal property. Some of these shelters—such as movie ventures, coal royalties, master recordings, gems, and Bibles—have been diminished as viable tax shelters for individual investors because of prior changes in the tax law or because of a toughened Treasury tax posture. Recent case law has also denied tax deductions where an unreasonable price for a motel was agreed upon by the parties, where oil drilling actually occurred in the subsequent year despite agreement to commence drilling in the current year, and where payment for prepaid feed represented a deposit rather than a binding payment. Aside from the Treasury's intensified efforts to uncover abusive tax shelters and take appropriate action, restrictive provisions have been incorporated in the 1976 TRA which had diminished the attractiveness of most tax shelters. However, the provisions of the 1981 ERTA permitting increased depreciation deductions and tax

---

[685] Reg. 1.871-7(c)(3).
[686] Reg. 1.871-7(d)(2)(iv).
[687] Code: 871(d).

[688] Code: 897, effective for dispositions after June 18, 1980.
[689] Code: 881.

credits and nullifying the effects of the tax preferences on the maximum tax on personal service income has made certain tax shelters more attractive. Investments in real estate, oil and gas property, and leased personal property are among those which have greatly benefited from the recent tax changes. On the other hand, reducing the maximum tax rate for individuals from 70 percent to 50 percent will also reduce the amount of tax savings derived from tax shelters.

The massive changes made in the 1981 ERTA will require investors to reevaluate their investment strategy. New projections should be made to see whether greater after-tax income can be obtained from tax shelters or from tax-exempt securities and taxable bonds and stock. Any investment, including tax shelters, should be judged on their risk-reward ratios. In the past many tax shelters were poor investments but could still result in a substantial after-tax rate of return on investment because of favorable tax treatment. This included leverage, whereby an investor could get deductions of $3 to $4 for every dollar invested because of nonrecourse loans; substantial deductions in the first years through prepaid interest expense, prepaid feed, or construction period expenses; deferral of tax until the shelter is sold or a complete escape of tax if the investor were to die holding the tax shelter; and for many tax shelters long-term capital gain on ultimate disposition.

Below is a discussion of some of the relevant provisions incorporated in the 1976 TRA, 1978 RA, and 1981 ERTA and their effect on specific tax shelters.

.01 "At risk" capital.   Increased leverage generally can no longer be obtained through nonrecourse financing whereby the debtor is not personally liable.[690] The effect of this provision is to limit the total amount of allowable deductions to actual cash or property contributions and recourse financing. Previously, nonrecourse financing would result in a higher tax basis, resulting in greater depreciation deductions in the early years and, more importantly, in larger investment credits. This is still true for commercial real estate, especially qualified rehabilitated buildings.[691] Investment credit in qualifying personal property, such as breeding cattle, personal property leasing, and motion picture film, may be limited to the amount the investor is "at risk" (cash outlay plus recourse financing).[692] Increased invest-

---

[690] Code: 465(a).
[691] Code: 46(a)(2), as amended by 1981 ERTA: 212.
[692] Code: 46(c)(8), as amended by 1981 ERTA: 211(f).

ment credit can no longer be obtained in personal property investments from the use of nonrecourse financing unless the lender is a
bank, insurance company, or other lending institution. All tax shelters, other than real estate, will be affected by these at-risk limitations with respect to losses and investment credit.

.02 **Upfront deductions.**   Prior to the 1976 TRA, the Treasury permitted a deduction for one year's prepaid interest expense where
there had been no distortion of income. Cash-basis taxpayers are in
effect now placed on an accrual basis and can only deduct prepaid
interest ratably over the duration of the loan.[693] (See **48.05.**) This
will affect most tax shelters involving financing. In the same vein,
interest and taxes incurred during the real estate construction period
will now have to be capitalized under transitional rules.[694] Real
estate taxes and interest expense can still be deducted during the
construction of low-income housing.[695] The costs of producing
motion picture films cannot be deducted when incurred, but are
deferred until income is earned.[696] Farming syndicates can deduct
expenses for feed, fertilizer, seed, and other farm supplies only when
consumed.[697] In addition, the cost of planting, cultivating, maintaining, and developing a citrus or almond grove, an orchard, or a vine-
yard must be capitalized where incurred prior to the productive
stage.[698]

.03 **Tax preferences.**   In the past, the tax preference items created
by the tax shelters were not considered important because of the exemptions and deductions allowed in computing the minimum tax on
tax preferences, but had a substantial effect on maximum tax on
personal service income. (See **57** and **59** respectively.) With the
repeal of the maximum tax on personal service income in 1982,
investors, such as professionals and corporate executives, no longer
will need to be concerned that the tax preferences could substantially increase the tax in their earned income. Future shelters will
depend more on accelerated depreciation, intangible drilling expenses, and tax credits, but investors should not ignore the economic
aspects of the shelter. They must bear in mind that they are now
sheltering only "50 percent" income rather than "70 percent"
income and, therefore, can suffer a greater after-tax loss from the
investments. In addition to obtaining less tax benefit for each dollar

---

[693] Code: 461(g).   [696] Code: 280.
[694] Code: 189.   [697] Code: 464(a).
[695] Code: 189(d) as amended by 1981   [698] Code: 278(b).
   ERTA: 262.

of loss thrown off by the tax shelter, the investor should also consider that the Treasury may question the validity of the tax shelter if it lacks a profit potential.

.04 Capital gains on disposition. The maximum capital gains rate of 20 percent for post-June 9, 1981, transactions increases the tax benefits of certain tax shelters and must be contrasted with other shelters that generate ordinary income on disposition subject to tax rates up to 50 percent (70 percent pre-1981). Investors no longer have to be concerned that the deductions created by the tax shelter may be offset against income subject to a maximum tax rate of 50 percent and can be recaptured at 70 percent tax rates. Gain on sale of residential property, other than certain low-income housing, will be taxed as ordinary income to the extent of accelerated depreciation.[699] This ordinary income treatment previously applied to sale of commercial real estate, leased personal property, motion picture film, and breeding cattle. A gain on sale of oil and gas property will also be taxed as ordinary income to the extent of excess intangible drilling costs.[700] In lieu of a sale, many investors have made charitable contributions of the oil and gas property. A charitable contribution deduction will not be allowed to the extent ordinary income would have resulted from a sale of the property.[701]

.05 Increased basis at death. Due to the inability of disposing of a tax shelter during lifetime without incurring substantial tax liability, many investors had retained their tax shelters until death. At death, the deceased investor's estate or beneficiary would obtain a new tax basis for the property equal to its market value and thereby escape tax for the excess deductions previously allowed. The ability of the estate or beneficiary to obtain a new increased basis for the shelter has been retained with the repeal of the basis carry-over rules.[702] For many investors this will represent the only means of avoiding the adverse tax effects of a burned-out shelter other than investing in another shelter to offset the income flowing from the burned-out shelter.

68 DEFERRED ANNUITIES

A variation of the variable annuity policy has recently received a good deal of publicity. The main selling points of these deferred

---

[699] Code: 1250(a).
[700] Code: 1254(a)(1)(A).

[701] Code: 170(e).
[702] Code: 1023.

annuities appear to be high guaranteed interest rates in the first years of the policy, deferral of income taxes on the income earned by the investments, and flexibility in receiving the deferred income and the principal contributed by the investor. The terms of the policies will vary among the different insurance companies.

One type of annuity is the savings annuity whereby an investor will contribute $30,000 or more in savings bank certificates, or certificates of deposit. The insurance company takes title to these certificates and the income is not taxed to the investor until he receives his annuity payments. Because the certificates do not mature for a period of time, the investor has less flexibility in making withdrawals.

Investment annuities, on the other hand, give more flexibility to the investors. Funds are contributed to the insurance company in the form of cash, mutual fund shares, or securities. These annuities also provide for high guaranteed interest in the earlier years and either a lower interest rate thereafter or an interest rate dependent on the yield from investments in the investor's custodian account. An initial contribution of securities by the investor will result in gain or loss to the investor. Any gains realized after the insurance company takes title are taxed to the insurance company, but the costs are passed on to the investor by a charge to his custodian account. For this reason investment of long-term, high-yield bonds is better than low-yield stock. The income earned on the investments is passed through to the investor as a tax-free return of investment on the theory that the annuity has not started, but this results in larger income when the investor starts receiving annuity payments. For these services an investor may be charged an original sales charge plus annual handling charges varying from 0.5 percent to 2 percent. Penalties may also be charged for premature distributions.

Inherent in the investment annuity policies and other deferred annuities is the requirement that the investor must make the investment decision or must hire investment counselors to make them. Any additional costs for investment advisory services are borne by the investor. Originally, the Treasury approved these investment annuities, but it has since ruled that the investor would be treated as the owner of the assets held in the custodian account if he had full control over future investments.[703] In this event, the investor would

---

[703] Rev. Rul. 77-185, C.B. 1977-1, 12. A court action to prohibit the Treasury from enforcing this ruling has failed, but Congress may still act in this matter. Investment Annuity, Inc., 609 F. 2d 1 (CA-DC, 1979), Cert. Den. The Treasury has ruled that the investor is currently taxable on the wraparound annuity contract in Rev. Rul. 80-274, C.B. 1980-2 CB, 27, and Rev. Rul. 81-225.

be taxed on the income generated by the investments as if he retained ownership.

The announcement by the Treasury with respect to investment control casts clouds over subsequent annuity policies issued with this provision. In other respects this type of annuity offers deferral of income till later years when the investor may be in a lower tax bracket and, in the meantime, the investor receives additional income from funds that otherwise would have been used to pay the income taxes imposed on the investment income. Any distributions prior to the annuity date (i.e., the date annuity payments commence), are treated as return of principal and, in effect, the tax deferral increases the income yield of the investments less the additional costs incurred in entering into the deferred annuity arrangement. As stated previously, annuity payments made after the annuity date are taxed under the normal annuity rules,[704] and the percentage of the annuity payments that will be subject to tax will increase if prior principal payments were made. A lump sum payment to the investor's beneficiary upon the investor's death before the annuity date would be tax-free, similar to a payment of life insurance.[705] However, the insurance proceeds would be subject to estate taxes.[706] Before investing in these deferred annuities, an investor must compare the economic and tax results with other types of investments, including tax-exempt bonds.

---

[704] Code: 72.
[705] Code: 101 (a).

[706] Code: 2042.

Index of Citations

COURT DECISIONS

184

Subject Index